Standing Soldiers, Kneeling Slaves

Standing Soldiers, Kneeling Slaves

RACE, WAR, AND MONUMENT
IN NINETEENTH-CENTURY
AMERICA

KIRK SAVAGE

PRINCETON UNIVERSITY PRESS
PRINCETON, NEW JERSEY

Second printing, and first paperback printing, 1999
Paperback ISBN 0-691-00947-3

The Library of Congress has cataloged the cloth edition of this book as follows

Savage, Kirk, 1958–.
Standing soldiers, kneeling slaves : race, war, and monument
in nineteenth-century America / Kirk Savage.
p. cm.
Includes bibliographical references and index.
ISBN-13: 978-0-691-00947-6
ISBN-10: 0-691-00947-3
1. United States—History—Civil War, 1861–1865—Social aspects.
2. Slaves—Emancipation—United States. 3. Public
sculpture—United States—History—19th century.
4. United States—Race relations. 5. National characteristics,
American—History—19th century. I. Title
E468.9.S28   1997
973.7'1—dc21   97-9731

This book has been composed in Sabon

The paper used in this publication meets the minimum requirements
of ANSI/NISO Z39.48-1992 (R1997) (*Permanence of Paper*)

http://pup.princeton.edu

Printed in the United States of America

3 5 7 9 10 8 6 4 2

For Charlotte, Rose, Sara, and Elizabeth

———————————————

CONTENTS

List of Illustrations   ix

Acknowledgments   xiii

CHAPTER ONE
Introduction   3

CHAPTER TWO
Exposing Slavery   21

CHAPTER THREE
Imagining Emancipation   52

CHAPTER FOUR
Freedom's Memorial   89

CHAPTER FIVE
Slavery's Memorial   129

CHAPTER SIX
Common Soldiers   162

CHAPTER SEVEN
Epilogue   209

Notes   215

Index   259

ILLUSTRATIONS

1.1 J. C. Nott and George R. Gliddon, *Types of Mankind* (Philadelphia, 1854), 458. (Courtesy of Swem Library, College of William and Mary) — 10

1.2 Apollo Belvedere, Roman imperial copy of a Greek bronze, Vatican. (Alinari/Art Resource, New York) — 11

1.3 Sheet music cover for *Songs of the Virginia Serenaders* (Boston, 1844). (Courtesy of Harvard Theatre Collection, Houghton Library, Cambridge, Mass.) — 13

1.4 Henry Kirke Brown, *Choosing of the Arrow*, 1849, bronze statuette. (Courtesy of Denver Art Museum collection) — 14

1.5 John Rogers, *Slave Auction*, 1859, plaster. (Collection of the New-York Historical Society) — 16

2.1 *Am I Not a Man and a Brother*, circa 1787, Wedgwood brooch, jasperware set in silver. (Courtesy of the Mint Museum, Charlotte, N.C.; Delhom Collection, 65.48.DC.EPy.W528) — 22

2.2 *Am I Not a Man and a Brother*, 1837, woodcut. (Library of Congress, Washington, D.C.) — 22

2.3 *Illustrations of the American Anti-Slavery Almanac for 1840*, woodcut. (Library of Congress, Washington, D.C.) — 24

2.4 Pietro Tacca, Monument to Grand Duke Ferdinand, 1620, Livorno, Italy. (Alinari/Art Resource, New York) — 26

2.5 Edward W. Clay, *Practical Amalgamation*, 1839, lithograph. (Courtesy of the Library Company of Philadelphia) — 27

2.6 Hiram Powers, *Greek Slave*, 1847, marble. (Courtesy of Yale University Art Gallery, New Haven, Conn.; Purchase—Olive Louise Dann Fund) — 29

2.7 Henry Kirke Brown, model for House pediment of U.S. Capitol, 1855, plaster (now lost). (Library of Congress, Washington, D.C.) — 33

2.8 View of South Carolina State House, circa 1860, woodcut. (Courtesy of South Caroliniana Library, University of South Carolina, Columbia) — 37

2.9 Henry Kirke Brown, model for pediment of South Carolina State House, 1860–61, plaster (now lost). (Library of Congress, Washington, D.C.) — 37

2.10 Brown, model for pediment of South Carolina State House, 1860–61. Detail of left wing. (Library of Congress, Washington, D.C.) — 38

2.11 Brown, model for pediment of South Carolina State House, 1860–61. Detail of right wing. (Library of Congress, Washington, D.C.) — 39

2.12 Brown, model for pediment of South Carolina State House, 1860–61. Detail of central section. (Library of Congress, Washington, D.C.) — 39

2.13 George Cruikshank, *Emmeline about to Be Sold to the Highest Bidder*, illustration in H. B. Stowe, *Uncle Tom's Cabin* (London, 1852), 290. (Courtesy of Darlington Library, University of Pittsburgh)   40

2.14 *Slavery As It Exists in America; Slavery As It Exists in England*, 1850, lithograph. (Library of Congress, Washington, D.C.)   44

2.15 F. M. Coffin, *The Slaves in the Cornfield*, illustration in W.L.G. Smith, *Life at the South, Or Uncle Tom's Cabin As It Is* (Buffalo, 1852), 38. (Courtesy of Foster Hall Collection of the Center for American Music, University of Pittsburgh)   45

2.16 T. Addison Richards, *Harvesting the Rice* and *A Carolina Rice Planter*, illustrations in "Rice Lands of the South," *Harper's New Monthly* 19 (November 1859): 729, 738. (Courtesy of University of Pittsburgh Library)   46

3.1 John Quincy Adams Ward, *Freedman*, 1863, bronze statuette. (Photograph © 1996 Detroit Institute of Arts, Gift of Mr. Ernest Kanzler)   53

3.2 Currier and Ives, *Emancipation of the Slaves*, circa 1863, lithograph. (Library of Congress, Washington, D.C.)   56

3.3 *Harper's Weekly* 7 (July 4, 1863): 429. (Courtesy of University of Pittsburgh Library)   58

3.4 William Wetmore Story, *Libyan Sibyl*, 1862, marble. (Metropolitan Museum of Art, New York, Gift of the Erving Wolf Foundation, 1979)   60

3.5 Edmonia Lewis, *Forever Free*, 1868, marble. (Howard University Gallery of Art, Washington, D.C.)   63

3.6 Henry Kirke Brown, Lincoln Monument, 1869, Prospect Park, Brooklyn. (Library of Congress, Washington, D.C.)   68

3.7 Louis Verhaegen, Charles Avery Monument, 1860, Allegheny Cemetery, Pittsburgh. (Courtesy of Henry Pisciotta)   71

3.8 Verhaegen, Charles Avery Monument, 1860, Allegheny Cemetery, Pittsburgh. Detail of relief panel. (Courtesy of Henry Pisciotta)   71

3.9 Henry Kirke Brown, model for monument to Lincoln, 1866–67, plaster (now lost). (Library of Congress, Washington, D.C.)   74

3.10 Randolph Rogers, *Lincoln and the Emancipated Slave*, circa 1866, plaster. (Courtesy of University of Michigan Museum of Art, Ann Arbor; Gift of Randolph Rogers, 1885.3)   76

3.11 Thomas Ball, stereograph of plaster model for monument to Lincoln, circa 1866. (Library of Congress, Washington, D.C.)   78

3.12 *Arrotino*, Hellenistic marble, Uffizi Gallery, Florence. (Alinari/Art Resource, New York)   80

3.13 Vinnie Ream [Hoxie], *Abraham Lincoln*, 1871, marble, U.S. Capitol. (Library of Congress, Washington, D.C.)   82

3.14 Randolph Rogers, Rhode Island Soldiers' and Sailors' Monument, 1871, Providence. (Rhode Island Historical Society, Providence)   85

3.15 Randolph Rogers, model of emancipation relief, 1870, plaster (now lost). (Rhode Island Historical Society, Providence)   86

4.1 Thomas Ball, Freedmen's Memorial to Abraham Lincoln (Emancipation Monument), 1876, Lincoln Park, Washington, D.C. (Library of Congress, Washington, D.C.)   91

4.2 Harriet Hosmer, model for Freedmen's Memorial to Lincoln, 1866, plaster (now lost). (Courtesy of Watertown Free Library, Watertown, Mass.)   95

4.3 Hosmer, design for Freedmen's Memorial to Lincoln, in [London] *Art-Journal* 7 (January 1, 1868): 8. (Courtesy of Frick Fine Arts Library, University of Pittsburgh)   99

4.4 Clark Mills, model for National Lincoln Monument, circa 1868, plaster (now lost). (Library of Congress, Washington, D.C.)   105

4.5 Thomas Ball, model for Freedmen's Memorial to Lincoln, circa 1874, plaster (now lost). (Library of Congress, Washington, D.C.)   115

4.6 Ball, *Emancipation Group*, 1879, Park Square, Boston. (Library of Congress, Washington, D.C.)   121

4.7 Augustus Saint-Gaudens and Stanford White, Lincoln Monument (*Standing Lincoln*), 1887, Lincoln Park, Chicago. (Library of Congress, Washington, D.C.)   123

4.8 Saint-Gaudens, Lincoln Monument (*Standing Lincoln*), 1887, Lincoln Park, Chicago. Detail of statue. (Library of Congress, Washington, D.C.)   123

4.9 Harriet Hosmer, *African Sibyl*, design for portion of Lincoln Monument, circa 1890 (now lost). (Courtesy of Watertown Free Library, Watertown, Mass.)   127

5.1 A. Hoen and Co., *Genl. Lee on Traveler*, 1876, lithograph. (Library of Congress, Washington, D.C.)   134

5.2 Edward Valentine, model for Lee monument, circa 1877, plaster. (Valentine Museum, Richmond, Va.)   142

5.3 Moses Ezekiel, model for Lee monument, circa 1877, plaster (now lost). (Courtesy of American Jewish Archives, Cincinnati, Ohio)   143

5.4 Charles Niehaus, model for Lee monument, circa 1886, plaster (now lost). (Library of Congress, Washington, D.C.)   144

5.5 Antonin Mercié and Paul Pujol, Lee Monument, 1890, Monument Avenue, Richmond. (Eleanor S. Brockenbrough Library, The Museum of the Confederacy, Richmond, Va.)   147

5.6 Photograph of Monument Avenue, circa 1907, in Richmond Chamber of Commerce, *Richmond, Virginia, 1907*, n.p. (Valentine Museum, Richmond, Va.)   149

5.7 Photograph after hoisting of the Lee statue, May 29, 1890. (Library of Virginia, Richmond, Va.)   153

5.8 Monument to faithful slaves, 1896, Fort Mill, South Carolina. (Author)   156

5.9 Detail of figure 5.8, relief panel. (Author)   156

5.10 Detail of figure 5.8, relief panel. (Author)   156
6.1 Richard Morris Hunt and John Quincy Adams Ward, 7th Regiment
    Memorial, 1869–74, Central Park, New York City. (Courtesy of
    the Art Commission of the City of New York)   163
6.2 Confederate Soldier Monument, 1909, Livingston, Alabama. (Library
    of Congress, Washington, D.C.)   165
6.3 Winslow Homer, *Defiance: Inviting a Shot before Petersburg*, 1864,
    oil on panel. (Photograph © 1994 Detroit Institute of Arts, Founders
    Society Purchase with funds from Dexter M. Ferry Jr.)   171
6.4 Photograph of dead Confederate at Petersburg, circa 1864. (Library
    of Congress, Washington, D.C.)   172
6.5 Thomas Nast, *Patience on a Monument*, in *Harper's Weekly*
    (October 10, 1868): 648. (Courtesy of University of Pittsburgh
    Library)   175
6.6 George H. Mitchell and Lorado Taft, Union Soldiers' and Sailors'
    Monument, 1891, Yonkers, New York. (Courtesy of Wayt Thomas)   179
6.7 Sandusky County Soldiers' Monument, 1885, Fremont, Ohio,
    illustration in *Proceedings at the Unveiling of the Soldiers' Monument
    on the Site of Fort Stephenson, Fremont, Ohio* (Fremont, Ohio:
    Democratic Messenger, 1885), frontispiece. (Courtesy of Franklin and
    Marshall College Library)   185
6.8 Bullard and Bullard, architects, design for National Emancipation
    Monument, 1889, lithograph. (Library of Congress, Washington,
    D.C.)   191
6.9 Augustus Saint-Gaudens and Charles F. McKim, Shaw Memorial,
    1897, Boston Common. (Library of Congress, Washington, D.C.)   194
6.10 Office of H. H. Richardson, design for Shaw Memorial, circa 1882,
    pen and ink. (Department of Printing and Graphic Arts, Houghton
    Library, Harvard University, Cambridge, Mass.)   198
6.11 Saint-Gaudens, plaster cast of sketch model for Shaw Memorial,
    date unknown. (Courtesy of Saint-Gaudens National Historic Site,
    Cornish, N.H.)   199
6.12 Saint-Gaudens, relief panel of Shaw Memorial, 1897, bronze.
    (Library of Congress, Washington, D.C.)   200

ACKNOWLEDGMENTS

I OWE MY INTEREST in public monuments to a wonderful course taught by
Nicholas Penny in London in the summer of 1979. Inspired by his syn-
thetic approach, I have been thinking about them off and on ever since.
The issues at the heart of this book emerged several years later in graduate
school with the help of a superb group of advisors at the University of
California at Berkeley. Dell Upton steered me to Monument Avenue and
gave me important criticism at every stage of my dissertation; Paula Fass
made me see the importance of race; Anne Wagner made me think about
Habermas and gave me a series of probing questions about the commemorative process; Margaretta Lovell guided both my thinking and my writing with great tact and acumen.

Doing justice to their comments and criticisms took me far beyond the
dissertation. In that long, hard process of creating a book, many of my
ideas evolved from the classes I taught. My students at the University of
Pittsburgh and the College of William and Mary consistently helped and
challenged me to think about the material in new ways. They are too
many to name individually, but they all worked together to create an
atmosphere of inquiry and constructive criticism that enabled me to take
my work in more interesting directions.

Many other people and institutions have been generous and indispensable in their help. My initial research at the predoctoral stage was supported by grants from the University of California at Berkeley and by a
three-year Mellon Fellowship in the Humanities. My subsequent work
was supported by summer research grants from the University of Pittsburgh and by a two-year Material Culture Fellowship from the Commonwealth Center for the Study of American Culture at the College of William and Mary. Another grant from the Richard D. and Mary Jane Edwards Endowed Publication Fund at the University of Pittsburgh helped
defray the costs of reproductions. Several scholars have very kindly
shared their own research materials with me: Thomas Brown, William
and Aimee Cheek, Janet McCall, Merl Moore Jr., William Parrish, Louise
Pettus, Henry Pisciotta, Michael Shapiro, and Chris Thomas. Others
have helped out in a variety of ways both logisticial and intellectual—
taking a photograph, discussing a paper, doing last-minute research, offering a home away from home. These would include, to name only the
most obvious, Michele Bogart, Jennifer Craven, Melissa Dabakis, Jay Fis-
ette, George Henderson, Roberta Kefalos, Pam Kennedy, Angela Miller,

Matthew Roper, Stephen Savage, Dan Sherman, Tom Somma, Wayt Thomas, Sara and William Thomas, Anne Weis, and James and Harriet Wrenn. I have also had the good fortune to work with outstanding professional staff at many research institutions. I cannot name them all, but I would like to single out a few institutions whose staff did favors above and beyond the call of duty: the Country Music Foundation Library, the Massachusetts Historical Society, the South Caroliniana, the Valentine Museum, and the Watertown Free Library.

I am grateful more than I can say to my editor at Princeton, Deborah Malmud, for her faith in the project and for her sensitive readings of the manuscript. I got many other careful and instructive comments from several people who read all or part of my manuscript in its later stages. These readers include Vivien Fryd, Peter Karsten, Angela Miller, and, above all, my wife Elizabeth Thomas, who has always been my first and best reader. Without her ideas, insights, and clear guidance at every stage of the project from beginning to end, this book would not be here. And without the joy that she and our three daughters Charlotte, Rose, and Sara, have given me, I would never have been able to bring the book to completion.

Standing Soldiers, Kneeling Slaves

CHAPTER ONE

INTRODUCTION

THE UNITED STATES OF AMERICA originated as a slave society, holding millions of Africans and their descendants in bondage, and remained so until a civil war took the lives of a half million soldiers, some once slaves themselves.[1] This book explores how that history of slavery and its violent end was told in public space—specifically in the sculptural monuments that increasingly came to dominate public space in nineteenth-century America.

The shift from slavery to freedom precipitated by the Civil War was the cataclysmic event and the central dilemma of the century, one that continues to shape American society even today. That event reverberated throughout public space in countless ways, some obvious and others subtle. The war provoked the greatest era of monument building ever seen in this country, yet the role of the public monument in defining the war's legacy is a subject that has been considered only in fragments, if at all. The fragments tell us little because their significance depends on how they are put together. Doing that means interweaving three large themes: the meaning of race, the experience of war, and the function of the public monument. All three—race, war, and monument—were pivotal to the nation as it emerged from its long tradition of slavery. Passing through this epochal transformation, all three combined to reshape the American sense of its nationhood.

The Civil War did not simply emancipate four million individuals whose lives and histories had been shaped in slavery. That act of emancipation shook the life of the nation and everyone in it. The death of slavery required nothing less than "a new birth of freedom," to use Lincoln's famous phrase from the Gettysburg Address, a reinvention of the very meaning and practice of liberty. Slaves could not shed bondage like a suit of clothes; they had to find new identities, new ways of work, new routes into society. Nor could the larger society suddenly shed its tradition of slavery without facing fundamental challenges to its own institutions and identity. What would freedom come to mean in a society still attached to the very concept of racial difference used to justify slavery? Would new barriers between the races have to be erected, or could race itself be rethought, reimagined? Far from solving an ideological crisis, the abolition of slavery precipitated a new one—a momentous struggle over the idea of race and the terms of citizenship in a nation supposedly dedicated to equality.

That struggle dominated the politics of the period we call Reconstruction. Yet Reconstruction was not merely a contest over public policy— voting rights, land distribution, and so forth. Change of that kind could not be realized without a more profound cultural transformation. Reconstruction demanded nothing less than that the nation and its people reimagine themselves. Public monuments were at the center of this highly abstract, and yet terrifying, conflict—a conflict that lasted long after Reconstruction's official demise.

Public monuments were meant to yield resolution and consensus, not to prolong conflict. The impulse behind the public monument was an impulse to mold history into its rightful pattern. And history was supposed to be a chronicle of heroic accomplishments, not a series of messy disputes with unresolved outcomes. Even now, to commemorate is to seek historical closure, to draw together the various strands of meaning in a historical event or personage and condense its significance for the present in a speech or a monument. It is true that the *process* of commemoration often leads to conflict, not closure, because in defining the past we define our present. Yet in choosing to remember "historical" events or heroes we still hope to plunge them into a past secured against the vicissitudes of the present.

Public monuments are the most conservative of commemorative forms precisely because they are meant to last, unchanged, forever. While other things come and go, are lost and forgotten, the monument is supposed to remain a fixed point, stabilizing both the physical and the cognitive landscape. Monuments attempt to mold a landscape of collective memory, to conserve what is worth remembering and discard the rest. Today public monuments are everywhere, so much a part of the landscape of our daily life that we hardly even notice them. But in the middle of the nineteenth century the public monument still meant something vital and precious. Public monuments were much rarer, and many of the types of monuments we now take for granted simply did not exist. Before the Civil War one could stroll through most streets or squares without ever encountering a bronze statue of a departed hero or even a simple stone shaft marking a historical event.[2]

The "new birth of freedom" proclaimed by Lincoln at Gettysburg in 1863 ushered in a new era of the public monument as well. The national soldier's cemetery Lincoln helped consecrate that day was the first of its kind, and the modern war memorial, dedicated to the ordinary soldier, originated around the same time. In the decades following the war, the number and variety of monuments erected throughout the country multiplied exponentially. Increasingly they commemorated the common man and, sometimes, woman. While monuments retained their traditional virtues of permanence and fixity, they became ever more popular—in more than one sense of the word. In an earlier century, public monuments had been part of a cult of rulership; now they claimed to be revelations of the popular will. Made of imperishable stone or metal, and erected prominently in shared civic space—parks, town squares, public buildings— public monuments were meant to be a genuine testimonial of the people's memory, an eternal repository of what they held most dear.[3]

Slavery constituted perhaps the single most difficult challenge facing "the people" as they struggled to build a democratic memory of their collective past. Slavery could hardly even be acknowledged in public space without exploding the myth of a democratically unified people from the very outset. The abolition of slavery after the Civil War did not solve the problem but only intensified it. Once abolished, slavery forced itself into the domain of memory, there to be reckoned with in one way or another—suppressed, integrated, romanticized. Emancipation introduced into national memory a new people (some four million ex-slaves) and a new history (*their* history of enslavement).[4] "The people" now included slaveowner and slave alike, multiple and opposing histories united under the same banner of the nation. While the democratization of monumental space tied it ever more closely to the image of the people, the question of who constituted the national people grew more divisive. Ultimately the war turned on the question of who belonged to the nation: who had a claim on the national possession of liberty, and what did the possession imply. The monuments of the war inevitably forced these issues to the surface; representational decisions had to be made, and they had public consequences. At the very time, therefore, that a resurgent nationality was sparking a new monumental era, the meaning of nationality was changing in dramatic and unpredictable ways. It is this conjunction of events—and the cultural and artistic problems arising from it— that my book investigates.

TODAY we are acutely aware of public space as a representational battleground, where many different social groups fight for access and fight for control of the images that define them. Recent controversies over the Vietnam Veterans Memorial in Washington, the John Ahearn bronzes in the Bronx, and the Arthur Ashe statue in Richmond—to name just three— have put the problem on the front page of newspapers and in the halls of government. Public space in the nineteenth century was also torn by conflict, though the terms of the conflict and the access to it were rather different. The battles fought and the decisions made in that era had a profound impact on the lives of people then and, at the same time, created an enduring landscape of public monuments that continues to shape our public experience and expectations today.

In the expansive era of the nineteenth century, monuments were not bestowed by the state on the citizenry, or at least they weren't supposed to be. It was the reverse claim that animated the whole monumental enterprise: monuments were supposed to arise spontaneously by popular demand, only then to be donated to the state for safekeeping. What gave monuments their peculiar appeal in an era of rising nationalism was their claim to speak for "the people." Monuments were "true" only insofar as they seemed to display the people's heart. Most monuments therefore originated not as official projects of the state but as volunteer enterprises sponsored by associations of "public-spirited" citizens and funded by individual donations. These voluntary associations often had direct links to officialdom, but they achieved legitimacy only by manufacturing popular enthusiasm (and money) for the project. Sponsors usually worked hard to sustain the fiction that they were merely agents of a more universal collective whose shared memory the project embodied. For example, the sponsors of Lincoln's tomb monument in Springfield, Illinois, asked "to be regarded as only the *channel* through which the promptings of the popular heart may find expression,—the instrument to mould its offerings into forms of enduring strength and beauty."[5] Hence the importance of the "popular subscription," in which rich and poor, young and old, were canvassed alike for their financial contributions; and the rituals of cornerstone laying and dedication, where great crowds gathered and symbolically erected the monument. Sponsors had to publicize their enterprise from beginning to end; to marshal the resources and support needed to place a monument prominently in public space, they really did have to summon the symbolic and financial participation of a "public" that the monument would represent. The more widely the monument campaign appealed, the more enthusiasm it seemed to generate, the more convincingly its public would come to resemble the democratic vision of one people united by one memory.

Nowadays, in the academy at least, we are inclined to question this equation. We think of collective memory—and indeed the "people" who supposedly share this memory—as complicated fictions, manufactured to serve ideological ends. Monuments emerged within a public sphere that communicated between actual communities of people and the abstract machinery of the nation-state. Monuments were one space in which local communities based on geography or interest or both could define themselves and speak to or for the larger collective. The relationship between the local community and the more abstract collective was complex and at times, I will argue, quite strained. Monuments did not simply serve the official demands of the state. Nor did they simply channel spontaneous popular sentiments, as the sponsors liked to claim in their standard rhetoric. The process of commemoration was in fact reciprocal: the monument manufactured its own public, but that public in turn had opinions about what constituted proper commemoration. In practical terms, the designers of public monuments—mostly sculptors, as it turns out—usually had to satisfy a committee of elite citizens who were themselves competing for popular approval with other philanthropic projects and even other monument proposals. The designer could not impose an official version of history but could only propose one possible version, which then had to win a place in this peculiarly competitive public arena.

In the process, elite and popular interests inevitably intertwined and reshaped one another. This was simply the nature of the public sphere in the nineteenth-century United States. A truly vernacular "folk" memory might be nurtured outside the public sphere, in quilts or tales or traditional rituals, but once memory turned public it became altogether different structurally: a composite creation of many different groups and voices acting and reacting in relation to one another. Some groups had more control over the process than others, but no one had enough mastery to set the agenda or dictate the result. The process included both the production of public monuments and their subsequent use. The public monument, after all, was not just a rhetorical space where people debated image and symbol, but was also a real physical space where publics could gather and define themselves at ceremonies and rallies. In the late twentieth century we are all too familiar with the competition among groups for representation in this public process. The difference is that now many groups openly stand for themselves and their own interests, while in the nineteenth century almost everyone claimed to speak for the people as a whole. Collective memory was just as much a brew, but it had to be presented as the product of a united people.[6]

There is good reason to believe that even in the nineteenth century people saw through this popular fiction of the public monument; they were not so naive as their rhetoric seems to suggest. They fought over the sponsorship and design of public monuments precisely because they knew what power the monuments had to define the will of a people. But a funny thing happened once a monument was built and took its place in the landscape of people's lives: it became a kind of natural fact, as if it had always been meant to be. The monument's rhetorical claims of popular status became self-fulfilling prophecy. Begun as a project designed by particular actors for particular political ends, the monument was transformed into the image of the people—even if some part of the people took the unusual step of contesting that image. Public monuments exercised a curious power to erase their own political origins and become sacrosanct, a power that is still evident today whenever people rise to defend

monuments from change or attack.[7] The individuals and interest groups
that vied for representation in monumental space understood that there
was a great deal at stake in the form and content of public monuments.
They were competing not merely for the right to speak for the people but
for the chance to etch the people's voice in stone, where it would remain
forever.

The irony is that now, in the late twentieth century, we must work so
hard to recover that voice once thought to be eternal. If many monuments
from the past seem mute to us, they do still have stories to tell. But those
stories are not necessarily what the monuments were intended to tell us.
To make the monuments speak again we must question the often bland
surface they show the world. We must investigate who were the people
represented in and by monumental space, and how they competed to construct a history in the language of sculpture and in the spotlight of the
public sphere.

Throughout the nineteenth century, sculpture remained the public
monument's central medium of expression. Monuments were architectural, of course, some more conspicuously than others, and the architecture was usually inscribed with texts, some laconic and others expansive.
But the primary burden of the commemorative content fell on the sculptor, to condense the meaning of the monument into the deceptively simple
language of human form. Collosal statues of heroes, bas-reliefs of great
men in action, sleek female allegories for abstract principles—these were
the stock in trade of the public monument.

The medium's obsession with ideal human form made the whole subject of slavery extremely difficult for sculptors to represent. More than
any of the other arts, sculpture was embedded in the theoretical foundation of racism that supported American slavery and survived long after its
demise. For racism, like sculpture, centered on the analysis and representation of the human body. The concept of race emerged in late eighteenth-
and early nineteenth-century natural science as a way of explaining visible differences between bodies. Certain differences, notably of skin color,
facial structure, and hair type, came to be correlated with moral and intellectual capacities thought to be inherited and therefore shared by the
"race." The invention of the scientific notion of race transformed the intellectual understanding—indeed, the very perception—of the human
body.[8] Sculpture helped effect this transformation of the human body and
was in turn transformed by it. Sculpture's relation to the human body
had always been more direct and intimate than painting's: the sculptor's
main task was not to create illusions on a flat surface but to reproduce
three-dimensional bodies in real space. Sculptors could even create exact
molds of the human face and body in plaster, which gave their art a
unique scientific and documentary power that lasted even after the advent

of photography.[9] This helps explain why racial theorists looked to classical sculpture specifically as an empirical model of white racial superiority. Blumenbach, Camper, Cuvier, and other pioneers of the modern concept of race discussed and measured the ways in which the bodies and particularly the heads of darker races departed from the supposedly perfect lines and proportions of antique sculpture. The sculpture of antiquity thus became an authenticating document of a normative white body, a "race" of white men.[10]

One of the more notorious examples of the scientific appeal to classical sculpture appears in the most widely discussed racial treatise of the antebellum period, *Types of Mankind* (1854) by J. C. Nott and George R. Gliddon. At the end of the book, as a kind of coup de grace, the authors provided a "comparative series of likenesses" in which an engraved profile of a bust of Apollo was placed above a caricatured face of a "Negro" and a head of a chimpanzee (fig. 1.1).[11] The burden of the book and the image was to prove that mankind was divided into a hierarchy of racial types whose characteristics were permanent and unalterable. The image is a deck peculiarly stacked against the "Negro": the engraver has filled his face with a grotesque pattern of curving lines to represent its dark skin tone; and this caricatured head has been placed underneath an image not of an ordinary white man but of Apollo, a god. What is quite literally a comparison of god, man, and animal is nevertheless meant to be read as a comparison of white man, Negro, and animal.[12]

How was this semiotic sleight of hand possible? It has everything to do with the peculiar status of sculpture as definitive of the human body. The head of Apollo illustrated here is taken from what was perhaps the most celebrated classical sculpture of them all—the ancient statue in the Vatican known as the Apollo Belvedere (fig. 1.2). It is hard now to appreciate the power that this antique piece and a few dozen others like it once held in Western culture: this sculptural canon constituted nothing less than a benchmark in the concept of the human.[13] The Apollo in particular was a widely recognized standard of male beauty and, by implication, a lesson in the relationship of physical beauty to intellect and culture. As sculpture, this head managed to sustain a dual status. It was at once an ideal representation and the real thing, imaginary god and canonical measure of humanity. The viewer's ability to see the head as both at once (an ability the authors were certainly counting on) is testament to sculpture's peculiar power to invest stone or metal bodies with real living force. The "likeness" of the god therefore became an authentic document of superior physical form, and the label "Apollo Belvidere" brought with it the prestigious associations of high culture and classical civilization; all of these qualities were now regrouped not under the banner of antiquity but of whiteness—a whiteness emphasized by the engraver's minimally

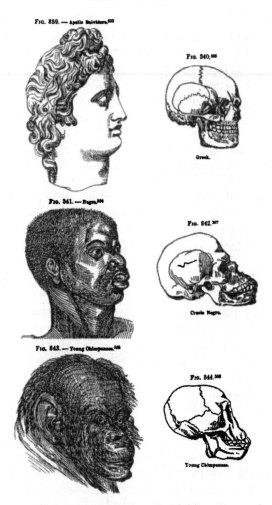

FIG. 339. — Apollo Belvidere.

FIG. 340.

Greek.

FIG. 341. — Negro.

FIG. 342.

Creole Negro.

FIG. 343. — Young Chimpanzee.

FIG. 344.

Young Chimpanzee.

1.1 J. C. Nott and George R. Gliddon, *Types of
Mankind* (Philadelphia,1854), 458.

hatched rendering of the white marble out of which this head was actually made. The upshot of this complex, though instantaneous, act of
viewing is that "white" and "man" become conflated, and the Negro
drops to a liminal status, wavering between the realm of man and the
realm of animals.[14]

Nott and Gliddon's illustration is far from an isolated example. It was
in fact based on a similar illustration from an earlier French text by Virey,
a student and popularizer of one of the pioneering racial taxonomists of
the Enlightenment, Buffon.[15] The Virey illustration used a head of Zeus,

1.2 Apollo Belvedere, Roman imperial copy of
a Greek bronze, Vatican.

which carried its own associations of naked might. The shift to Apollo
subtly (and effectively) shifted the axis of comparison from brute power
to more specifically aesthetic and intellectual qualities. In both cases, classical sculpture served as the benchmark of whiteness and, indeed, served
that function over and over again in the writings of the racial taxonomists. The importance of the aesthetic dimension of racial theory cannot
be overemphasized, and sculpture served as the aesthetic standard.[16] It
hardly needs to be stated that these theorists did not generally apply the
same rigorous standards of comparison to actual European heads and
bodies, but this was because it was taken for granted that white Europeans were the legitimate progeny of the ideal classical type.

It is hard to fathom today how a canon of ancient sculpture could be
used as scientific evidence, especially when that very canon has since
been discredited by art historians and archaeologists as a collection of
mostly inferior copies of lost originals. But such was the sway of this
canonical sculpture that plaster casts of the most important pieces were

disseminated across the Western world in a wide variety of instructional contexts, even in medical schools.[17] The high-cultural understanding of the human body was, in part, an understanding of classical sculpture and its continuing tradition in the practice of modern sculpture. The phenomenon I am describing was dynamic. Natural philosophers used classical sculpture to visualize and articulate a new racial construct, but the resulting theory transformed the understanding of classical sculpture by racializing it. This had a significant impact on modern sculpture, for nineteenth-century sculptors, whether deliberately neoclassical or not, worked in the shadow of classical sculpture. They drew after plaster casts, they lifted famous poses or gestures, they strove to emulate the supposedly classical qualities of restraint and decorum. Broadly speaking, classical sculpture still served as the benchmark of the sculptural and thereby defined what was not sculpture—most fundamentally, the body of the "Negro," the black antithesis of classical whiteness.

For the most part, then, the black body was relegated instead to the "lower" realm of representation reserved for it in Nott and Gliddon's illustration, the media of graphic illustration and popular caricature. In the early nineteenth century, African Americans or their mimics became much more visible in these media. In political cartoons, songbook covers, and illustrations of blackface performance, the ragged "darky" of the plantation and the uppity "coon" of the city became stock figures. These stereotypical black bodies—whether they represented black Americans or whites masquerading as such—were still conceived and pictured as the grotesque inversion of what Bakhtin called the "classical" or "canonical" body.[18] The canonical body, in his formulation, is a closed contour, without holes or protrusions; this conforms to the ideal figure in sculpture, which sculptors would often say could be rolled downhill without breaking (a principle honored in the breach, as the extended arm of the Apollo Belevedere demonstrates). By contrast, the grotesque body is characterized by swaying contours, wildly scattered limbs, protruding buttocks, spread-eagle legs, all devices that break the erect, contained profile of the canonical body. One of the best illustrations of the canonical/grotesque polarity in popular culture comes from the world of minstrelsy, where a sheet music cover of the 1840s contrasts the ideal body language of the standing white gentlemen with the comic motions of their seated blackface impersonations (fig. 1.3). The principle of opposition used here is very similar to the principle operating in the "scientific" illustration, where the vertical profile of the canonical face is contrasted with the supposedly jutting jaw of the more animal-like Negro. The body codes distinguishing the two types can be traced as far back as ancient theater, where the comically swaying bodies of slave characters were contrasted with the erect postures of the hero.[19]

1.3 Sheet music cover for *Songs of the Virginia Serenaders* (Boston, 1844).

This connection between the caricatured black body and the slave types of ancient theater is a reminder that race alone does not account for the peculiar status of African Americans in American sculpture. The point becomes clearer if we compare the representation of African with native Americans. Although racial thought demoted both groups to inferior status, the two "races" played very different roles in science as well as sculpture. The cranial measurements Nott and Gliddon relied upon to document racial difference showed little difference in size between Ameri-

1.4 Henry Kirke Brown,
Choosing of the Arrow, 1849,
bronze statuette.

can Indian skulls and African or African American skulls, yet it is consistently the "Negro" who appears in the text as the definitive sign of racial inferiority and thereby the standard of comparison for the white man.[20] In antebellum sculpture, while the figure of the Negro almost never appeared, the figure of the Indian appeared regularly, and often in classicizing pose or appearance. When sculptor Henry Kirke Brown in 1849 modeled a small bronze figure of an Indian with an arrow, he based it on the pose of the Apollo Belvedere (fig. 1.4).[21] Nor was the Indian confined to the darker material of bronze; Indian figures appeared repeatedly even in white marble, despite all its associations of purity and antiquity. Thus the opposition of "lower" race and the classic did not apply evenly across racial types. Both the native American and the African American were marginalized but their social histories, and their representations in culture were quite different. The dividing line between them, of course, was slavery. The African American body was indelibly scarred by it, whether literally by the whip or figuratively by a racist culture that specifically singled out African bodies for enslavement.[22] Sculpture in the classical tradition was devoted to the human body in its most noble and divine form. The body, in effect, was a metaphor for mastery, and slavery was

the very antithesis of that ideal. This is why the Indian, though marginalized by civilized society, still had an ideal dimension. He could be represented as courageous and independent, a symbol of a vanished or vanish-
ing American antiquity. The Negro as slave functioned more readily and
more evenly as a sign of lack—lack of power, lack of decorum, lack of
self-restraint, lack of humanity.[23]

Orlando Patterson's comparative study *Slavery and Social Death* use-
fully conceptualizes the slave as a liminal figure, poised on the boundary
between society and chaos, between man and animal. The situation of the
"Negro" in Nott and Gliddon's image perfectly illustrates this liminal
status. The subject of slavery actually permeates their text and especially
the anecdotal examples they use to buttress their cranial "data," so it is
not surprising that his opposition of white and black stands equally well
for the opposition of mastery and slavery. It is important to remember,
however, that Patterson's idea is a theoretical schema, in a sense concep-
tualizing the master's point of view—which is why the comparison with
Apollo could so well illustrate it.[24] In the varied textures of their actual
existence slaves were not liminal; they were fully human of course and
also part of society, important members of the master's household or of
the overall plantation community. Patterson's theoretical schema perhaps
helps account better for the representation of slavery than for its lived
reality.[25]

The reason, then, that African Americans loomed as the unspeakable
reality that sculpture barely dared to approach was not so much that
slavery was politically divisive, even though "politics" in this partisan
sense was certainly a factor.[26] The deeper reason is that the age-old status
of the slave combined with the newer concept of race created an extremely powerful cultural formation that rendered the African American
virtually the embodiment of what was *not* classically sculptural. In antebellum America, black slaves could sometimes be *imagined* as sculpture—for example, in Harriet Beecher Stowe's abolitionist novel *Dred*,
where she introduced the hero as "a tall black man, of magnificent stature
and proportions" whose "skin was intensely black, and polished like
marble."[27] Even more directly, in an essay on Sojourner Truth, Stowe
likened the ex-slave to the *Negro Woman at a Fountain*, a now lost statuette executed in the 1840s by Charles Cumberworth, who was active in
France and England.[28] In both cases she was describing escaped or fugitive slaves, heroic figures who had broken the bonds of the system that
debased them. They were heroes insofar as they refused to allow slavery
to define them, and the appeal to sculptural metaphors to describe them
simply confirmed that heroism. But these remained metaphors, rather
than actual works of sculpture: it was inflammatory enough merely to
describe a figure like Dred, but far more so to make the figure into marble

1.5 John Rogers, *Slave Auction*, 1859, plaster.

or bronze where it would stand, legitimated by all the weight of classical
sculptural tradition, as an incarnation of black humanity. Simply to represent black slaves in sculpture was in a sense to emancipate them.[29]

Before 1860 there are no known images whatsoever of African Americans, slave or free, in marble or bronze, the more permanent and prestigious materials of the sculptor's art. Portraits of African Americans did
appear in simplified linear form on slate gravestones dating to the eighteenth century; three such images of slaves or servants exist in the African
American section of Newport, Rhode Island's Common Burying Ground,
and there may possibly be other examples in cemeteries that have not
come to light.[30] One much better known work has survived in the form of
a small-scale plaster, about twelve inches high. This is John Rogers's
Slave Auction of 1859 (fig. 1.5).[31] The piece demonstrates well how
sculptors could use an essentially colorless medium to represent racial
"color." Since sculpture was understood then to be monochromatic,

sculptors could not represent skin color directly. But skin color was by no means a straightforward or consistent marker of racial identity; it was (and still is) shorthand for a whole array of racial characteristics encompassing face and hair, which the sculptor could exploit to the fullest. Thus in Rogers's work, the "black" man is identified not only by his position in front of the auctioneer's stand, but by the full lips and the compact curled hair. He stands erect, unbound and unchained, his trouser legs insistently vertical, his arms crossed defiantly, while separated from him by the auctioneer's stand is the softer, curvilinear grouping of mother and children, the mother characterized by conspicuously "whiter" hair and physiognomy. Like Stowe's Dred, the male figure embodies the idea of resistance, belying through the language of his body the debasement implied by the auctioneer's action; Rogers remarked about his model that "he would be a capital fellow in a Harpers ferry insurrection." The artist never intended the work for monumental sculpture. The piece belonged to a "lower" genre, that of the small-scale "image" as it was called, cheap desktop-scale works in plaster that were usually sold by Italian artisans who carried them around on trays from door to door. Rogers decided to have his hawked on the streets of New York by a "good looking negro" instead of an Italian, and by doing so the work attracted the attention of some local abolitionist newspapers and acquired a limited public reputation.[32]

Before the war one sculptor did expend a great deal of time and effort trying to introduce the figure of the slave into "high" sculpture in public space. This was Henry Kirke Brown, the modeler of Indians; his repeated efforts in the 1850s form the subject of chapter 2. Not until the 1870s did black slaves begin to appear on major public monuments in the United States. The sudden and unforeseen destruction of slavery brought about by the Civil War made this change possible, but it did not suddenly erase the dilemma slavery posed for sculpture. African Americans could not simply be included in sculpture once slavery ended; the very enterprise of sculpture would have to be reconstructed to make room for them and their history. The challenge facing sculpture paralleled the challenge facing society after the Civil War. Four million newly emancipated slaves could not just be absorbed into the preexisting fabric of society and culture: the fabric itself had to change. Yet in the immediate aftermath of the war, even that seemed possible. A new nation was born, and with it the promise of a new interracial order that would bury slavery forever. It was a time when the likes of William Dean Howells, writing in 1866, could actually suggest that the heroic image of an escaped slave be enshrined as a war memorial in the small towns of the nation's heartland.[33]

During this extraordinary moment in American history, the moment of "Reconstruction," many of America's most important sculptors did try to overcome the drag of accumulated tradition and fashion an interracial order in sculpture. Their efforts to bring the African American body into public sculpture largely failed. Most of their designs were never erected in public space, and today survive only as photographs or written descriptions buried in archives. Some designs, however, were seriously considered and even heavily publicized. One was erected prominently, at the close of Reconstruction: Thomas Ball's notorious image of Lincoln standing above a freed slave, adopted for the Freedmen's Memorial to Lincoln in Washington, D.C., of 1876 (fig. 4.1) and later for a replica in Boston. In this bizarre monument to emancipation, the black man enters sculpture only to reencode the racial hierarchy established in "scientific" illustration. Kneeling on the ground, the African American once again becomes the foil by which we measure the superiority of the white deity above him. But if this outcome seems predictable, the decade-long process of experimentation that preceded it is surprising. As we will see in chapters 3 and 4, the proliferation of monumental schemes commemorating the end of slavery not only reveals a time of great sculptural ferment but also illuminates the larger cultural contest in which monumental sculpture played a key part. If the theme of black slavery and its abolition could not enter sculpture without sculpture's reconstruction, that theme could not enter monumental sculpture without reconstructing the very image of the people.

During these critical years following the war, emancipation became the single most important commemorative subject. But sculptors struggling to represent emancipation in public monuments were out on the cultural forefront, working to visualize what was still unfolding, still unwritten. They were coming to grips with a new social paradigm that seemed clearly defined in principle but was yet to be absorbed into the hearts and minds of the national citizenry. Their task was profoundly paradoxical, at once conservative and progressive. They were charged with conserving the memory of something that had not yet taken form, that might never take form. Meanwhile the ex-Confederates were engaged in an opposite, though equally paradoxical, quest. As we will see in chapter 5, they were trying to commemorate their slaveholding secession without commemorating slavery, as if their whole war had had nothing to do with it. If the winners were trying to rewrite the future into the past, the losers were trying to rewrite the past in order to change their future.

Out of all this ferment, sculpture and its image of the people were both ultimately reconstructed, but not in the way the politics of Reconstruction demanded or in the way critics like William Dean Howells envisaged. As I argue in chapter 6, the destruction of slavery bore fruit not in a genuine liberation of the black body but in a transformation of the *white* hero and the *white* body. It was the very failure to create a real interracial order in sculpture that enabled the rise of new forms of public sculpture commemorating Anglo-American heroism. A whole new type of public monument emerged dedicated for the first time not to the illustrious hero but to the ordinary white man, the generic citizen-soldier who had fought in the war on both sides (see figs. 6.1–6.2). This redefined what commemoration was all about and what war memorials were meant to be. In 1866 Howells had proposed that the memorials of the war should be about emancipation; within a few years it was taken for granted that they were about soldiers—common white soldiers. While emancipation came to be inscribed not on the bodies of African Americans but on the body of Abraham Lincoln, so the moral imperatives of citizenship came to be inscribed on the bodies of white soldiers—profoundly reshaping the image of the soldier and the nation in the process.

The emergence of the common-soldier monument is part and parcel of the very process that has redefined race by making it the special property of minorities. To understand the far-reaching changes in nineteenth-century public monuments we must, in a sense, undo that process. We must no longer accept the standard histories of public sculpture in the United States that leave the issue of its racial content to the margins, to works like Ball's Emancipation Monument. The standard histories so completely accept the racial content of mainstream sculpture that they do not even see it. The history of the Emancipation Monument is indeed important—and it has never been properly told—but that history cannot be completed without the much larger story of how public sculpture itself failed to be emancipated.

To write this history, we must recognize, along with other recent scholars, that whiteness is itself a racial category. Whiteness, in Cornel West's words, is "parasitic" on blackness: the ruling category is unnecessary, even meaningless, without its negative counterpart.[34] Decades ago, Winthrop Jordan in his landmark study White over Black demonstrated how English colonists did not arrive in the New World as "white"; they gradually adopted this term to separate themselves from the "blackness" they had imported in the form of African slaves. More recently, David Roediger and Noel Ignatiev have examined the process by which nineteenth-century Irish immigrants overcame their identification with oppressed blacks and learned instead to be "white."[35] My study confirms that in the public sphere the creation and recreation of whiteness is inseparable from the creation and recreation of blackness. The marginalization of African America went hand in hand with the reconstruction of white America. African Americans could not be included or excluded in the landscape of public sculpture without changing the fabric of commemoration itself, without ultimately changing the face of the nation.

The story of the marginalized cannot therefore be understood without rewriting the history of what became dominant. This is why the current literature that seeks to document exclusion—from public art, public sculpture—does not go far enough.[36] The recognition of the racist power relations that drive such exclusions is a necessary first step. But that recognition does not amount to an analysis of the racial formation of dominant culture. If the subject of race teaches us anything, it must teach us to revise the history of what is *included* in the dominant culture. Recent books such as Toni Morrison's *Playing in the Dark* or Eric Sundquist's *To Wake the Nations* have put the issues of slavery and race at the heart of our national literature. It is high time that we do so with those forms of public art that have done so much to define the mission of the nation and the identity of its heroes.

A STUDY of this sort requires travel down many byroads, into military history, slave economies, art criticism, race relations, local politics, and so on. The documentary material I draw on is equally varied, offering information not only on artists but on the myriad cast of characters involved in public commemoration—politicians, ministers, intellectuals, veterans, activists of all kinds. If the nets of my investigation are spread wide, the results are nevertheless focused on the art forms of commemoration in the public sphere. By and large, these forms were sculpture—a medium with its own rules, idiosyncrasies, and possibilities. My working method therefore includes some detailed discussions of the medium and a few extended readings of particular works. Ultimately, the historical investigations of this book are successful only if they yield a new visual understanding of those concrete forms. It is my hope that, having gone through this process of historical and visual analysis, the reader will look with new eyes at the commemorative landscape that surrounds us and embodies our collective purpose.

CHAPTER TWO

EXPOSING SLAVERY

WHEN ARTISTS after the Civil War faced the great challenge of representing a society recently emancipated from slavery, they brought to the task
various assumptions and images that had been deeply ingrained by the
system of slavery and by the long campaign to abolish it. Most of the
artists working on public monuments in the first years after the war had
established their careers in the 1850s, when the conflict over slavery was
at its peak. We cannot understand the problems they faced, or the solutions they devised, without understanding the intense representational
battle fought over slavery itself. The images of slavery and emancipation
deployed during this battle had a lasting hold on popular and artistic
imagination alike.

The most influential and widely circulated imagery of slavery came out
of the abolitionist movement, first in Britain and then in the United States.
Recognizing the power of imagery to advance their cause, British abolitionists in the late eighteenth century devised an emblem that would become the single most common visual representation of a black slave. This
image of a young black man, kneeling and in chains, imploring "Am I
Not a Man and a Brother," originally appeared as a sculptural cameo
mass-produced by the Wedgwood factory in a size appropriate for wearing as jewelry (fig. 2.1).[1] The few earlier European emblems of slavery
had shown slaves as mere victims of their labor, chained to a yoke or
stooping to move a giant boulder.[2] The new image changed the focus
from submission to supplication. Neither crushed by the weight of oppression, nor driven by it to defiance, the Wedgwood figure was calculated to inspire a benevolent sympathy.

Benjamin Franklin wrote Wedgwood that "it may have an Effect equal
to that of the best written Pamphlet in procuring favour to those oppressed people."[3] British abolitionists agreed, and after they succeeded in
ending slavery in their colonies, one of them advised Americans:

> Thou must do as we have done in England. A sculptor came among us with
> images, in black marble, of an African child kneeling in chains. Almost every
> abolitionist purchased one, and when a man came to us to vote for him as
> member of parliament, we held up the image and asked, "What hast thou
> done for *this*?"[4]

2.1 *Am I Not a Man and a Brother*, circa 1787,
Wedgwood brooch, jasperware set in silver.

2.2 *Am I Not a Man and a
Brother*, 1837, woodcut.

This was probably a small-scale figure inspired by the Wedgwood design, but in any case its sculptural presence was critical to the abolitionist strategy. As they performed their sculptural puppet show, abolitionists literally acted out their own intervention on behalf of the "African child," the helpless slave.

American abolitionists translated this sculptural image into the medium of the popular print (fig. 2.2). Reproduced on an astonishing array of household materials and objects, from books and broadsides to pincushions and pen wipers, the kneeling, chained slave became one of the most familiar images in antebellum America.[5] "Remember the slave," abolitionists demanded. The function of the image in its various domestic uses and settings was to force the slave's plight into constant view, so that it would never be forgotten even where slavery had long since disappeared. Printmakers supplemented this canonical image with a wide range of pictures of cruel masters and suffering slaves (fig. 2.3). Helped by steam-powered presses introduced in the 1830s, antislavery imagery became so pervasive that almost any visual representation of slavery could be suspected as abolitionist. Crude woodcuts depicting slaves on an auction block, used to advertise slave sales in Southern newspapers, were labeled "incendiary" antislavery propaganda when they were merely reprinted in abolitionist periodicals.[6] Certain conventional signifiers such as chains and the liberty cap, which had been more generalized symbols of tyranny and freedom during the Revolutionary era, now became closely linked with the antislavery cause. By the 1850s, for example, the sculptor Hiram Powers was being denounced as an abolitionist simply because his allegorical figure of America had broken chains under foot.[7]

The power of the abolitionist imagery was so strong that it made it very difficult for those sympathetic to slavery to create any convincing alternative imagery of the institution. In fact, it was problematic for the proslavery forces to make any visual representation of their system at all. By the mid-nineteenth century much of the traditional imagery of slavery had already been appropriated by abolitionists. The traditional images had not flinched from the essential power relations of the system: slavery entailed the subjection of one person's body to the will of another, always under the condition or threat of violence. The representation of slavery as extreme domination had its roots in antiquity and flourished in baroque Europe in public monuments to rulers. In Pietro Tacca's 1620 monument to Grand Duke Ferdinand in Livorno (fig. 2.4), the contorted, abased, immobilized figures of the captive slaves—who in this case are Turks—recall the archetypal images of suffering published in emblem books of the period. Their misery actually worked to glorify the heroic body of the captor above them, an opposition reinforced by the contrasting colors of the sculptural materials of bronze below and marble above. Stripped of

Illustrations of the American Anti-Slavery Almanac for 1840.

Nurtures Hospitality.—New-York some months ago. [The Slave steals out of the Slave State, and his chains fall. A Free State, with another chain, stands ready to re-enslave him.]

"Our Peculiar Domestic Institutions."

Burning of M'Intosh at St. Louis, in April, 1836.

Showing how slavery improves the condition of the female sex.

The Negro Pew, or "Free" Seats for Black Christians.

Mayor of New-York selling a Coloured Vaccine to a coloured Man.

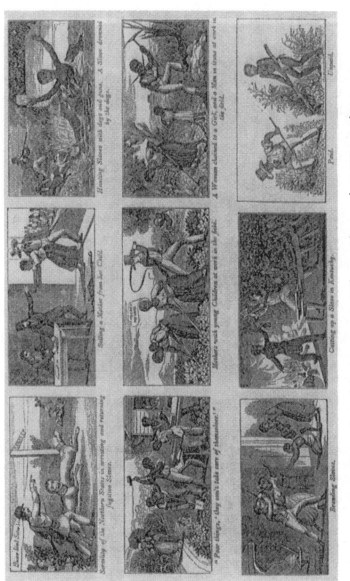

2.3 *Illustrations of the American Anti-Slavery Almanac for 1840, woodcut.*

2.4 Pietro Tacca, Monument to Grand Duke Ferdinand, 1620,
Livorno, Italy.

their own power and honor, the slaves served as attributes of those same
qualities in the master-monarch.[8] This formula still echoed in painted
portraiture of masters with their slaves in eighteenth-century America.[9]
But by the nineteenth century that image of domination had been transformed into a critique of slavery. In the slaveholders' world, signs of coercion—manacles, neck collars, chains—now had to be suppressed because
of abolitionist associations. As soon as images began to suggest the subjection of one body to another, they were already straying into abolitionist territory.

    The easier alternative for the proslavery side was to attack abolition-
ism rather than to refashion the image of slavery. Antiabolitionist prints
began to appear in the early nineteenth century, and they relied heavily on
the tactic of caricature, aimed especially at free blacks. Some of the most

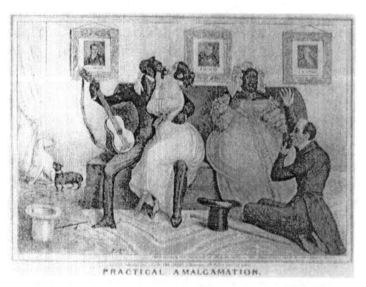

PRACTICAL AMALGAMATION.

2.5 Edward W. Clay, *Practical Amalgamation*, 1839, lithograph.

enduring visual stereotypes of African Americans emerged in this campaign. Perhaps most common were the "uppity" blacks who aped genteel
manners in absurdly distorted ways, who marched pompously in silly
uniforms, who took jobs belonging to whites, who seduced white women
(fig. 2.5).[10] Instead of picturing slavery's blessings, these images represented the terrors of emancipation. The sexual scenes were the most powerful weapon because they conjured up an image of emancipation as
moral and racial anarchy, with whites and blacks rushing lasciviously to
"amalgamate" despite their supposed racial enmity.

By avoiding the problem of representing slavery, these images only
compounded it. They supplied a vocabulary of racist caricature meant to
drag the image of African Americans down to a level where they seemed
fit only for slavery. But the proslavery argument at midcentury was moving in the opposite direction, determined to prove that Southern slavery
was not degrading blacks but actually elevating them. Since the 1830s
proslavery apologists in the South had been articulating ever more emphatically the "positive good" thesis, as it has come to be known from
famous speeches in 1837–38 by South Carolina Senator John C. Calhoun; Calhoun and others argued that slavery was not an evil but a Christian institution, which exerted a civilizing influence on the Africans
brought under its shelter.[11] Under American slavery, their argument
went, the African had changed "from an ignorant and idle barbarian . . .
into an industrious, orderly, quiet, and useful laborer."[12] The racist caricature, on the other hand, trafficked in the age-old stereotypes of the slave

as feckless, lewd, irresponsible, and lazy; these stereotypes had always been invoked to rationalize the violence and cruelty of the master class.[13] While the old stereotypes still persisted in the modern system of slavery, of course, they were no longer quite compatible with its ideological needs. Forced to defend themselves against the abolitionist critique, slaveholders had to make the practice of slavery seem consistent with the ideals of a modern democratic republic that no longer sanctioned the outright coercion and violence traditional to slave systems. A new image of slavery, and a new stereotype of the slave, were needed. This is where the medium of public sculpture, ironically enough, had a potential role to play.

Sculpture in the United States had not been appropriated by the abolitionists, despite the great success of the Wedgwood cameo in Britain. There was essentially no abolitionist sculpture, certainly nothing that occupied public space. Rogers's *Slave Auction*, as we have seen, appeared very late and only then in the privatized, lower-status medium of the small plaster image. The figure of the black slave was so antithetical to the theory and practice of ideal sculpture that even sculptors sympathetic to the cause steered clear of it in their work. The only antebellum work in marble that came close to abolitionism was the *Greek Slave* (1844) by Hiram Powers, one of the most celebrated and discussed works of art in the nineteenth century (fig. 2.6). While the *Greek Slave* was not commissioned as a public piece—Powers made it for sale as parlor sculpture—it took on a public life when it was widely toured and viewed by hundreds of thousands in the 1840s and 1850s.[14] The work did not depict an American slave, of course, but a young Greek woman captured by Turkish slavers in the war of the 1820s, and offered on the auction block for use in a harem. However, despite the Orientalized narrative, the prominence of the chains draped across the slave's genitals could not but fail to inspire abolitionist interpretations.[15] One critic in the *Christian Inquirer*, for example, saw behind the fiction of the *Greek Slave* the reality of white-skinned Creole women being auctioned in the slave markets of New Orleans: "Every day does our own sister city of New Orleans witness similar exposures, with a similar purpose. Let no one keep down the natural promptings of his indignation by the notion of wooly heads and black skins."[16] The racial boundaries of American slavery were in reality so blurred, the critic argued, that even the canonical white beauty of the *Greek Slave* might be contemplated at an American slave market. The lesson of the *Greek Slave*, then, was the essential depravity of all slavery, which not even racial prejudice could completely obscure. Elizabeth Barrett Browning suggested a similar lesson in her 1850 poem on the statue, in which she urged the "fair stone" to appeal "From God's pure heights of beauty against man's wrong" and to "Catch up in thy divine face, not alone / East griefs but west, and strike and shame the strong, / By thunders

2.6 Hiram Powers,
Greek Slave, 1847, marble.

of white silence, overthrown."[17] Here, it seems, she hopes that the very purity and silence of the marble—qualities prized as much in ideal sculpture as in bourgeois womanhood—will voice the crime of slavery and shame a race that is, like the statue, caught in its own "white silence."

Given the pervasive influence of abolitionist imagery, it is hardly surprising that abolitionists tried to claim the work for their own. What is more surprising is that Southerners refused to denounce it, despite the inflammatory motif of the chains. Some of Powers's most important patrons, in fact, were wealthy South Carolina slaveholders; one of them bought an early version of the work and others praised it as a masterpiece.[18] Slaveholders did not try to suppress it even though they were busy censoring anything that whiffed of abolitionism in the popular press. The statue was successfully toured in several Southern cities, not only in South Carolina but all the way to the white-slave center of New Orleans.[19] White Southerners obviously refused to view the work as an allegory of their slave system. For them, as for most viewers North and

South, the sculpture had a different reference altogether. It was the very archetype of the ideal. Transcending the shocking reality of the subject, it evoked a "higher" spiritual truth: the purity of the soul despite the violation of the body, the strength of Christian resignation in the face of material suffering.[20]

To make his slave ideal, Powers had to treat the sculptural body very carefully. First of all, he made it the very exemplar of whiteness. The neoclassical visage, with the facial angle prominently displayed by her turned head, recalled the archetypes of whiteness used by racial theorists and thereby removed the figure as far as possible from the popular conception of blackness. Second, Powers made the figure female. Had this been a nude man in chains, his victimization would have emasculated him. As ex-slave Frederick Douglass explained, "human nature is so constituted that it cannot honor a helpless man, although it can pity him; and even that it cannot do long, if the signs of power do not arise."[21] In a patriarchal society a helpless woman like the *Greek Slave* is not a despised creature; a helpless man is. Under extreme domination, she has not forfeited but in fact has *proved* her womanly virtue, which is why the statue could become in so many viewers' minds an allegory for woman in general.[22] Third, Powers had to purge the white female body of the material signs of enforced labor or sex. This was a body at once substantial and ethereal, which he fashioned by devising a subtly balanced treatment of the nude female form. The delicately interlocked contours of the figure move the eye slowly upward, while the extremely sensitive finishing of its marble skin displays the underlying form of bone and muscle and flesh without rendering the kind of exterior detail that would make the surface too erotically tangible.[23]

Powers's work thus becomes a phantasm of slavery: in it the degraded status of the slave is reversed and rendered ideal. Structurally speaking, the *Greek Slave* is not really a slave at all. In Powers's narrative, she has not yet experienced the "social death" that Patterson argues is essential to slavery.[24] American slaves were stripped of their old African names and identities but still remained stigmatized by their association with barbarism. The situation of the *Greek Slave* is in no way comparable. Though stripped naked, she retains a locket and a cross on the stump beside her, two critical cues to her social and religious identity. She has lost the protections of family and marriage but her purity lives on in the white beholder's recognition that she came from a world where those institutions were valued, and that she retains a claim on them in some way through her faith in God. The *Greek Slave*, in effect, belongs to the social and cultural world of the white audience. The structure of American slavery has been inverted: the slave is the perfected image of the audience, while the slaveowner is the dark other. It was not the immorality of slavery per se that charged this narrative but the indignity (and excitement) of that racial inversion; she/us is stripped by *them*.

For Southern slaveholders, the great lesson of Powers's *Greek Slave* was that in the medium of high sculpture abolitionists did not necessarily control the imagery of domination. The reality of slavery could be transcended; the figure of the slave could be idealized. Even if Powers accomplished this by an outright inversion of the slave's status, he still managed to make that inversion credible to an immense public audience. The question that remained was whether black slavery itself could be idealized. To us this possibility seems patently absurd from the outset, but to the proslavery faction their very survival depended on it. It was the political and aesthetic challenge that underlay all their claims to civilization. The political challenge was whether the notion of slavery's degradation of body and spirit could be replaced by the modern notion of slavery's "blessings"; the aesthetic challenge was whether the black body could be freed from its conventional debasement without somehow suggesting an allegory of emancipation.

It was in South Carolina, the center of proslavery activism, that this dual challenge finally bore fruit in a remarkable public project designed to expose the Southern system of slavery to posterity's view.[25] Just before the Civil War the state embarked on a huge sculptural undertaking, the largest outside Washington, D.C., for its lavish new State House in Columbia: a central pediment on the building's front devoted to black slaves laboring in the rice and cotton fields. Never completed and therefore virtually unknown today, this project was unprecedented in several respects. It was the first and last ambitious effort by the proslavery culture in America to represent its defining institution in public art. Black field laborers, so lowly in social standing that their very humanity was called into question, were suddenly to be elevated to the highest point of the proudest building in the staunchest slave state of the Union. The irony of the undertaking only deepens when we learn that the sculptor, Henry Kirke Brown, was actually a Northern abolitionist, morally committed to making the figure of the "Negro" visible in public sculpture. How are we to explain the paradox of an abolitionist sculptor working on the eve of Civil War, in the very hotbed of proslavery politics, to create the first image in public sculpture affirming slave labor? Answering that question will expose some of the basic paradoxes of slavery and its representation in antebellum America.

BOTH political and aesthetic convictions drove Henry Kirke Brown to the subject of slavery. As an abolitionist he wanted to use his art form to make slavery more publicly visible, more difficult to ignore in official life. He hoped "that something in Art might awaken a national feeling in regard to [the slave's] importance."[26] As an advocate of a distinctively "national" sculpture, he found the figure of the black slave intriguing because it was a distinctly American type that had not been seen before in sculpture. From the beginning Brown's position was paradoxical: he wanted to represent in permanent form the very institution he hoped would disappear; he wanted to profit artistically from the Americanness of slavery while he hoped to make America free of it.

Brown was an extremely ambitious sculptor who, like Powers, had gone to Italy in the 1840s to establish a career in ideal marble sculpture. But unlike Powers, Brown came back to the United States determined to produce a more recognizably national sculpture. Brown himself characterized his artistic repatriation this way:

> I feel that my humble mission is here, and I begin to rejoice in my freedom from old masters both ancient and modern; I have received from them my patrimony and have gone out into the world to work for myself, and to work back if possible into the simple boyish love of nature which I came near losing sight of.[27]

The mixing of metaphors here, of both maturation and regression, release from tradition and return to nature, owes much to an already established rhetoric of America as New World nation. That it was also a rhetoric of slavery and freedom—Brown the New World artist struggling for emancipation from "old masters"—shows how deeply the political issue permeated American cultural discourse of the time. Yet creating a new American sculpture did not mean discarding the "patrimony" of the classical tradition. That tradition still directed Brown to the human figure as the basis of sculpture and it shaped how he saw, posed, and modeled the figure, even when he went so far as to sketch real Indians in their "natural" environment.[28] What Brown wanted to avoid was not Greek taste, but Greek goddesses and slaves. He wanted to do away with mythological figures and classically draped allegories identified as such by conventionalized attributes. Instead he wanted to find legitimate sculptural forms to represent American subjects in American costumes holding American tools and American goods.[29] In this campaign the subject of the black slave took on the quality of an obsession.

Brown's first attempt to represent slavery came in an elaborate design he modeled in 1855 for the House pediment of the U.S. Capitol in Washington, a design that survives today in a studio photograph of the small-scale plaster model (fig. 2.7).[30] The pediment for the new Senate wing had already been commissioned to the expatriate sculptor Thomas Crawford, but the pediment for the new House wing remained unspoken for and it was clearly an unrivaled opportunity for an ambitious sculptor to put his stamp on this most important of national structures. For Brown it was the

2.7 Henry Kirke Brown, model for House pediment of U.S. Capitol, 1855, plaster (now lost).

chance to make a grand design "representative of the life of the nation."[31] In his model he ruthlessly pared away classical signifiers and substituted instead a range of recognizably contemporary types who staked their claim to national existence by engaging in productive work. His one allegorical figure, the central statue of America, has no props and attributes and signifies beneficent nationality simply through the gesture of her upraised arms, which extend a sheltering curtain of drapery. The male figures in the wings represent what Brown called "the material interests" of the nation. Farmer, fisherman, and hunter represent the means of subsistence on the right, with the farmer (identified by the plow) occupying the highest and most central position within the hierarchy. On the left are represented interlocking components of trade: an explorer leaning on a globe; a child holding a sailboat, who (according to Brown) "is the promise of commerce and navigation"; a seminude black man sitting on the archetypal cash crop, a bale of cotton; and a fur trapper kneeling by his prey. The pediment thus assembles a regionally diverse array of material interests which embraces not only yeomen agriculture and Eastern commerce but also the contributions of the Western frontier (the outermost figures) and of the plantation South (the black man).[32]

Yet within this apparently unified scheme the figure of the black man creates a profoundly disjunctive note. He is a slave among free laborers, his status clearly indicated by his nudity, his pose, and his physical link to the cotton crop, which undergirded the whole Southern system of slavery. The only comparable figure on the pediment is Brown's "distressed foreigner" who nevertheless kneels under the protection of America, in the expectation of citizenship, while the slave has no such prospects, no such relation to the central grouping. Brown chose a male slave to relate the figure to his male-defined arena of production, even though it was well known that female slaves also worked as agricultural laborers; by doing so he drew a sharp contrast between his figure and the *Greek Slave*, whose implied use value is for pleasure not for economic production. It is interesting to compare his figure of the producer-slave with that of the farmer-citizen, the only other agricultural producer depicted in the group. They share a unique compositional role: in both figures one upper arm exactly lines up with the angle of the pediment and therefore reinforces and contains the triangular shape of the whole. But of course the farmer *stands*, his weight firmly planted, his hand propped securely on his hip, while the slave *sits*, bent over on himself, chin on hand, his legs crossed, his right arm wrapped behind his back. The pose recalls both the traditional image of suffering found in emblem books and the slave type familiar from ruler monuments, with one important difference: Brown's figure is unbound.[33] It seems that Brown, choosing to dispense with the conventional devices of restraint, has instead represented the slave immobilized by and in his own body; he would have to uncoil completely simply to get up. Brown thus avoids the obvious abolitionist signifiers of chains or manacles and at the same time arrives at a solution to the problem of representing enslavement that is thoroughly sculptural because it is contained within the body's form. By thus encoding alienation within the slave's body, the sculptural signs make a political point: the slave has produced a major source of national wealth like the other figures, but unlike them he is cut off from the economic and civic rewards of that productive act.

When Brown offered his design to the official in charge of the construction of the Capitol, according to Brown that official simply placed his finger on the figure of the slave and said "I think no Southerner would consent to it." To which Brown retorted, "But that is an institution of the country, how else can it be represented?"[34] In effect Brown was offering a clever gambit. If Southern masters truly believed slavery to be a blessing for all, Brown reasoned, those masters should be proud to see it exposed in public alongside commerce, yeomen agriculture, and the other institutions of American economic life. But, of course, at the same time Brown was not merely exposing the institution of slavery but representing it in a particular way. True, the figure of the slave was not untraditional in its formal type, but Brown had recontextualized the figure in a completely untraditional way. By linking the image of the downcast slave with figures of independent men actively engaged in their own work or in the civic life of the polity, Brown's design juxtaposed the institution of slavery with the free-labor vision of a republic of self-determined producers. To make the point clear Brown omitted any intermediate categories of labor that might have presented conceptual difficulties. There was no representation of factory work in the urban North, no suggestion of wage labor (with the possible exception of the "distressed foreigner," who in any case is in a transitional state). A proslavery viewer might well have argued that Brown had stacked the deck against him: the figure of the slave appeared so anomalous only because the design misrepresented American capitalism as a whole and failed to show Northern production in its proper light.[35]

Brown's design never did come to light, though, because it was summarily rejected and, even after Brown tried to accommodate the Capitol officials by replacing the offending figure of the slave with the figure of a miner, he still did not get the commission. Here the matter might have been dropped forever had not Brown's career path taken an unpredictable shift. The sculptor had apparently made connections with South Carolina art patrons as early as the 1840s, when he was still in Italy. In the 1850s, while in Washington, he expanded his connections among these planter-politicians of the most extreme proslavery state in the

Union.[36] They were also some of the most important early supporters of American sculpture; they had helped launch the careers of Hiram Powers and Clark Mills, two of the best-known American sculptors at mid-century. They had admired the *Greek Slave* and brought it to South Carolina.[37] They also had grand designs for their new State House in Columbia—the building project that for years had been absorbing nearly half of South Carolina's entire state budget.[38] For reasons that may never be known, Brown was asked in the spring of 1859 to work on this project, at first on the modest task of creating portrait medallions of two famous spokesmen for slavery, Robert Hayne and George McDuffie. To lure Brown, the supervisor of construction dangled the possibility of more ambitious work, specifically the commission for the ninety-foot-long pediment on the building's facade (fig. 2.8).[39] Without any comparable commissions from official Washington on the horizon, Brown decided to travel to Columbia to begin work on this conspicuous proslavery undertaking.

What happened next is impossible to reconstruct with any certainty from the fragmentary record that survives. But Brown's longtime friend, the abolitionist William Morris Davis of Philadelphia, recalled in an essay written twenty years later that while Brown was in Columbia he worked out a design on his own initiative for the huge pediment project. In Davis's story, Brown worked "solitary and alone, in the secret chamber of his studio" in accordance with a "vow" he had made years earlier "to place the Negro Slave in marble or bronze on Southern soil."[40] The design he created emblazoned plantation slaves across most of the pediment's surface (fig. 2.9). When he presented the design to the committee in charge, Davis reported that "silence fell upon the assembled judges as they looked on the bold conception." They asked Brown to elaborate on the design, and according to Davis, Brown explained that monuments "are prized as faithful records of the times in which they were made." So:

> In this spirit I have wrought to transmit to your posterity a faithul record of the times in which we live. I have endeavored to record in enduring form the institutions and productions of your native state, and a testimonial to present and future generations of your conviction that the institutions thus portrayed are the most favorable to an advanced civilization, as well as a more perfect human government. This you believe, and are prepared to defend. I simply give art expression to your convictions.[41]

Whether Brown actually couched the argument in these terms we can never know. Nor do we know who the actual judges were. But we do know that he won the approval of the men who mattered—powerful slaveholders like Wade Hampton and John Preston, who had formed their ideas about sculpture from works like the *Greek Slave*. Brown had finally captured the sort of career-making commission sculptors dreamed

THE NEW STATE HOUSE, COLUMBIA, S. C.

2.8 View of South Carolina State House, circa 1860, woodcut.

2.9 Henry Kirke Brown, model for pediment of South Carolina State House, 1860–61, plaster (now lost).

2.10 Brown, model for pediment of South Carolina State House, 1860–61.
Detail of left wing.

about. He even moved with his wife to Columbia in 1860 to oversee the
execution in marble, which he expected would take several years to complete and would finally free him of personal debt.[42]

Brown's model (again, known only through photographs) is a startling
and unprecedented leap from his earlier pediment proposal (figs. 2.9–
2.12). Instead of downplaying the subject of slavery in the South Carolina
project, he actually multiplied the figures of slaves (to eight in all) and
made them the major subject of the composition rather than a lone dissonant note within it. Of the two registers in the pediment, the allegorical or
"ideal" in the center and the contemporary or "real" in the wings, the
register of the real is entirely defined by slaves, with the sole exception of
one white horseman. The slave in this design no longer serves as the sign
of negation, of alienation from the social order, but appears as active
contributor to the commonwealth, his body shown engaged in productive
labor rather than restrained from it by outside force or by inner misery.

In these remarkable scenes slaves attend to two of South Carolina's
most important cash crops, rice on the left (fig. 2.10) and cotton on the
right (fig. 2.11). Seven male slaves appear, alternating between fully
clothed and shirtless figures. The two outermost figures, wedged into the
narrowest part of the pediment, stretch out and slumber, while the remaining figures kneel or bend over their tasks. They are engaged specifically in the harvest—the removal of the marketable crop from the fields
and its preparation for transport and hence trade. On one side a man
kneels to pick the cotton and two others carry off a bale of it; on the other
side a man cuts rice stalks with a scythe and another stacks the sheaves.
In addition, one black woman holding a basket of cotton appears on the

2.11–12 Brown, model for pediment of South Carolina State House, 1860–61. *Above*: Detail of right wing. *Below*: Detail of central section.

right; the model of production is still male dominated and the female figure probably is included only because the presence of slave women in the fields was so undeniable. Finally, a white man on a horse, posed like the ancient equestrian Marcus Aurelius, gestures in command on the left. Brown seems to have inserted the equestrian figure, awkwardly shrunk to fit inside the pediment, to stand for the governing paternal elite; the lone white male among a group of black slaves, this diminutive figure becomes the dissonant note within the composition.

2.13 George Cruikshank, *Emmeline about to Be Sold
to the Highest Bidder*, illustration in H. B. Stowe,
Uncle Tom's Cabin (London, 1852), p. 290.

In the allegorical section at the apex of the pediment (fig. 2.12), Brown
eschewed the disciplined simplicity of his Capitol design and jammed the
panel with signifiers of all kinds—a lion, an eagle, a palmetto tree, shields,
sunbeams, an anchor, a sword. Brown may have hoped thereby to supplement and stabilize the meaning of the slave scenes so that his proslavery patrons would feel reassured. In the center is a figure of Hope, on the
right is Justice, and on the left Liberty, identified by the liberty pole with
cap on which she leans.[43] This last allegory is the most peculiar and daring of the group, since it is a reappropriation of an emblem that had
become commonly associated with abolitionism. The liberty pole and cap
appear for example on an antislavery society emblem of 1840, and in a
Cruikshank illustration for *Uncle Tom's Cabin*, juxtaposed ironically
with a slave on the auction block (fig. 2.13).[44] The association was so

common in fact that Secretary of War Jefferson Davis worked assiduously in the 1850s to keep the liberty cap off any decoration of the U.S. Capitol.[45] The slaveholder elite routinely invoked the concept of liberty in their public defenses of slavery; they argued that enslaving black laborers not only freed whites from the forms of industrial servitude common in Europe and the North, but freed the blacks themselves from responsibility and cares. Yet this may be the only time that slaveholders adopted the standard visual symbol for this concept so often broadcast in speech.

In one sense Brown's gambit seemed to remain unchanged. He was challenging the convictions of the proslavery elite; if slavery was indeed the "safe and stable basis" of their institutions, as South Carolina's own Calhoun had argued in his "positive good" speech, why should they be afraid to emblazon their State House with it? What was uttered in public rhetoric inside government buildings should be utterable in public sculpture on government buildings. Yet the new pediment clearly changed the stakes enormously. Brown was not merely showing the presence of slavery, as he had in the Washington design. Here he was creating perhaps the first work in the history of western art that sought to represent slavery as integral to the social order. Slaves, of course, had appeared in visual representation as actors in daily life or as symbols of the ruler's power, but the bold assertion of the South Carolina pediment—slavery as a productive system central to the socioeconomic structure of civilization—has no obvious parallels in earlier representational traditions.[46] Any elements extraneous to the slave economy were rigorously excluded from his design. Gone are the hunters, fishermen, and yeomen, indeed any types whose work would suggest economies of self-sufficiency, even though South Carolina certainly had plenty of these types especially in the upcountry. Instead the pediment focuses solely on the plantation economy, supported by slaves, with its production of staple crops for export. It is the crop that explains the figures' roles and integrates their disparate actions into one coherent productive system. Harvest is the chosen narrative because this makes palpable the link between the slaves' labor and the production of surplus value. This explains why the left scene is devoted to rice even though rice fields occupied a relatively small swath of the state: those few lands produced well over half the nation's whole crop and created an enormously rich and powerful planter class in coastal South Carolina.[47] The slaves pictured here create the surplus wealth, which in turn maintains an elite able to acquire the refinements of a superior society and civilization; in a real if indirect way, the labor of slaves on plantations made possible the very pediment on which they were represented.

It is difficult to exaggerate how unorthodox this pediment was. It was not simply the appearance of the slave in Southern public sculpture that was startling, but the assertion of the civic importance of slave labor, which had profound implications. This assertion hardly sat comfortably with the old stereotype of the slave as childlike and incapable, a stereotype to which the master class still resorted precisely to deny its dependence on the slave. Masters often liked to think of the slave as a ward, whom they indulgently tolerated, rather than a skilled worker, on whom they depended.[48] Indeed, in the traditional ruler image of the bound, captive slave, the ruler of course does not depend in any way on the slave's ability to act; the ruler's dominance immobilizes the slave altogether. In Brown's pediment the slave's activity is crucial, becoming the necessary complement of civilization.

It is interesting and not too surprising that the one official description of the pediment I have been able to find continues the old tradition of denial by refusing to acknowledge even the presence of slavery in the pediment. Even though the officials had accepted a design representing slave labor, they were still unable or unwilling to articulate the fact of that labor. The description, quoted in *Harper's Weekly* in December 1860, notes that the pediment will consist of fourteen colossal figures "representing the State and its principal agricultural industry—the cotton and rice culture, with its accessories."[49] Of course, it is through this term "accessories" that the laborers are at once suggested and erased, as if the cotton and rice grow themselves with just a little outside help. But this elision does point to a real absence of signifiers of slavery within Brown's design. To put it more plainly, how can we be sure that the figures are slaves? There are no chains, ropes, whips, brands. The conventional markers of slavery, as we have seen, tend toward the negation of the human body's abilities or in some other way suggest physical violence to the body. In a work ostensibly justifying modern slavery Brown could not apply markers associated either with the abolitionist critique of the system or with the older celebration of slavery as the conqueror's prerogative in warfare. Brown instead relied on the racial markers of "color" available to the sculptor—hair, lips, nose, profile. In South Carolina blackness was virtually equated with slavery. Whites were a minority there: the state population had the highest percentage of slaves of any in the Union (57 percent in 1860). Moreover, the proportion of free blacks to the total black population was very low (2.4 percent in 1860).[50] Brown's images of blacks engaged in the production of cash crops would be read automatically as slaves. Slavery here is the invisible extension of race, an extension made through the viewer's awareness of the social context.

Brown's decision to bypass the obvious attributes of slavery did not solve his representational problems, however. He still had to find a way to introduce the bodies of slave laborers into public sculpture without either degrading them or emancipating them. He had to sustain the nobility of the whole while marking the inferior status of the majority of his figures. Mockery and caricature were not appropriate options in this case. Indeed, the decision to hire a Northern sculptor to represent slaves on such a conspicuous monument can only be explained as a deliberate effort by a segment of slave society to distance itself publicly from those characteristic stereotypes of the slave, which ultimately undermined the prestige of the institution itself. The South Carolina elite wanted instead to articulate a new kind of ideal slave system, productive and harmonious, molding the slave into an "industrious, orderly, quiet, and useful laborer." But this was completely uncharted representational territory.

One of the only popular images that tried explicitly to represent the blessings of slavery did so by imagining slavery without labor: blacks dance and frolic in the foreground as the masters in the background explain that their system frees the slaves from responsibility and overwork (fig. 2.14). Depicting slaves actually at work was far more problematic. While there were some neutral images of slave labor made for private consumption, public imagery was much rarer.[51] For a proslavery audience in particular, the issue was explosively dangerous since it threatened to expose the basic paradoxes of slavery, which the proslavery ideology worked so hard to overcome. The problem lay in the nature of labor itself. Hegel is perhaps the first philosopher to have theorized what free-labor abolitionists took for granted: that work begets consciousness. "Thus precisely in labor," Hegel argued, "where there seemed to be merely some outsider's mind and ideas involved, the bondsman becomes aware, through this rediscovery of himself by himself, of having a being and a mind of his own."[52] For the slaves work was at once an outside burden, imposed by the master's will, and an internal expression of skill and productivity, sometimes even creativity.[53]

This dialectic of slave labor could easily split into opposing paradigms. On one end of slavery's spectrum, that usually associated with gang labor in large plantations, work seemed to dehumanize, transforming slaves according to many contemporary observers into something like beasts of burden. This is how the old iconography of slavery represented labor, by showing the slave yoked liked an ox or stooped to engage in a crushing task best left to beasts. On the other end of the spectrum, that associated with the more privileged agricultural or artisanal class of slaves, work seemed to humanize, to demonstrate that slaves had the competence and temperament to be free. Abolitionists, in their polemical imagery, could work either possibility into an indictment of slavery. The *American Anti-Slavery Almanac for 1840* (see fig. 2.3), for example, includes an image of black men busily engaged in woodworking, blacksmithing, and gardening while a white couple looks on and remarks stupidly, "Poor things,

2.14 *Slavery As It Exists in America; Slavery As It Exists in England*, 1850, lithograph.

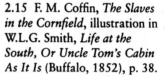

2.15 F. M. Coffin, *The Slaves in the Cornfield*, illustration in W.L.G. Smith, *Life at the South, Or Uncle Tom's Cabin As It Is* (Buffalo, 1852), p. 38.

'they can't take care of themselves'"; nearby is an image of two field workers, one labeled "paid" and the other "unpaid," with the slave distinguished by his lack of energy, the concentration on his unseen supervisor rather than his task, and the lack of clothing that would mark him as a social being. For a proslavery audience the representation of slave labor could easily fall into this dual trap. On the one hand, an artist trying to create a "positive" image of slave labor risked evoking the humanizing dignity of work and thus, by extension, the injustice of withholding work's customary reward. On the other hand, the artist who dehumanized the act of labor risked evoking the traditional specter of slavery's oppression.

The few images of slave labor in popular media that do not come out of abolitionism tend to avoid the problem by resorting to comic or picturesque devices. In *Uncle Tom's Cabin As It Is*, a rejoinder to Stowe's abolitionist novel, black slaves appear as childlike beings who must be cajoled or tricked into labor by an infinitely patient, if exasperated, white overseer. The picture that emerges subverts any claim for slavery as a rational system of production; appropriately the illustration accompanying the work scene shows several black men leaning on a fence, their hoes resting, apparently doing nothing (fig. 2.15).[54] By contrast, a reportorial stance is taken in an 1859 *Harper's New Monthly* article on the rice-growing region of South Carolina, which did create more of a space for

2.16 T. Addison Richards, *Harvesting the Rice* and *A Carolina Rice Planter*,
illustrations in "Rice Lands of the South," *Harper's New Monthly* 19
(November 1859): 729, 738.

representing slaves actually at work.[55] Yet they are not called slaves,
and—unlike the novel—the text suppresses all direct reference to slavery.
Here the emphasis is on picturesque signifiers of racial difference, which
both articulate and justify the black laborers' separation from the social
order. The article concludes with an image of a rumpled banjo player,
humorously entitled *A Carolina Rice Planter*, as if to resituate the laborer
we have just seen at work in a comic and colorful universe (fig. 2.16). This
Africanized world, and the labor performed within it, thus appear alien,
which is why the national audience (Northern and Southern) might ignore the humanizing potential of honest work openly depicted.

A representation positively affirming slave labor and its central place
within the social order could not caricature or exoticize its subject. It was
left to face a highly problematic negotiation between the alternatives of
humanization and brutalization. The question of slave labor thus revealed the basic conceptual instability in the notion of the slave. The master class treated the slave as a liminal figure, standing on the threshold
between the world of humans and the world of brutes. This explains why
the stereotypes of the slave could be so wildly ambivalent, pointing in

opposite directions (docility and craftiness, emasculation and potency).[56] But Brown's task was to fix the status of the slave for all eternity in an ideal representation. To affirm the social blessings of slavery in a democracy ostensibly dedicated to the advancement of mankind, the South Carolina pediment had to represent the slaves' integration into humanity as fully as possible without denying their enslavement, without in effect freeing them.

How did Brown manage this? First of all, he did create a hierarchy within the composition by placing the allegorical figures upright in contrapposto stance in the highest part of the pediment, while making the slave figures stoop, kneel, or recline depending on their position inside the angle of the pediment. The bodies of the allegories display the canonical signs of effortless balance, of mastery without exertion: gently swaying hips, flowing drapery folds integrating the figure, gracefully extended arms. By contrast the black bodies are marked by sharp angles in the limbs, even in the two figures at rest, and by drapery that is more stiff and functional; the black bodies do not assume postures of mastery because they are slaves to the labor they must perform. There is no doubt that the allegorical figures in physiognomy read as white and that they associate the qualities of civilization with both whiteness and mastership. But white mastership is not directly represented, except in the figure of the horseman who is so oddly marginal. The absence of white supervision in the composition actually accords with changes occurring in the modern slave culture, as the task system increasingly supplanted the gang system of labor. Under the task system, slaves had a measure of autonomy because they worked on their own and could rest or do their own labor once their specific tasks were completed; the system had long been used in the rice plantations and was beginning to make inroads even in the cotton fields.[57] To Brown's patrons it might have seemed peculiarly appropriate that the world of the black laborers and the world of the white allegories would appear distinct but complementary, each one depending for its very existence on the other. The opposition of blackness and whiteness in the composition thus metamorphoses into one of labor and civility, with all the intermediate categories of work and life that might upset the polarity systematically suppressed.

If these slave figures thus become typical of labor itself, Brown's solution to the problem of representing labor was to neutralize the opposing possibilities of humanization and brutalization through carefully balanced juxtapositions. In the peculiar oscillation between shirtless and covered figures, for example, Brown was asserting a mean. Too little clothing in the group might suggest backwardness and want; too much might suggest a degree of socialization and competence that was incongruous with enslavement. The resulting combination of nudity and clothing recalls the images we saw in the 1840 antislavery almanac of unpaid and paid black labor. Yet where the broadside intensifies the allusiveness of each image, Brown's composition seeks to contain their dangers by offering them as natural complements of one another. Then there is the juxtaposition of figures at work with figures at rest. This is dictated in part by the shape of the pediment, which demands reclining figures to fill the narrow wedges at the end, yet Brown had nevertheless managed to construct active end figures in his Washington design. Perhaps again he was hoping to strike a balance: no space for rest might represent labor as an intolerable burden while too much space for rest might suggest exhaustion or endemic laziness.

So far we have been working from the visual evidence of the sculpture itself to reconstruct the problems Brown faced as he approached the peculiar demands of this project. Brown's intentions, in a moral or psychological sense, are unknowable, and they were probably, in any case, confused and contradictory. Certainly the pressures on him, as he engaged in this vast apology for slavery, were enormous. His old abolitionist friends could not understand what he was doing and turned against him. Nor did he feel safe and welcome in South Carolina. When he began to model the pediment in 1859, John Brown attempted his slave insurrection in Virginia; one of the stonecutters at the State House apparently made some remarks sympathetic to the man and for this he was arrested, paraded through the streets of Columbia with his hands held by two slaves, whipped by them on the bare back, then tarred and feathered from the waist upward. The sculptor and his wife had to caution their Northern correspondents not to write anything in letters that might cast suspicion on them. In 1860 Brown was apparently poisoned by a domestic slave and for a time became deaf and blind. How the pressures of all these circumstances worked on him and through him can only be imagined.[58]

Whatever Brown's motivations were, his pediment was designed to win the approval of a proslavery audience. This does not mean, though, that an antislavery reading was impossible, for by exposing slavery in public sculpture its contradictions threatened to surface as well. The only extended critical reading of the pediment that survives is in fact an abolitionist one, written by Brown's friend William Morris Davis. Davis had a falling-out with Brown in 1860 over the Columbia project, but they patched up their friendship after Brown abandoned the project at the start of the Civil War and returned North. Davis's essay dates from the 1880s, and though it is retrospective and celebratory, it illuminates despite itself the instability of meaning—the undecidability—at the heart of the whole project. His account begins with the proslavery interpretation, noting that Brown's admirers in Columbia believed that the reclining slaves gave the lie to tales of overtasking masters and showed the enslaved laborer content with his lot. But "a Northern mind might read the lesson differently," Davis explains; the Northern mind "might question, whether Justice presiding over enforced and unrequited toil, should not naturally end in ragged, aimless, and improvident sloth: or that liberty, wresting the harvest from the reapers hook, should not as naturally terminate in death-like stupor and exhaustion."[59] Davis does not hesitate to shift the meaning of the reclining slaves, so that they become overtasked rather than relaxed, improvident rather than content; this shift in turn changes the reading of the rest of the pediment and its overall moral lesson. Nor does he stop there: the laboring figures are "giants in brute strength, human only in form, engaged in robbing the land of its fertility . . . as unrequited labor tends to sloth and slumber, even so unmanured soil tends to barrenness." The black men thus metamorphose into primitive brutes, degraded by the backward conditions under which they labor; never mind that the pediment displays a range of tasks and activities, some involving skill and finesse as much as strength. "The pervading feature of the composition," Davis sums up, "is of a degraded humanity performing its offices through brute strength alone."[60]

The irony, of course, is how closely this old abolitionist's reading conforms to the negative images of the black man traditionally held by the slaveholders, images that Brown's pediment ostensibly sought to revise and improve. The abolitionist attack on slavery had peddled in the same universal stereotypes of the slave, the major difference being that abolitionists blamed the slaves' vices on the institution whereas the owners blamed them on the slaves themselves.[61] For Davis, slaves could not be anything but improvident and aimless. He ignored the well-known fact that a slave-controlled economy did exist; many slaves—especially under the task system widespread in South Carolina—worked for themselves in their spare time, marketed their own goods, and made money, which they kept and sometimes even passed on to the next generation. To turn the pediment into an abolitionist lesson, therefore, Davis had to draw erroneous inferences about black bodies that he would most probably not have drawn had those same bodies, in the same poses and costumes, been identified as white.

Brown's alternating images of nudity and clothing, work and rest, when combined with the dramatically charged motif of blackness, were bound to produce contradictory readings. While a proslavery viewer might see happiness and efficiency, an antislavery viewer could see overwork and idleness; while the proslavery viewer might see a happy mean between indulgence and oppression, the antislavery viewer could see a system tending toward both evil outcomes at once. What is striking is how little seems to separate one reading from the other, how easily the lesson of the pediment could flip from an affirmative statement to a negative one, from pro to con.

It is now possible to explain why the choice of an abolitionist sculptor to work on a proslavery program was not so unthinkable after all. To work, the pediment had to concede as far as possible the humanity of the black slave. The political challenge facing the pediment's sponsors, to reconfigure slavery as a humane and productive institution that deserved a legitimate place in the modern world, converged with the sculptor's aesthetic challenge, which was to refashion the enslaved body to suit the high ideals of sculpture. Jointly, they attempted an impossible feat of inversion: to make a moral and aesthetic affirmation out of the overwhelming negation wreaked by slavery. Powers's *Greek Slave* managed the feat only by fantasizing the enslavement of whites, turning a white nightmare into a spiritual and erotic journey. But Brown had to make an affirmation of black slavery itself, a task that had never been attempted in sculpture before. In the end Brown could not solve the problem because he could not clarify the dual position of the slaves who labored and rested in the fields. He could not prevent the beholder from shifting their significance, tilting too far toward humanization or too far toward brutalization. Neither could the slaveholders ultimately fix their ideology in plastic form; they could not so drastically alter the ambiguous status of the slave without in fact abolishing slavery. To condense the ideology of slavery into an eternal image, in other words, meant abolishing the necessary paradox of the slave.[62]

The pediment was never built. While Brown seems to have stayed on good terms with the governor and the planter elite, the outbreak of civil war forced a halt to the project. In the spring of 1861 he decided to return North; remarkably, he left with the goodwill of his hosts, who regretted that the war had interrupted his work. But he returned home a changed man, more fiery in his opposition to slavery than ever before. He reconnected with his abolitionist friends, and soon he was criticizing Lincoln for being soft on the issue. Meanwhile, in South Carolina, all of Brown's small-scale and large-scale plaster models, all the figures that had been roughed out in marble, were destroyed when Sherman invaded Columbia in 1865 and burned the city.[63]

We cannot know how the pediment would have been received if it had been erected under a slaveowning order, or how it would have adapted to the new social order post abolition. What we do have, as a kind of coda to the project, is an afterthought by Brown's son and biographer, Henry Kirke Bush-Brown, speculating on what might have been had his father's dream been realized. The pediment, according to Bush-Brown, "would expose what was true in those slave days, and would be none the less true now that the negro does the work as a free citizen."[64] The irony of this observation, made in the early twentieth century, seems lost on its writer. What he is remarking on is the pediment's lack of clear reference to the structural reality of slavery—the systematic violence of its social order and the profound helplessness of the enslaved person. With slavery abolished, the pediment could actually be reinterpeted as a representation of the enduring racial hierarchy of a supposedly "free" society. Either way, slave or free, the pediment would have stood as a testament to the plain truth that white glory was still wrung from the sweat of black labor.

IRONICALLY, on the eve of the Civil War, the image of slavery and the image of freedom came together. Antislavery and proslavery ideologies converged over the body of the black slave. For both sides, that body was tainted by barbarism and vice. Yet both agreed that it was a body deserving elevation, an appointed place—however limited—in the terrain of the ideal. This helps explain why Brown could move so readily from one camp to the other. After the war, he shifted sides yet again. He still pursued his dream of making the "Negro" visible in public sculpture, but he turned his attention from the subject of slavery to the subject of emancipation. This time he was not alone. He was joined by a host of other sculptors who had grown up with slavery and who were now inspired by slavery's destruction to represent the great promise of social transformation that seemed to lie ahead.

CHAPTER THREE

IMAGINING
EMANCIPATION

ON JANUARY 1, 1863, the Emancipation Proclamation took effect. From a legal standpoint it was a peculiar document since it applied only to slaves in Confederate territory, and left slavery protected in Union-held areas. In effect it declared the enemy's slaves free and kept its own in bondage. Still, the proclamation was by no means an empty gesture. It did promise emancipation on a massive scale, for the millions of Southern slaves who could escape the Confederacy or who could hang on and wait for the Union army to liberate them. The proclamation thus confirmed what many already suspected and what the slaves themselves had begun to take into their own hands. The Civil War, which originated as a fight to restore "the Union as it was," now threatened the institution of slavery itself. From this point on, the Union's soldiers became an army of liberation, and the slaves of the South were invited to join it. The nation appeared to be heading irreversibly toward a final settlement of the question whether it was to remain a slave society or banish slavery once and for all.[1]

Later that year, in an art exhibition in New York, there appeared a two-foot-tall statuette fashioned in response to Lincoln's proclamation. Entitled the *Freedman* (fig. 3.1), it was made by the young sculptor John Quincy Adams Ward, Henry Kirke Brown's favorite pupil. Despite its modest size and its fledgling artist, the *Freedman* created an immediate sensation and fired the imagination of critics for years to come. The piece shows a seminude man poised on a tree stump, holding a broken manacle—an apparent fugitive from slavery, one of the many Lincoln hoped would escape to the Union ranks to secure the freedom promised by his proclamation. The design seems to emerge out of the experiments of Ward's mentor, specifically Brown's 1855 model of the slave seated on a cotton bale—as if that downcast figure had now sprung to life. The pose and action of Ward's figure break decisively from the iconography of abjection, particularly from the familiar abolitionist image of the black man in chains, kneeling on the ground and begging to be treated as a man and a brother. The *Freedman* does not plead or grieve. He has gotten up

3.1 John Quincy Adams Ward, *Freedman*, 1863,
bronze statuette.

off the ground and broken his own chains, still clenched in one fist. His
head turns alertly, the brows knit, the gaze intent on something in the
distance. No longer passively awaiting salvation from above, this figure
exudes an active force working to shape his own destiny.[2]

The work appeared initially in the form of a plaster model, shunted
into a dimly lit, crowded corner at the National Academy of Design's
annual spring exhibition. If not for Lincoln's proclamation and the official turn in wartime policy, the model would not have been exhibited at
all.[3] It might easily have been lumped into the same marginal and ephemeral category as John Rogers's plaster *Slave Auction*, except that critics
noticed a radical difference from the beginning. Ward's piece was not
dismissed as genre, or as polemic. With its heroic nudity, it belonged to
sculpture's classical tradition; its folded and subtly twisted midriff even
echoed an antique work from the canon, the Torso Belvedere. Audiences
accustomed to seeing the black body represented as the antithesis of
sculpture (recall Nott and Gliddon's invidious comparison to the Apollo
Belvedere) must have been surprised, to say the least, to see such a figure.
Many critics sensed that this marked a profound shift not only in the

prevailing image of the black but in the very definition and practice of sculpture. To accommodate the black body to the classical sculptural tradition, that tradition had to be reinvented—or at least reconceptualized. The *Freedman* seemed to promise a new sculptural order, an escape from the white marble fantasies of neoclassicism like the *Greek Slave*; it put the classical tradition in touch with the demands of contemporary reality. "It is a negro, and nothing more," wrote the *Independent*, and at the same time "it makes the nearest approach . . . to the statuary of the Greeks of any modern piece of sculpture we have seen." The combination of ethnographic realism and classical perfection—of blackness and Greekness—struck many as both a moral and artistic triumph.[4]

It took only a slight stretch of the imagination for some of these critics to conceive of this little figure as a monument in public space. Several writers actually made the suggestion that the *Freedman* be enlarged to heroic size and erected permanently to mark the new era of freedom promised by the Emancipation Proclamation and the Gettysburg Address. James Jackson Jarves, for example, envisioned it in the Capitol as a companion to Horatio Greenough's statue of George Washington, an interracial conjunction that would complete the meaning of American democracy by "commemorat[ing] the crowning virtue of democratic institutions in the final liberty of the slave."[5] Ward's sculpture seemed to embody, in the simple form of a single black man, the abstract idea of a new national order.

Encouraged by the critical acclaim, Ward had the plaster model reproduced in bronze and sold on a limited scale to subscribers.[6] The *Freedman* thus became the first representation of an African American in the medium of bronze. After this, however, the piece fell into obscurity. Despite the calls from Jarves and others, the *Freedman* never was enlarged and erected as public sculpture. Moreover, its example turned out to be unrepeatable. It did not mark a turning point in American sculpture, nor did it even herald a new representation of the African American body in sculpture. Emancipation entered public sculpture instead through the body of the white hero Abraham Lincoln. Despite the efforts of numerous sculptors like Henry Kirke Brown to introduce the figure of the African American into the monumental equation, the bodies of the emancipated themselves for the most part did not even materialize. This chapter will examine why—why the claims made on behalf of the *Freedman* went unfulfilled, and a different order of sculpture arose to take its place.

WARD was the first of several important sculptors to probe the uncertain terrain of emancipation, to condense its complex struggle over human rights into the narrow sculptural language of human form. At the time the outcome of the war was very much in doubt and slavery was still protected in Union territory. Ward was certainly not thinking of the *Freedman* as a public monument. He was not engaged in commemoration but in anticipation. He wanted to be timely, perhaps even daring, so he chose a smaller, more experimental scale. This allowed the work to acknowledge more frankly the obvious questions of emancipation's prospects.

That uncertainty about the future is most evident in the unusual pose and action Ward gave the figure. The figure, as we have seen, breaks clearly from the emblematic image of the slave kneeling in abjection. Yet neither does the figure stand erect, as the classical hero would. The *Freedman* remains somewhere between the two sculptural poles of abjection and triumph. The action of the figure, at first glance so simple, becomes oddly indeterminate on closer inspection: he is neither relaxing into the seat nor getting up from it. Bent forward, the body balances edgily between repose and movement. The taut right forearm, veins bulging from the skin, pushes down on the stump in a strong vertical, transferring the brunt of his weight through the other arm to the leg planted in front. The abdomen too is pulled in and tensed, keeping the body's weight from sinking down into the seat. This conspicuous torso, framed by the taut muscular contours of the limbs, gives the whole body the effect of a compressed coil ready to spring up. The face staring upward only emphasizes the sense of anticipation; its precise intention or expression remains open to interpretation. The important point is not what he is thinking and feeling, but *that* he is thinking and feeling. It is this evidence of an alert, acting subject within the poised body that gives its ambiguous pose a concrete potential for liberation.

The material props, too, suggest that the *Freedman* is neither entirely beyond the world of slavery nor entirely within the world of freedom, but rather between the two. While the broken chains attest to the man's strike for freedom, slavery is still suggested by the manacle that continues to bind his left wrist This ambiguity explains the curious slippage, in some of the original reviews from 1863, from the title "freedman" to the rather differently resonating label "contraband," the term that came into wide use in 1862 to designate the thousands of fugitive slaves who were streaming into Union forts and being treated as war booty.[7] A narrative of flight during wartime does seem to conform well to the spare cues Ward has given: having broken his own chains, the fugitive awaits—or awakens to—the recognition of freedom he will get only when he reaches the Union lines. Ward, it seems, deliberately set the figure within the paradoxical legal space created by the Emancipation Proclamation, which only freed slaves held where the proclamation was not recognized as law. In this space the fugitive must free himself, and his entry to the official "freedom" granted by Lincoln's proclamation is, ironically, the life of a contraband, a possession of war.

3.2 Currier and Ives,
Emancipation of the Slaves,
circa 1863, lithograph.

FREEDOM TO THE SLAVES

Ward himself steered clear of the label "contraband," presumably to
avoid drawing attention to its dehumanizing implications, so much at
odds with the notion of emancipation. But his own more dignified title
also dissatisfied him. He had this to say about his sculpture when he sent
it to the academy for exhibition:

> I shall send tomorrow or next day a plaster model of a figure which we call
> the "Freedman" for want of a better name, but I intended it to express not
> one set free by any proclamation so much as by his own love of freedom and
> a conscious *power* to brake things—the struggle is not over with him (as it
> never is in this life) yet I have tried to express a degree of hope in his under-
> taking.[8]

Though Lincoln's proclamation obviously occasioned the subject matter,
Ward wanted to distance his representation from the act itself because he
intended to focus attention on the black man as an agent of his own
liberation. He avoided the standard representation of emancipation that
was already beginning to appear in pictures and prints: there is no figure
of Lincoln or female allegory of liberty smashing the chains and raising
the slave to freedom (fig. 3.2).[9] As a title, however, the *Freedman* has two
drawbacks. With its stress on the past participle, it places the black figure
once again in the passive position, acted upon rather than acting; and it

suggests a closure that Ward deliberately resisted. This figure, like the race he represents, is supposed to be seen in the midst of a historical struggle for freedom whose final outcome is still undetermined.

Thus the *Freedman*'s very nudity—its most conspicuous and celebrated feature—becomes a double sign, pointing at once to vulnerability and to heroism. The lack of clothes suggests the precariousness of the man's position as he tries to move from one world to another, yet that same lack allows the "ideal" display of the male body, so much appreciated by contemporary critics. Nudity enabled Ward to push in two directions simultaneously: toward the evocation of the antique and toward a scrupulous realism of surface detail. Ward apparently modeled the figure from life,[10] and he took great pains to make "nature" visible in the surface of the bronze as it registers the minutiae of joint, muscle, and vein—not to mention the racial signifiers of hair, nose, and lips. Like his mentor Brown, Ward had spent some time in the South working for slaveholding patrons, and it was there that he supposedly had opportunities to observe slaves closely.[11] Ward's "naturalism" stood out to contemporaries because the marble sculpture of the day—the *Greek Slave*, for instance—tended to produce smooth or doughy surfaces, the anatomy more submerged beneath the stone skin of the figure. The shift in medium from marble to bronze not only signaled a shift in the "color" of the subject but also allowed Ward to exploit the superior surface detail of cast metal. It is that very detail of vein and flexed muscle that encourages us to read the body as I have—to grasp the precise tension of the pose, to enter imaginatively into the kinetic sensations of this moment.

Yet this same fidelity to detail that makes us imagine plausible narratives of the body raises two vexing issues. One is the very flawlessness of the detail, the absence of all scars by which the bodies of slaves were so frequently marked and which did appear in other types of representation (fig. 3.3).[12] The perfection of the body's surface shows the limits of Ward's realism, which remained comfortably within the classical notion of sculptural form as a language of "higher" truth distinct from commonplace reality. "Art means the selection and the perpetuation of the noble and beautiful and free," Ward was later quoted as saying; the equation of freedom with the ideals of art helps explain why slavery was so difficult to represent in art and why the representation of emancipation meant purifying the body of slavery's scars.[13] Second, the concreteness of Ward's representation might easily make us wonder why the figure is undressed in the first place. After all, tattered clothing was rapidly becoming the representational convention for fugitive slaves in the before-and-after prints and photographs of this period. It seems absurd that contemporary critics could maintain that this classically nude figure was "the direct expression of a fact."[14] The reason the *Freedman*'s

3.3 *Harper's Weekly* 7 (July 4, 1863): 429.

nudity did not jar critics is that for them the black man lacked a determinate social identity that demanded clothing. For a statesman or a soldier, realism and nudity were mutually exclusive—which is why Greenough's seminude Washington, for instance, had received so much abuse. One of the basic paradoxes of mid-nineteenth-century sculpture is that nude flesh, the essence of the classical sculptural tradition, could not be shown in the representation of the contemporary hero. It is no accident that Ward's most important early works, the *Freedman* and the *Indian Hunter*, were mostly nude studies of racially defined others. He was working out his brand of realism on the male bodies of the socially marginal, where his attention to nude flesh could be made plausible and acceptable. The *Freedman's* nudity at once connected the figure to the highest sculptural tradition while marking its difference from the standard white hero.[15]

The *Freedman*, then, embodied a peculiar kind of realism. The piece was obviously not an allegory of liberty in the traditional sense—a generic figure holding a conventionalized attribute like a liberty pole—yet it was not a portrait of an actual fugitive either. It escaped generic classification, which is why the novelist and critic William Dean Howells singled it out in his *Atlantic* essay of 1866, "Question of Monuments."[16] Indeed, the *Freedman* makes sense not in the conventional categories of mid-nineteenth-century sculpture but instead as a kind of sculptural analogue of the literary realism Howells championed; like Howells's model of good fiction, it navigated between the extremes of brutal fact and improbable romance. What we are seeing is not so much a "real" freedman as a generalized representative of the new black man poised on the threshold of freedom. The sculptural cues of pose, props, and clothing all reinforce the idea that the social identity and prospects of this new man remain uncertain, undetermined. Yet that indeterminacy does not only mean lack—of material goods, political rights, social position. The *Freedman* in his very indeterminacy also carries heroic potential, a possibility for transformation into a fully formed, fully acting social being. If he has not yet won the struggle for freedom in the largest sense, he has not yet lost it either. As shaped by Ward, this freedman has exchanged one problematic status for another—the institutionalized alienation and dehumanization of slavery for the difficult rebirth and rehumanization of emancipation.

Here gender is crucial, for it is only the male in nineteenth-century society who had the claim to citizenship and, with it, full economic and political agency. This drama of emancipation[17] could not be represented with such meaning on or through the female body because, as we have seen in our discussion of the *Greek Slave*, that body remained wedded to narratives of dependence or entrapment or victimization. The story of escaped female slave Sojourner Truth, for example, inspired Ward's contemporary, then celebrated sculptor William Wetmore Story, not to portray Truth herself but to create an appropriately distanced piece of ideal sculpture—an ancient and enigmatic *Libyan Sibyl* (1861) brooding passively over the tragic fate of the African race (fig. 3.4). Or Anne Whitney's frankly erotic plaster statue of *Africa* exhibited in 1864, an ideal figure of Grecian profile with only the slightest suggestion of black African features in her wavy hair, rouses from an evidently deep slumber, as if trying to shake off the paralyzing weight of centuries of oppression.[18] Story's *Libyan Sibyl*, in particular, earned considerable notoriety as an antislavery work, helped in part by an article written by Harriet Beecher Stowe in 1863; in a sense it represented the ideal marble alternative to Ward's narrative realism.[19] Removed both in time and space from the historical moment of emancipation, and from the racial configuration of American slavery, the *Sibyl* could not even claim to represent the black American experience. As Story himself said, it was "Libyan African of course, not Congo"—meaning that his North African type deliberately differed from the Central Africans who populated the slave ships to America.[20]

In Ward's hands, by contrast, the drama of emancipation liberated the black male not only from physical enslavement but from the conventional poles of oppressive representation: the "whitened" ideal represented by the *Libyan Sibyl* or *Africa*, on the one hand, and the grotesque caricature

3.4 William Wetmore Story, *Libyan Sibyl*, 1862, marble.

of popular and scientific illustrations, on the other hand. This helps explain why Ward's apparently simple achievement of making the black
man a sculptural subject impressed critics to no end, and why in that
achievement some critics saw a turning point in sculpture itself. Ward's
figure, they argued, showed how to transcend the sterile tradition of conventional ideal sculpture because it managed to reconcile the demands of
truth to reality with the demands of classicism. "Here was the Greek's
conception of art—repose and simplicity—applied to a modern fact," the
New York *Evening Post* argued.[21] The point the critics stressed repeatedly is that the *Freedman* approached the classical ideal of form and proportion without being a mythological subject or in any other obvious
way mimicking Greek sculpture. Hence the irony that this marginal subject, generally debased in the representational practices of American culture, "more nearly approach[ed] the classic" than neoclassical subjects
themselves.[22]

It is crucial to stress here that both the artist and his audience were
white—in other words, the production as well as the reception of this

image took place within a privileged community of people who, whatever their particular racial beliefs, saw the black man as *different* from themselves.[23] In this context, insofar as Ward's figure was true to reality (i.e., "a negro, and nothing more") he was different; insofar as he was ideal or classic (i.e., conforming to white European models) he was similar. It was this simultaneous assertion of racial difference and human similarity that so impressed critics like James Jackson Jarves, who saw the figure as the symbol of "a new people," "the African race of America." The reception to the *Freedman* suggests that it did not erase racial categories but showed how they might—at least in visual imagination—be brought into harmony rather than opposition. Africans could become Americans, so the *Freedman* seemed to declare.

A more recent critic, Michael Hatt, has argued that the *Freedman* posed a question that it ultimately could not answer: "Is this general humanity or specific blackness?"[24] Yet the *Freedman* impressed critics of the 1860s precisely because it did seem to answer the question Hatt poses as a paradox. The simple answer to this either/or question was both. And Ward's achievement was to make it look simple, as if it were merely what true sculpture demanded of its subject. Still, racial difference did remain problematic in one crucial respect—in the erotic potential of the figure's nudity. In that eroticism there were troubling implications for the new black man's masculinity.[25]

If the *Freedman*'s humanity was generally celebrated by critics, his *masculinity* was received rather differently—called into question by the very nudity that seems to confirm his manhood so vigorously. The critics of the 1860s register the figure's equivocal masculinity in various ways. One claimed that the figure "spoke powerfully for the manhood of the negro"; another depicted the figure as only beginning to sense "a faint conception of his manhood, his soulhood."[26] The *New York Times* pointedly framed the issue this way: "The final question will be, whether he makes a good and sufficient fight. When the difficulties are fairly shown, is there yet manhood enough in the figure to overmatch them?"[27] The figure's uncertain hold on "manhood," read in this instance as a political problem, becomes the basis of its erotic tension as well. Without a fixed masculine identity, a clear place in the world of men, the figure is ripe for erotic fantasy. The problematic space he occupies between social worlds is the sort of liminal space often eroticized because it is removed from social convention; indeed the liminality of the space makes possible the nakedness of the figure to begin with. While contemporary reviewers certainly did not engage in any obvious erotic fantasy, they did allow themselves to revel in the display of anatomy. Ward "exposed a lusty negro with firm and expanding muscle," the *Evening Post* reported, in terms that would have been considered strange and improper if applied to a white hero.[28] Even the defenders of Greenough's seminude Washington, for instance, did not revel in its anatomy but focused soberly on its moral significance.[29]

Thus the *Freedman*'s masculinity read at once as extreme and insufficient. The lack of a socially fixed masculinity in the figure permitted Ward to represent more flagrantly its erotic masculinity. This is not simply a matter of naked anatomy but the tactile approach to the anatomy Ward's technique and composition invite. The subtle turns in the figure—notice how the arms and the legs are paired in nearly perpendicular planes—and the sensuous voids in the composition created by the spaces between torso and arms, trunk and legs, all lead our eye to wander through and around the figure, as if to caress it; and indeed small bronzes like this were meant to be explored by hand as well as by eye.[30] This was precisely the sort of erotic scrutiny foreclosed in realist representations of contemporary white male bodies.

As a turning point for sculpture, then, Ward's little figure turns out to be highly problematic. Though it appeared to many viewers as a declaration of reform for American sculpture, it could not readily be repeated. Its careful synthesis of lifelike detail and ideal form could not be so obviously duplicated on the clothed surfaces of white male bodies, nor could it be understood as a legitimating precedent for nudity in modern subjects since its erotic potential had to be actively suppressed in the more canonical representations of great men. On a semiotic level, its ability to suggest complex meanings without recourse to allegory or other neoclassical devices also seemed to be limited by the peculiar status of the subject. In the more typical subjects of public sculpture which Ward was soon to pursue—individual heroes with socially fixed identities—the *Freedman*'s suggestiveness was very difficult to emulate. The sculptural problems that the *Freedman* appeared to overcome continued to bedevil sculptors for decades.

Moreover, the liminality of the *Freedman* made it a peculiar precedent even for the sculptural representation of the black body. Shortly after the *Freedman*'s exhibition, events seemed rapidly to overtake its story, to render it obsolete. The fortunes of the Confederacy began to turn sour that summer of 1863 with the defeat at Gettysburg, and a few weeks later fugitive slaves and free blacks mustered into the Union army fought their first major battles and displayed their heroism to a skeptical white public. The black man, it seemed, was no longer between worlds; he was standing erect, in uniform, armed and ready to fight for the cause of freedom. Slavery's disintegration was accelerating, so that by January 1865 Congress had passed a constitutional amendment to abolish it forever. By the

3.5 Edmonia Lewis,
Forever Free, 1868,
marble.

end of the year the amendment took effect. Emancipation had seemingly been won, and black "contrabands" like Ward's freedman had made the victory possible.

In that moment of victory a new optimism appeared and intruded into sculpture in the work of Edmonia Lewis, one of the growing colony of expatriate women sculptors working in Rome. Daughter of a Chippewa woman and a black man, she was the only sculptor of identified African American descent working in this period.[31] In her marble group *Forever Free* (fig. 3.5), originally modeled in 1866–67, the freedman does indeed stand erect, holding aloft broken chains and looking up to God. The emotional and historical distance from Ward's figure seems clear enough, but Lewis's bodies remain liminal in certain crucial respects. The partial nudity of the man, the shackles which bind wrist and ankle, and the kneeling woman—whose pose is virtually identical to that of the abolitionist emblem—all combine to locate the narrative in the first joyful flush of freedom (the *Morning of Liberty,* as the group was titled in its early stages).[32] Though no longer slaves, their identities are still defined by slavery and its characteristic signifiers; new identities await them as they lift their thanks to God. Even their racial characteristics are mutable, as the Africanized physiognomy of the man is counterbalanced by the flowing hair of the woman, who might "pass" for white. Lewis's chief patrons were white abolitionists, and she originally intended the work as a tribute to Boston abolitionist William Lloyd Garrison. Her group seemed to remain little known outside the Boston abolitionist circle. It was after all a private work, for a single patron, never reproduced as far we know and never shown in a major exhibition for another century.[33] Its marble medium and generalized modeling aligned it with an old-fashioned style that was beginning to be superseded by Ward among others.

By contrast, Ward's figure—despite its smaller scale and its apparently dated narrative—acquired a public reputation that lasted for several years. In the mid-1860s critics argued that it should reach the largest possible audience: Jarves suggested enlarging the piece for the Capitol building, while Henry Tuckerman advised that it be reproduced small-scale in a cheap material so that it would "be seen and possessed by the great mass of the people."[34] Howells in the essay "Question of Monuments" (1866) also envisaged a wide distribution. He called the *Freedman* a "sublime parable . . . the full expression of one idea that should be commemorated." The *Freedman* was the only piece of sculpture Howells mentioned in the essay, and he recommended it specifically as a prototype for a new kind of war memorial that "would better celebrate the great deeds of our soldiers" than the traditional martial images of battle heroes."[35] Both Howells and Jarves transformed Ward's open-ended piece into a commemorative artifact: the liminal figure becomes a finished "parable," bringing suitable closure to the long historical episode of slavery. Yet Ward's piece does not commemorate in this way, nor did he intend it to. Instead of fixing the meaning of the past, it raises questions about the future; in this narrative the black man's struggle is beginning, not ending.

The *Freedman* posed a series of questions about the fate of the black body, in sculpture and society. The task of public sculpture was to supply answers, not questions. Not surprisingly, Ward's figure never became public sculpture, never even found a private patron to enlarge it to life size. Writing in 1894, art critic Charles de Kay could still claim that the piece was Ward's "strongest work" while lamenting that "race prejudices" had consigned it to oblivion.[36] The piece did still have some life in popular culture. It appeared in 1890 as a print, without credit to Ward and under the title *Unshackled*, in the landmark history of black troops in American wars, *The Black Phalanx*.[37] Yet Ward himself never returned to the subject of the black male body, and only once again, in 1891, did he execute an African American figure, a black girl who serves as a subsidiary figure in a monument to abolitionist Henry Ward Beecher. The *Freedman* remained, in many senses, a singular achievement.

EMANCIPATION, as we have seen, was not a historical event that could be tidily defined, demarcated, and commemorated. Even after the final abolition of slavery in 1865, the bitter struggle over the meaning of freedom and how it translated into social and political rights continued to intensify. Herein lay the basic dilemma for all sculptors who would face the problem of representing emancipation in public monuments. The subject defied the sort of historical closure they were asked to deliver. The public sculptor's task was not comparable to the printmaker's or even the painter's. Their images did not have to endure in public space, and so they had more license to represent the passions of the moment. But the public monument's terrifying finality put the sculptors of emancipation in a distinctly problematic position. They were testing the limits of what was culturally possible before anyone had a clear idea of what those cultural limits were.

Therefore, the theme of emancipation did not enter public sculpture as a subject in its own right. It entered public sculpture through the commemorative subject of Abraham Lincoln, as a means of locating—and "closing"—his unique historical achievement. In virtually all the numerous projects to build monuments to Lincoln in the 1860s and 1870s, emancipation figured in one form or another. As a sculptural theme, emancipation is simplified but obviously diminished once it becomes inseparable from the historical figure of Lincoln. Making Lincoln the primary historical agent tends to trivialize the role of slaves and other African Americans in bringing about their own liberation; a complex social phenomenon is shrunk to fit a great-man (and specifically great-white-man) model of history. The temporal horizon of emancipation is similarly shrunk to fit into a completed past that can be sealed off for commemoration. Such shrinkages are part and parcel of the business of commemoration, and they held true not only in white-sponsored monuments but even in some African American rituals as well. African Americans in Norfolk, Virginia, for example, celebrated their emancipation on the anniversary of Lincoln's proclamation taking effect (January 1) even though the proclamation actually had had no effect on slaves there, because the city was in Union hands and thus exempt.[38] The impulse to commemorate dates and heroes defined by the orthodox narrative histories of the dominant culture remained strong, even when those definitions worked to marginalize the very people doing the commemoration.

Yet within this reductive framework there was still room for sculptors to stretch the subject of emancipation into important new representational territory. In fact, insofar as sculptors chose to bring the black body into the representation at all they were in novel territory. The introduction of the black body into public sculpture, even within the limiting framework of a monument to Lincoln, raised some of those open questions about emancipation and society that commemorative monuments were supposed to suppress. The universe of possibilities suggested by the *Freedman*, while obviously shrunk by the commemorative subject of Lincoln, did not disappear altogether.

To grasp this point we need a few remarks about the public monument as a sculptural genre, with its constraints as well as its possibilities. In the nineteenth century monuments were expected to double as high art and popular expression. They were usually thought of as architectural landmarks, and so they were often envisaged and described with terms such as shaft, pile, and column. What is curious, though, is that Americans as often as not turned to sculptors to design monuments, even when the commemorative work was couched in terms frankly architectural. The sponsors of the Lincoln Tomb in Springfield, Illinois, in their fund-raising appeals anticipated a grand "Memorial Structure," a "mighty shaft," yet they chose the design of sculptor Larkin Mead, who did give them an obelisk but surrounded it with several large groups of bronze statuary.[39] Sculpture was essential because it transformed the landmark into a meaningful object. History, the stuff of commemoration, was taken to be a chronicle of great acts performed by great human actors, and the sculptor's task was to recreate those actors in stone or metal. In a rather literal way, preserving the memory of a hero meant preserving his image for posterity. In the comportment of his body and the lines of his face, the traces of his moral example and achievement were thought to be readable. Hence Charles Eliot Norton in his 1865 essay on monuments asserted the primacy of sculpture, particularly portrait statuary, and argued that almost all the major architectural types of monuments were really vehicles for it. And Howells, while proposing less orthodox monumental types such as parks or town halls, still believed that they had to include "some significant piece of statuary" to be properly commemorative.[40] The canonical examples of monuments often cited by critics were those that combined grandeur of site and mass with significant sculpture, like Rauch's monument to Frederick the Great in Berlin or the Edinburgh monument to Sir Walter Scott.

Though sculpture was considered essential to both the artistic and the expressive aims of the monument, its possibilities were nevertheless highly restricted. Meaning had to be compressed into a narrow compass: the language of pose, gesture, expression, attributes, and accessories. When faced with the task of representing the significance of complex events, sculptors tended to condense expression into a few standard sculptural formulas. Consider the rather elaborate explanation offered by Henry Kirke Brown for his simple figure of Lincoln, cloaked and holding a scroll [fig. 3.6]:

> In any view of the late rebellion the Southern interest in human slavery was its foundation and its motive power and, in consequence, the destruction of that institution by the President's proclamation was the final blow to it, and the basis upon which the war was closed. It has therefore appeared to me proper to represent the late President unfolding the sublime purpose of emancipation to the people—symbolized by the scroll he holds in his hands—upon which may be engraved the body of the proclamation and the finger of his right hand pointing to those ever living words "forever free." I have introduced as accessories two wreaths, indicating the army and the navy, and also the arms of the United States, as identifying his acts with the country. On the reverse side of the monument may be represented the arms of the City of Brooklyn.[41]

Brown does not have to justify the standing pose, which identifies Lincoln as a man of action, or the surrounding cloak, which adds a hint of classical drapery as well as mass to the body; these are the long familiar generic devices of portrait sculpture, and they were especially appropriate here because Lincoln's figure was thought to be ungainly and intrinsically unsculptural. Instead Brown begins with a sweeping (and acute) analysis of the historical significance of the war and then condenses that lesson into a simple sculptural device, the scroll in Lincoln's left hand highlighted by the pointing gesture in his right. Reading the monument to grasp Brown's lesson, we must move from the general meaning of the heroic body to the specific meaning of the scroll and finally to the decorative accessories on the pedestal that connect those meanings to the nation and to the locality sponsoring the monument. Though Brown frowned on abstract devices such as allegories, his hierarchical procedure for conveying complex historical lessons in a few simple steps was in all respects exemplary.

The repertoire of signifying devices in portrait sculpture was so limited that certain solutions were continually recycled. Thus virtually all the Lincoln statues erected in the 1860s and 1870s—standing figure holding scroll, seated figure in act of writing—had precedents in one previous sculptural subject, the figure of George Washington.[42] While critics seemed to demand the clarity and conventionality of such sculptural language, they also deplored its repetitious banality. Norton believed that very few sculptors had the talent to carry off portrait sculpture successfully, and Howells found the typical sculptural solutions so impoverished that he could cite only the example of the *Freedman* as an alternative. The basic problem was how to make the subject of contemporary

3.6 Henry Kirke Brown, Lincoln Monument, 1869, Prospect Park, Brooklyn.

man convincingly sculptural, especially when he no longer looked or dressed like the canonical models of the body from antiquity. For sculptors and critics Lincoln was the very exemplar of this disparity: his figure was too tall and bony, his physiognomy cragged, his clothing a shambles. Summing up the standard opinions, critic Marianna Griswold Van Rensselaer wrote that "in physical structure and attire he might have seemed almost the embodiment of the sculpturally impossible."[43] How was a sculptor to produce anything eloquent from such intractable material?

For some sculptors and some critics, the black body held that promise of eloquence. Like Lincoln the black man was not canonical, but unlike Lincoln his contemporary likeness was not yet fixed, his identity not yet defined by conventional types of pose and gesture and attribute. In its very indeterminacy the black body was liberating. It opened up possibilities for commemorative sculpture that the figure of Lincoln alone could not contain, which explains why the conventional single-figure formula for Lincoln justified so cogently by Brown failed to satisfy many sculptors, including Brown himself.

The aesthetic problems of commemorative sculpture cannot be separated from the more obviously political pressures inherent in this public medium. The dividing line between the aesthetic and the political is in fact difficult to define since the generic characteristics of heroic sculpture themselves carry profoundly political significance. The whole notion of history as a tale of great men is made palpably glorious in the statues of heroes; that glory works to marginalize cultural constructions of the past that might represent other groups and other categories of historical experience. The intertwining of heroic history and heroic sculpture is precisely what Brown took for granted in his discussion of the Brooklyn statue. The choice of Lincoln as the commemorative focus, and the representation of him as a heroic body, rested on presuppositions which were so self-evident that they surely did not strike the sculptor as politically charged. But within that undisputed framework important political dilemmas still arose and intruded into the consciousness of the public sculptor, all the more so because the sculptor, unlike say a writer of history, had to secure the approval of a commissioning body and the public it claimed to represent.

Nowhere was this more true than in the field of monuments to Lincoln. After his death dozens of monument associations formed in cities across the country and competed with one another for funds and legitimacy. In addition to the local associations, there were at least four groups going by the name of National Lincoln Monument Association or Lincoln National Monument Association, all vying in public to stake out this preeminent commemorative territory.[44] This outbreak of commemorative fever was unprecedented in American history. Certainly nothing comparable had taken place after the Revolutionary War or after Washington's death. There was of course an extraordinary confluence of events that helps account for this: the first presidential assassination in the United States, coming right on the heels of a traumatic civil war—the bloodiest war in American history before or since. The monument campaigns of 1865–66 cast their scope over the whole historical panorama; they sought to commemorate not simply the figure of Lincoln but the era he helped to define.[45] In effect they sought to give some shape to the incredible events of the previous years, which had changed the destiny of the nation and the personal lives of everyone in it. But in the process of seeking closure through commemoration they opened up questions about the present. The various associations and the sculptors vying for their commissions were forced to imagine, articulate, and embody a Lincoln for the post-Lincoln nation—a historical founder for what the new nation had come to be, or was in the process of becoming.

For sculptors thrust into this momentous task, the subject of the emancipated, or emancipating, black body held enormous promise on both aesthetic and political fronts. It offered a means at once of transcending the formulaic solutions of portrait sculpture and of connecting Lincoln's presidency with the new order apparently dawning in Reconstruction. Yet the subject held risks that were equally impressive. Against the strong tradition of dehumanizing representation in both popular and scientific media, the sculptors of emancipation threatened to legitimize the black body. Making the African American body a monumental subject would alter its marginality, would make African Americans newly visible and historically significant in the physical and cultural landscape. What was at stake fundamentally was the notion of an interracial monument. Such a monument was bound to be read not simply as an image of Lincoln's historical achievement but as a representation—literally a personification—of the new interracial order emerging after slavery.

THE first interracial monument dealing with emancipation actually appeared just on the eve of the war, as the national election campaign got into swing. This was a marble relief panel located in a cemetery in Pittsburgh on the tomb of Charles Avery, a wealthy industrialist who was also famous as a philanthropist dedicated to antislavery causes (figs. 3.7, 3.8]. The panel is the first known instance of African American representation in marble or bronze. Designed by an obscure New York sculptor, Louis Verhaegan, for a town that was hardly a cultural center, the work was easy to miss. Although it was described effusively in the black newspaper *Christian Recorder* in 1869, the monument soon enough fell into oblivion.[46] Cemetery monuments, in general, occupied a marginal zone; Norton, for example, specifically excluded them from the category of the

3.7–8 Louis Verhaegen,
Charles Avery
Monument, 1860,
Allegheny Cemetery,
Pittsburgh.
Below: Detail of
relief panel.

public because they were usually sponsored by families for themselves. Avery's tomb was not a family affair, but the project of several important Pennsylvania Republicans who obviously intended to make a public statement. They lavished money on the project even though Avery himself had explicitly requested a modest burial, and by locating the tomb in the most prominent site of Pittsburgh's fashionable garden cemetery they created what was probably the first public monument in the region. The marble panel on the front of the pedestal has long been severely mutilated, but the early description and photographs indicate that in its original state the figure of Avery orchestrated an emancipation narrative. Avery had founded a black school in Pittsburgh and supported black missionary work in Africa. Consequently the panel represents a series of black figures changing from nude to clothed, downcast to upright; they are progressing from an abject state of slavery through education to the role of African missionary. Avery culminates the narrative, waving a Bible in one hand and pointing with the other to a ship that will take the black missionaries under his wing to Africa. It is a narrative of uplift from slavery achieved by white benefactors and Christian education, a narrative whose ultimate end was the uplift of Africa itself. On the great political question of abolition, the panel offered no obvious answer; certainly it could be read as abolitionist but it could just as easily be interpreted instead as a plug for colonization, the scheme advanced by Lincoln among others for the deportation of American blacks to Africa.[47] The panel seems to have been designed to appeal to a broad spectrum of conservative and radical antislavery viewpoints, precisely the coalition which the Republican Party was trying to put together for the 1860 election.

Although there is no reason to think that the Avery Monument was known to sculptors outside Pittsburgh, it prefigured the earliest efforts to find a sculptural solution to the postwar problem of Lincoln and emancipation. Like the Avery panel, these early solutions transformed the idea of emancipation into a personalized narrative of racial uplift orchestrated by the white hero. One simple image recurred often. This was the image of Lincoln standing above, and lifting or blessing, a crouching black figure below. When asked in 1866 to propose a design for a Lincoln monument in Philadelphia, John Rogers, the sculptor of small-scale genre groups, replied that "the design that strikes me without having had time to think of it much, would be to represent [Lincoln] as just risen from writing, and as receiving with one hand a petition from a crouching negro, whom he is raising with the other."[48] It is interesting that this was Rogers's first instinct, as if the image sprang from the most deeply ingrained assumptions about race and slavery. Of course by this time such images had already materialized and were circulating in popular prints, issued by Currier and Ives among others (fig. 3.2) Sculptors with more time to think and work on the problem also arrived at the same two-figure solution. Henry Kirke Brown, Randolph Rogers, and Thomas Ball all went so far as to produce models that were considered seriously by monument committees; as we shall see, only Ball's was ever erected.

The kneeling or crouching black slave refers us back once again to the abolitionist emblem, "Am I not a man and a brother?" We have already discussed the physical abasement of the figure, his contact with the ground. But the pose also establishes a peculiar relationship with the audience consuming the image and repeating its rhetorical question: the audience becomes the imaginary object of the slave's petition, the potential intercessor standing to receive the pleadings of the lowly. It is not much of a leap to materialize this unseen intercessor in the figure of Lincoln, thereby completing the image and bringing its narrative to closure. Yet that act of completion has enormous consequences for the representation of emancipation.

Consider the model proposed in 1866 or 1867 by Brown for a Lincoln monument in New York. The only surviving photograph shows a standing Lincoln pointing to heaven with his right hand and gesturing with his left toward a partially nude black male who kneels at his feet (fig. 3.9).[49] Lincoln looks down with a kindly gaze while the freed slave, his hands clasped over one knee in gratitude, looks back up. The upward tilt of his head exaggerates the receding slope of his forehead and thereby calls to mind the notorious facial angle used by racial theorists to measure intellectual inferiority. (In the abolitionist emblem this effect was avoided, whether intentionally or not.) Brown's kneeling figure seems oddly out of scale, only about two-thirds of Lincoln's height if imagined at full extension. Too small to be a man, too muscular to be a mere boy, he perhaps reads as an adolescent. He is barefoot, shirtless, slung with a canteen and some indeterminate drapery; his outfit seems intended to suggest the condition of a young "contraband," perhaps already in the unofficial service of the Union army. Whatever the precise status of the slave figure, Brown has rendered him less "manly" than Ward's "lusty negro" in order to emphasize more clearly the oppositions between Lincoln and the slave. The nudity of the *Freedman* was double-edged, a sign at once of ideal heroism and social deprivation. But the nudity of Brown's figure reads differently when juxtaposed with the clothed figure of Lincoln, standard-bearer of civilization. The ideal aspect evaporates and the black body reads more simply as difference, as lack. This contrast is reinforced by the multiple layers of Lincoln's outfit, each adding a literal and metaphorical weight to the figure, culminating in the massive cloak clasped around his neck that spreads behind him to create a sense of columnar stability and stature. The oppositions of posture, pose, dress, size, physiognomy, and, finally, race all combine to lock the two figures into unambiguous roles.

3.9 Henry Kirke Brown, model for monument to
Lincoln, 1866–67, plaster (now lost).

To Lincoln belongs human agency and divine favor; the slave is left only
with gratitude and potential. Lincoln is the benevolent white authority
who mediates between God and the lowly slave, while the recipient of
that kindness represents a thankful, though undeveloped, race.

Brown's solution not only transforms Lincoln into "Massa" but conceptualizes emancipation as an act of manumission orchestrated by the
Massa. Manumission—the master's voluntary release of individuals from
bondage—was a rite stretching back to antiquity that did not in fact sever
the relationship between master and slave but usually perpetuated it in
another guise. Patterson in his cross-cultural study argues that manumission was a gift exchange in which the master gave the slave the gift of
freedom in exchange for gratitude, patronage, and often continuing service from the ex-slave. In many cases the master continued to function as
the ex-slave's authority figure and mediator with outside society. In the
United States manumission was practiced but it occurred relatively rarely,
generally only with slaves most likely to retain ties of dependence.[50]

Brown's two-figure model can easily be seen to illustrate this relationship of master and slave in the act of manumission. Lincoln stands as the master figure who gives the slave the benefits of freedom and divine guidance, and the slave properly kneels to show gratitude and a recognition of his benefactor's higher authority. In the ancient Roman ceremony the slave crouched beneath an official who bestowed freedom with the light touch of a rod.[51]

The reason for this tradition of placing the manumitted slave in poses of obeisance in both rite and image was to reinforce the structures of authority and submission threatened by the act of manumission. The representation of the act upheld the power relations of slavery even as the act itself freed individuals from slavery; obviously such representation was necessary since manumission took place within the system of slavery and had to be reconciled with it. All of this should underscore why the adaptation of the formula to commemorate Lincoln was so much at odds with the principle of emancipation. The case for Lincoln's historical importance rested on the abolition of slavery itself and the permanent state of dependence it fostered; the whole point of emancipation was to make slaves independent citizens, participants in the American contract. Brown's design and others like it reinforced the notion of the freed slaves as a dependent class, beholden to the white authority that had generously bestowed freedom.

Brown and his abolitionist colleagues would probably have objected that such a reading runs counter to their intentions. Typically, abolitionists argued that blacks were not naturally dependent but that slavery had plunged them in a degraded condition, which emancipation could not immediately reverse. According to the *Freedmen's Record*, an antislavery organ published in Boston, "the freedman compared to the educated white man is a child needing instruction and guidance."[52] In this way of thinking Lincoln's act could be seen as the beginning of a national effort to "raise" the slaves from their infantilized state to the new standard required of free citizens. Thus the juxtaposition of standing Lincoln and kneeling slave was probably meant to suggest a narrative of uplift from slavery rather than continuing dependence after slavery. The problem with this argument is that it takes no account of the genre of commemorative sculpture in which this image would be created and read. A monument fixes a permanent image meant to define a historical event for all time. In marble or bronze, the black youth kneeling beneath Lincoln would not get up or grow up, or change the angle of his head, or put on a shirt or a pair of shoes. Even if we accept the abolitionist narrative of degradation and elevation—which certainly has problems of its own—the composition in monumental form works to disrupt the sense of historical flow and to freeze the narrative in a premature closure. The closure

3.10 Randolph Rogers, *Lincoln and the Emancipated Slave*,
circa 1866, plaster.

left by Brown's composition is the inscription of radical inequality, infantilized dependence on the part of the slave and the black race he represents
and masterly benevolence on the part of Lincoln and the white race he
represents.

While Brown reinforced this opposition between the two figures by
contrasting age and maturity, expatriate sculptor Randolph Rogers devised a polarity on the axis of gender. The design he proposed in 1867 for
the Philadelphia monument to Lincoln is the only known example of a
female slave paired with the president. The design has been lost but a
related plaster model does survive which, in the particulars of the two
figures, is probably very close to the Philadelphia version[53] (fig. 3.10).
This model features a standing Lincoln gazing down upon a crouching,
seminude woman whom he is lifting by the wrist with his left hand. Wearing a bandanna wrapped in the shape of a liberty cap (the *pileus* worn by
manumitted slaves in Rome), she gazes back up at Lincoln as she steadies
herself with her left hand. The physical touch between the two figures is
extremely significant. His hold of her wrist—rather than her hand—

erases any suggestion of romantic gallantry, which Rogers surely wanted to avoid; it places the action outside the familiar rubric of lady-gentleman contact. The gesture suits more the interaction of parent and child. Lincoln's clutch in effect replaces the manacle still visible on the woman's left wrist, the hold of the slaveowner exchanged for the hold of the emancipator. The other significant feature of the model is the drapery. The sculptor arranges Lincoln's coat and his limbs in a series of crisp, gently undulating verticals, while the slave's skirt is disposed in a repeating pattern of V-shaped folds, which visually anchor her to the ground. Hence the oppositions suggested by gender, pose, and gesture are extended to the costume and its abstract sculptural patterns.

Rogers's design insists even more blatantly than Brown's on the subordination of freed slave to emancipator qua manumitter. While the relationship is neatly condensed in the extraordinary hand gesture at the center of the composition, the controlling fact of the design is the juxtaposition of gender. No longer is the pairing a sculptural rumination on black manhood and its possibilities for development. The slave's nudity, for example, now takes on a new meaning. Her exposed breasts add a dimension of sexual allure and vulnerability absent in Brown's design. The narrative of elevation also has a new cast. The black woman could not become even in theory Lincoln's equal since women as a class were stripped of political rights. Even if we imagined the group transformed by the slave's rising to a "civilized" status—which means refusing to accept the closure already enforced by pose, gesture, and dress—the free black would still remain outside the polity by virtue of her gender alone. By deflecting the narrative from the complex of issues surrounding black masculinity and its social and political rights, the sculptor seriously undermines the prevailing abolitionist rhetoric of elevation.

One more design of note was proposed for both the New York and the Philadelphia projects, this one by another expatriate in Italy, Thomas Ball[54] (fig. 3.11). Ball's slave is once again male, stripped to just a loincloth and a liberty cap. The figure is bound by manacles but the broken chains that had connected them lie near his feet. Behind him, on Lincoln's left, is a whipping post, the archetypal sign of slavery's cruelty. The original plaster model, which was reproduced in studio photographs and stereographs, departs in a few interesting respects from the designs of Brown and Rogers. Lincoln does not touch the slave but reaches his left hand out over the man's body in a sort of benediction gesture; his right hand grasps a shield resting on the Emancipation Proclamation.[55] The slave does not look back up at Lincoln but stares out into space. Ball's slave is a man, fully grown, and his muscular presence in the composition foregrounds the issue of black masculinity. More than any of the other models, Ball's seemed to pose the problem this way: would the slave stand up and

3.11 Thomas Ball, stereograph of plaster model for monument
to Lincoln, circa 1866.

become a man and, if so, what kind of man? Would he come to hold the
conventional prerogatives that defined white manhood—in other words,
would the sameness of his gender overcome the difference of race—or
would both his rights and his manhood be called into question?

These were the very questions that underlay the whole legislative
agenda of Reconstruction: they defined the problem of equality. Ball had
to supply the answers in the peculiar language of sculpture, embedded as
it was in the form and action of the human body. His design seems to
embody the abolitionist ideal of uplift, with its tantalizing promise of
manhood and equality. But his narrative is less straightforward than

either Brown's or Rogers's, and the meaning of the slave's body is more difficult to read. In particular the slave's pose is quite peculiar, as anyone would soon find out by trying to hold it. Ball himself, according to his recollections written several decades later, took the pose and modeled the group in clay from a kneeling position by the use of mirrors. By so doing he "could appreciate exactly the position I required, and could not only see, but feel the action of each muscle."[56] If we as viewers follow the same procedure and try to approximate this uncomfortable position, we discover at once that the body is not in the process of standing up, as casual observers might assume. The figure crouches uneasily, leg muscles tensed, the left arm steadying his balance instead of pushing the body upward. To arrive at this strange and complicated pose, Ball must surely have studied two widely known prototypes on display in Florence, where he lived and worked. One was Bandinelli's group of *Hercules and Cacus* from 1534, located outdoors near Michelangelo's *David* in the Palazzo Vecchio. The figure of Cacus, who is about to receive a death blow from the hero above, also crouches on one knee, his head strained upward and his right arm steadying himself in a similar gesture. Of course the narrative energy of the group is entirely different, and Cacus's pathetically twisted torso has no parallel in Ball's design. Yet it is worth noting that this extreme image of lethal domination could supply much of the basic body language of Ball's solution.

The other prototype is the *Arrotino*, the one classical model of any relevance to Ball's problem (fig. 3.12). Often identified as a slave figure in the mid-nineteenth century, the *Arrotino* also appealed to racial theorists like Blumenbach as an example of a barbarian, an ethnic other.[57] Thus Ball had many reasons for appropriating the figure, but what is striking is how he has revised it. In the *Arrotino* the distribution of the body's weight is much different: the figure sits back on his right heel and stabilizes himself with his left foot planted in front; neither knee touches the ground. Ball's slave, with his weight thrown more forward on the knee and his back more horizontal, must exert considerable strain just to hold the head up as he does. The narrative thus shifts subtly but crucially. Unlike the *Arrotino*, Ball's slave must have been in abject misery, his face dropped toward the ground, only an instant before. What we see is the moment after, when the man has just raised his head as if awakening to the new fact of his freedom. It seems that Ball was trying to represent, in the language of the body, the very first moment of emancipation, that precise instant when the slave, still in an abject position, realizes his chains have been broken—sundered magically from above—and lifts his head in recognition. Needless to say Lincoln is the agent of this transformation: the slave is acted upon rather than acting in his own right. Yet the

3.12 *Arrotino*, Hellenistic marble, Uffizi Gallery, Florence.

slave does not respond to Lincoln but instead to his own new state of being. It is a narrative of coming to consciousness, of rebirth, set into motion by the unseen action of the white savior above.[58]

In one crucial respect Ball's design departs from the traditional manumission formula. The model does not represent a personal relationship between emancipator and slave; there is no direct interaction based on gratitude or patronage or dependence. As commentators then pointed out, the design is meant to be more poetic or ideal.[59] Lincoln's act of abolition and the slave's initial awakening are really two separate narratives brought together here to suggest cause and effect, yet without recourse to the realist fiction of an interaction between great man and lowly slave. The idealization of their relationship allows the slave figure a small internal space for self-consciousness, whereas the other designs forced the slave figures to direct their attention entirely to Lincoln. But that idealization also magnifies the unbridgeable distance between the two figures: Lincoln becomes a messianic figure of total consciousness while the slave is reduced to a newborn, just on the threshold of being. In the abolitionist narrative of degradation and elevation, the slave's ascent has hardly begun, only hinted by the lifting of the head.

Some observers later remarked that the slave figure itself was ideal, which was their way of observing that the physiognomy was less noticeably Africanized.[60] The old notion that the African body was intrinsically anti-ideal died hard. It is true that Ball began with a life model, presumably black, but rejected him in favor of self-modeling; the resulting physiognomy has some of the conventional cues of blackness familiar from visual representation (tightly curled hair, broadened nose and lips) but still remains racially indistinct. Ball in his autobiography recounted that the original model "was not good enough to compensate for the unpleasantness of being obliged to conduct him through our apartment. . . . As I did not require an Apollo," Ball explained, he used himself.[61] Ball's nonchalant reference to Apollo—accepted standard of male beauty—betrays the real distance between his conception of the black body and Ward's for the *Freedman*: for Ward the ancient canon and the black body occupied the same universe. Ball's visceral discomfort with the living black model is repeated by other white sculptors working on the African American subject for public sculpture. Brown referred to his model for the Lincoln group as "that thriving 'nigger'" and wrote his wife that he did not expect him to "show his miserable muzzle here again."[62] These comments point to an obvious disparity between the artists' informal characterizations of real black people and the formal narratives of elevation in which the black subject was supposed to take part. But the attitudes betrayed here were common even among dedicated abolitionists, and they help account for why each design insisted so systematically on the opposition between Lincoln and the freed slave.

Despite the great ambitions of these local monument campaigns to represent the whole historical era, in the end all the local projects through the 1880s resorted to the traditional single-figure portrait statue. None of the monument committees chose the designs we have been discussing, even though these designs were obvious attempts to connect Lincoln with the broader historical phenomenon of emancipation. In both the New York and Philadelphia projects the final designs represented emancipation merely as an attribute of Lincoln's fame. Brown's monument has a standing Lincoln, in the role of statesman, holding the scroll signifying the Emancipation Proclamation. This formula would be used over and again, most notably in the Vinnie Ream statue of Lincoln commissioned for the U.S. Capitol in 1866 (fig. 3.13)—the only truly "official" Lincoln statue of the nineteenth century. Rogers's work instead has a seated Lincoln, in the role of creative genius, as if composing the celebrated document.

The precise reasons for the dismissal of the earlier designs are now obscure. We have it on the authority of Brown's son and biographer that the kneeling-slave design "was rejected by the committee because of fear that the figure of a negro in a public monument would arouse the resent-

3.13 Vinnie Ream [Hoxie], *Abraham Lincoln*, 1871,
marble, U.S. Capitol.

ment of the Irish citizens."[63] If the story is true it shows that, despite the clear subordination of the black figure to the white one in the design, the sheer power of the medium of public sculpture to honor and ennoble its subjects overwhelmed the formal aspects of this composition. It should be remembered that, except for the obscure case of the Avery Monument, the figure of the black had not appeared anywhere in American public sculpture, and the mere appearance in any pose or guise was therefore enormously significant and threatening. This was precisely the point in time when white ethnic groups were beginning to mobilize and sponsor monuments representing themselves and their place in American society. The Irish in New York could point to an absence of Irish figures in public sculpture; the idea that their city might erect a monument to African Americans before erecting a monument to Irish Americans might well have galled them.

Although the information about Brown's design is uncorroborated, it would seem to speak volumes about the severe obstacles facing any kind of black representation in public sculpture—even when the subject seemed to cry out for it and even when the sculptor was careful to install a racial hierarchy in the representation. If even the manumission narrative, with its reinscription of the power relations and racial order of slavery, could not win the approval of a white public, what could? How much safer for sculptor and sponsor alike simply to include a small device like a scroll signifying the act of emancipation. Besides, the emancipated themselves could easily be imagined without actually being represented. In Vinnie Ream's version for the Capitol (fig. 3.13), a slight downward tilt of Lincoln's head was all that was required to suggest the presence of passive slaves. In the most widely reprinted description of the statue, the writer imagines Lincoln looking down "with anxious solicitude," ready to use his ample cloak to protect the now invisible bodies of "the defenceless beings who are to receive the inestimable boon of freedom."[64]

We know that the African American body represented a fundamental threat to public sculpture. But it was still possible for monument sponsors to contemplate African American representation if it was suitably subordinated to the claims advanced for white heroism. The Philadelphia case, which is the most amply documented of the local projects, is the best example. The committee there originally invited a few chosen sculptors to submit two designs, one for a conventional single-figure monument and the other for a two-figure group consisting of Lincoln and an allegory, the whole to represent Lincoln "as the defender of our nationality, or as the author of the Emancipation Proclamation."[65] There is no reason to believe that the committee at this point was even contemplating a black figure. Yet the only two designs the committee received, by Randolph Rogers and Thomas Ball, both substituted a slave figure in the place of the allegory. Ball's design came recommended by none other than Hiram Powers, and had already gotten some favorable publicity in the New York press and elsewhere.[66] We do not know why the committee rejected Ball's model, for only its response to Rogers's design survives (in draft form). But here the committee made clear that even though a black figure hadn't originally been contemplated, it was "entirely satisfied" with his crouching female slave figure and "would not have any of its details or its relation with [the] principal figure altered."[67]

This response is all the more striking given that the letter criticized almost everything else about Rogers's design—the stiff pose of Lincoln, his narrow shoulders, the tightly buttoned coat, and especially the inclusion of a demon being crushed beneath Lincoln's right foot to represent the vanquishing of rebellion. The committee thought it important to represent the strength of the Union "particularly as it is shown by the destruction of slavery when slavery threatened its dissolution." But it wanted the idea embodied in a form less likely to cause offense to the defeated side since the monument was to last for ages and the time was coming, it hoped, when "fonder feelings" between the two sides would reemerge.[68] This argument is notable for two reasons. First, the achievement of abolition is subsumed under the achievement of Union, a priority that Lincoln himself maintained. More important, it recognizes the potential for disparity between a permanent image and the changeable social conditions and sentiments surrounding that image. The white South and its many "Copperhead" sympathizers in the North (Philadelphia included) would not want to see themselves forever represented as demons ground beneath the martyr's feet. What might do for a popular print created in the passion of the moment would not do for a monument meant to last in perpetuity. Of course the same logic is not applied to the figure of the black. Would the emancipated like to see themselves forever represented stripped and subservient, even as they were supposed to be raising themselves up through education and free labor? Wouldn't the time soon come when the representation became obsolete, and didn't that outcome deserve as much hope as "fonder feelings" between victor and vanquished? The unqualified approval of Rogers's freed slave indicates two interrelated attitudes: first, that within the committee's notion of the "public" for the monument, African Americans had much less standing than their white political enemies; second, that the idea of black subordination was so deeply rooted in their minds that a future equality could not even be imagined.

In the end it is not clear why the committee settled for a single-figure design. Money may have been a factor, since the dual-figure design obviously would have cost more. Rogers apparently proposed the seated Lincoln himself after the severe reaction to his first design. One of the committee members later expressed regrets; after visiting Ball's studio in Italy, he wrote back enthusiastically about Ball's model, which had been revised somewhat and cast in bronze, but by then the decision to accept Rogers's new design had already been made.[69] Whatever the specific reasoning was, it almost certainly did not turn on the question of the black figure. The committee seemed to understand and to accept without question the opposition of Lincoln and the slave, along with the complex of attitudes that opposition implied.

Unexpectedly, then, the first image of emancipation appeared not in a monument to Lincoln but in a soldier monument—the very type of memorial Howells had had in mind for the *Freedman*. Yet when the image did appear, it was not the primary focus as Howells had intended, or as the Lincoln sculptors had envisaged in their projects. It was a subsidiary relief panel embedded within a huge multifigured monument which the state of Rhode Island erected to its soldiers in 1871 in the capital city of

3.14 Randolph Rogers, Rhode Island Soldiers' and
Sailors' Monument, 1871, Providence.

Providence (fig. 3.14). The sculptor once again was Randolph Rogers, and he initially proposed a design in 1866 shortly before he began working on the Philadelphia project.[70] That initial design laid out all the elements of the final monument—the figure of America triumphant at the top, the four servicemen around the middle, the allegorical bas-reliefs and name plaques below—except that none of the four reliefs dealt with emancipation. By 1870 the subject of one of the reliefs had changed from "History" to "Emancipation," and Rogers had sent a photograph of a preliminary version in plaster (fig. 3.15).[71] The figure was a female slave, nude from the waist up, identifiable as African American by the full lips and tightly curled hair. Displaying with open palms the manacles and

3.15 Randolph Rogers,
model of emancipation
relief, 1870, plaster
(now lost).

broken chains still clinging to her wrists, she looked upward, as if to
meet the gaze of God or some other unseen higher authority. She was, in
effect, a standing version of the crouching figure Rogers had contemplated for Philadelphia. Distinguished from the other three allegories by
her "color," she represented a unique interjection of racial difference into
the most conventionalized kind of sculpture there was—the allegorical. In
the final version, erected a year later, Rogers moderated the nudity and
changed the face slightly, but retained the same pose and content. When
the monument was dedicated, the high-relief figure on the back of the
pedestal was the first figure of an African American on a monument outside a cemetery. Despite its exceptional status, it has received virtually no
attention, local or otherwise, and it was still misidentified as "History" in
the most recent guide to the city's public sculpture.[72]

Rogers went on later to create one more subsidiary image of emancipation, in a soldier monument erected in Detroit (1872–81).[73] As in Providence, emancipation was one of four female allegorical figures, the only
one made to look African American. In Detroit, the figure is in the round

and therefore more difficult to ignore. She is not a slave but in every respect the equal of the other three allegories who, like her, hold out wreaths above soldier figures below. It is only her hair and physiognomy that distinguishes her and that associates her allegorically with emancipation. This figure was so exceptional that its allegorical status was even called into question. African American audiences reappropriated it as a portrait of escaped slave Sojourner Truth, who had lived and died in Michigan. According to *Ebony* magazine, "the sculptor denied that he intended to portray Sojourner, but the public seized on the 'African-type' figure as a fitting monument" in itself. For many years the figure was reproduced in black publications, one of the only works of public sculpture they could claim as their own.[74]

African American audiences could also admire a work by Austro-Italian sculptor Francesco Pezzicar that was sent by the Austrian government to the 1876 Centennial Exhibition in Philadelphia. It was a bronze figure of a standing black man, chest swelling and arms outstretched, holding in one hand a crumpled sheet signifying the Emancipation Proclamation. The figure was based on a European prototype, a commemorative medal struck in England in 1834 to celebrate the British act of emancipation. In freestanding sculpture such a work had never been seen before: a vital, active, erect black man reveling in his own freedom. There was no subtlety about it; it was a one-dimensional historical fantasy, unmarked by the ambiguity and uncertainty of Ward's *Freedman*. But it was also a bold assertion of political and spiritual independence. Made by a foreign sculptor for temporary exhibition, it had little chance of finding a permanent home on a public monument in the United States.[75]

THE burgeoning new interest in public monuments, which had seemed to promise a vast space for the representation of emancipation, yielded little in the end beyond the conventional formulas of heroic representation. The experiment of the *Freedman* proved impossible to emulate in monumental sculpture. We know that the logic of commemoration imposed heavy constraints on the subject of emancipation. To imagine emancipation, for the most part, was to imagine Lincoln. But even within this narrow compass sculptors still tried to innovate, to transcend the prosaic domain of portrait statuary and create an image that would speak to what the nation was in the process of becoming. Their most common innovation—the pairing of a standing Lincoln with a kneeling slave in what I have described as a narrative of manumission—turned out to be more of a look backward than a look forward; it embodied deeply paternalistic aspects of abolitionism. Ultimately even this solution was bypassed in favor of safer, and more conventional, signifiers of emancipation located on the body of the white hero; the black body melted back into invisibility. The image of Lincoln with a scroll or a pen in hand carried no commentary on the status of blacks in America or on the future of race relations in an emancipated world. Out of all this sculptural activity only one major monument to emancipation came to be erected, and the long history of how it emerged in public space is the subject of the following chapter.

CHAPTER FOUR

FREEDOM'S
MEMORIAL

ON THE NATIONAL STAGE, in the center of political power, a monument to "freedom" finally emerged. This was the Freedmen's Memorial to Abraham Lincoln, a project begun immediately after Lincoln's death and completed finally in 1876—neatly spanning the whole era of Reconstruction. Financed entirely by contributions from free blacks, the monument campaign was the most conspicuous attempt in public sculpture to capture the spirit of Reconstruction, to translate into the sculptural language of the human body principles of freedom that remained abstract and barely imaginable. While the nation attempted to redefine itself as a free interracial society, the Freedmen's Memorial—first on its own, then in concert with other national monument projects—sought to make the interracial nation a palpable reality in public space.

The commemorative projects discussed in the preceding chapter were more local in their scope, meant to boost the reputations of the big cities that sponsored them. The Freedmen's Memorial, and a few others like it, appealed explicitly to a larger collectivity, cutting across local and regional boundaries, and by doing so they opened up new possibilities for the imagination. The sponsors of national monuments were less likely to settle for a single-figure design and were more determined to realize grander ambitions, both in historical scope and artistic originality. It is in this arena that we see, for the first time, proposals for large-scale sculptural cycles devoted to African American history and emancipation. New possibilities opened up in part because locally defined constituencies like the Irish in New York had much less impact; the "public" was much bigger and more diffuse. Without the more clearly drawn parameters of local politics to fall back on, the makers of national monuments were forced in effect to invent their own public. But in that process of invention was the opening for real innovation. The right tactics could create room to nurture a public into existence that might bring something genuinely novel, something unpredictable, into public sculpture.

This effort was in itself a test of emancipation's strength. If historians have tended to focus on other tests, on measures of political or economic rights, they have overlooked the more subtle structures that hold such measures in place. The task of imagining new forms of interracial sculpture and new national publics to legitimate them put direct pressure on the most profoundly embedded racial attitudes and concepts. Sculpture, as we have seen, mapped the racial terrain of the human body, where the hierarchy of difference clung most tenaciously. The question was whether a national monument to freedom could succeed in remapping the terrain of race in a genuinely liberating way. This monumental project was not simply an ornament to Reconstruction, but rather an enactment of the cultural change that the nation had to bring about. The grand designs of Reconstruction were unlikely to succeed without the fundamental change that emancipatory sculpture promised and demanded.

It is important to restore the sense of historical possibility at this moment in American sculpture because the final result of the Freedmen's campaign—Thomas Ball's monument in Washington, D.C.—seems so predictable in hindsight. An early twentieth-century photograph of it (fig. 4.1) hauntingly evokes the distance between the African American public and its monumental image, between the monument's claim to uplift and the condescension of its imagery. For the bronze freedman functions not as an exemplar for the rumpled youth staring up at it but as a foil through which white mastery is revealed. Ball's emancipated man is the very archetype of slavery: he is stripped, literally and figuratively, bereft of personal agency, social position, and accouterments of culture. Juxtaposed against the fully dressed, commanding figure of Lincoln, the black figure's nudity loses its heroic aspect and works instead as negation—most drastically a negation of the conventional markers of masculinity now monopolized by the white man above. Frozen forever in this unfortunate juxtaposition, the monument is not really about emancipation but about its opposite—domination. Ball's work hardly lived up to the great ambitions of the sponsors or to the even greater rhetoric of Reconstruction. Most disastrously, perhaps, the monument failed to speak to the experience of those who actually paid for it and made it possible. None of these failures was foreordained, however; no one in 1866 could have predicted that Ball's design would emerge triumphant from the profusion of schemes circulating at the time. By retracing the tortuous series of events—artistic, political, and sociological—that led unexpectedly to Ball's monument, we can recapture what was at stake at this pivotal point in national representation.

From its extraordinary and much-publicized origins, the campaign for the Freedmen's Memorial was mired in contradictions. The story begins after Lincoln's assassination with a five-dollar donation entrusted by an ex-slave named Charlotte Scott to her ex-master for a monument to the martyr-president. The local newspaper in Marietta, Ohio, instantly publi-

4.1 Thomas Ball, Freedmen's Memorial to Abraham Lincoln (Emancipation Monument), 1876, Lincoln Park, Washington, D.C.

cized the act, and others took notice. African Americans from the area apparently augmented Scott's gift and began to create a real fund, but this homegrown fund-raising effort was soon supplanted and erased by larger forces. Word of the original gift reached a Union general who thought "such a monument would have a history more grand and touching than any of which we have account," and he persuaded the Western Sanitary Commission of St. Louis—a volunteer war relief agency—to sponsor the project and "make it known to the freedmen."[1] The commission seized on Scott's offering as a model gesture of black gratitude, made doubly sentimental by its transmission through the bond of master and slave. In the first broadside for "Freedom's Memorial," the commission reported that an "old negro woman" gave the money "'to build a monument to good Massa Lincoln.'"[2] That image of black deference to white patronage then became reproduced in the institutional structure of the campaign—and ultimately in the monument itself. African Americans, mostly soldiers, contributed the cash, while the white sponsors collected the money and decided how to spend it. There was never any possibility that the donors themselves might influence the design; the sponsors made clear that it was "the friends of the freedmen" who would "determine the character of the monument."[3]

After a few months $20,000 or so had been deposited with the Western Sanitary Commission, enough for a modest bronze statue. But a modest statue was not what the commissioners wanted; they were determined to erect nothing less than a great work of art. The commissioners let it be known that they were now working for $50,000 but actually hoping for much more, so that "the magnificence of the memorial may correspond to the distinguished excellence of the man." Toward that end they asked every freedman in the country to donate "one week's free work, or its equivalent."[4] They also redoubled their fund-raising efforts by appointing the distinguished black lawyer and activist John Mercer Langston to solicit contributions personally from African American communities in the South and Midwest. By this time, though, Andrew Johnson had vetoed the Freedmen's Bureau bill, and pessimism was already beginning to hurt the campaign. This did not stop the commissioners from adopting an elaborate design by expatriate sculptor Harriet Hosmer late in 1866, which they had exhibited in Boston and proclaimed in a published circular to be "the greatest achievement of modern art."[5]

As these few facts suggest, this was not a straightforward case of a monument to be erected by and for African Americans. The public for the monument was peculiarly fractured from the inception. The subscribing public—the black donors—were really addressing not their own but a separate public. They wanted to make a "dignified offering" (as Langston later put it) to the white public that constituted the civic realm; they wanted to demonstrate their own civic responsibility in a medium that brought notice and prestige. For them the grandeur of the design probably mattered little. As Frederick Douglass argued in the *Anglo-African*, no matter how humble the monument it "would express one of the holiest sentiments of the human heart."[6] The white sponsors, in turn, recast that "sentimental" civic project in the language of paternalism, making appeals to the freed slaves to "prove that they are capable of appreciating the greatness of their deliverance and of the sacrifice by which it has been sealed."[7] The sponsors, in other words, were not simply executing the wishes of their subscribing public. They were competing on a wider stage with other monuments to Lincoln, and they wanted theirs to outshine them all in artistic quality and emotional effect; their monument was supposed to capture the new era that seemed to be dawning with Reconstruction. And here is where the poor black donors played an indispensable role. Driven by a gratitude the white audience could not match, they gave the sponsors' project a distinctive aura that ennobled and expanded the white artist's intention.

It is surprising that the Western Sanitary Commission came to sponsor the project at all because its members did not have credentials in the abolitionist movement. Any of the prewar abolitionist societies would have been a more likely choice. The project fell into the commission's lap because its relief work for the many thousands of black refugees in the western theater during the war had pushed the agency unexpectedly into dealing with freedmen's issues.[8] The eminent men from St. Louis who promoted the commission's work lived and prospered in a slave state, and they had in one way or the other accommodated to the local institution. The most outspoken opponent of slavery among them was the founder, Rev. William Greenleaf Eliot, a leading Unitarian minister and college president. Yet, before the war, Eliot repudiated abolitionism as extremist and only favored gradual, compensated emancipation as a policy.[9] Wayman Crow, who was in the commissioners' circle and one of the most active in the monument campaign, was himself a slaveowner until 1853 when he manumitted his domestic servants. Harriet Hosmer was a close family friend of Crow and in his household came to have a benevolent view of slavery, which was only tempered years later under the influence of female abolitionist friends like Lydia Maria Child. Hosmer threw her energies into the "darkey monument" (as she sometimes referred to it) because she thought there lay her best chances of securing a major Lincoln commission.[10]

The structural division within the campaign between black donors and white organizers distinguished it from one other distinctively African American project for a national monument to Lincoln. This was the "Colored People's Educational Monument Association," led by Henry Highland Garnet, one of the nation's most famous black political activists. Garnet's group proposed to erect an alternative, utilitarian monument—a national school for freedmen in the name of Lincoln.[11] Though it enlisted contributions from everyone, black or white, the whole project was much more clearly embedded within the African American community, both in its institutional structure and in its goals and audience. But Douglass, longtime opponent of Garnet, still objected publicly. If African Americans wanted to build a monument to Lincoln to show the nation their gratitude, he argued in print, they shouldn't mix that civic project with their own pressing goal of self-education; it "*looks to me like an attempt to wash the black man's face in the nation's tears for Abraham Lincoln!*" [emphasis in original].[12] Douglass's opposition touched off a nasty exchange of letters between him and the monument managers printed in the *Anglo-African*. In that exchange Douglass broadened his attack, condemning the very idea of enlisting the aid of whites for a separate "colored" monument. It smacked of officially sanctioned separatism, he suggested: "what new plan or scheme is brewing with a view to make separation a substitute for equality, a colored nationality a substitute for complete incorporation in the American body politic?"[13] The debate is important because it shows what was at stake for African Americans in the whole monument business—nothing less than the terms under which they would enter civic space and find representation there in the body politic. We do not know what impact the debate had on actual African American communities but it surely must have hurt Garnet's campaign, for the project disappeared soon after the dispute was aired.

In 1865 there was one other national monument organization that tried to raise money in African American communities. This was the National Lincoln Monument Association in Springfield, Illinois, a group of prominent Illinois politicians who proposed a monument where Lincoln was buried. The association targeted African Americans and many other different groups for fund raising, in an effort to make the enterprise a legitimately "national" undertaking. Once again black soldiers contributed liberally, but other African Americans expressed a wish to build a monument by themselves or to have some portion of the tomb structure designated as their particular contribution. For them the whole point was to make their donation publicly visible; otherwise the act was lost and made meaningless.[14]

This seemed to be exactly the selling point of the Freedmen's Memorial, except that the adoption of Hosmer's design forced an abrupt change in the sponsors' strategy. Needing another $100,000 or more to execute the design, the commission suddenly opened its appeal for funds to a much wider public. A circular of December 1866 asked the citizens of New England (where the commission had raised most of its funds for relief during the war) and most particularly "the women of America" to complete the work begun by Charlotte Scott and her African American compatriots.[15] Shifting from race to gender, the new fund-raising appeal no doubt hoped to trade on the historic role played by women in the abolitionist movement; the sponsors were also simply trying to capitalize on the unique circumstances of a female founder and a female artist. The *Freedmen's Record*, organ of the New-England Freedmen's Aid Society, offered to help, but the commission's change of course received some damaging commentary elsewhere in the press.[16] The new public that the commission envisaged—an alliance of freedmen and their white supporters—did not materialize.

Despite the vagaries of the commission's campaign, the design by Hosmer that emerged from it did depart radically from the formula estab-

4.2 Harriet Hosmer, model for Freedmen's Memorial to Lincoln, 1866,
plaster (now lost).

lished by Brown, Rogers, and Ball. In the process, the design inspired at
least some critics to think that it might be the one work that adequately
responded to the challenge of representing the postabolition era. Hosmer's model fortunately survives in photographs and stereo form, and
a revised version was later engraved and published in the London *Art-
Journal.*[17] The original model, the one exhibited in Boston, is a multi-
tiered affair topped by a recumbent effigy of Lincoln on a sarcophagus
within an open, circular temple (fig. 4.2). Above the columns of the temple is inscribed an edited version of the final words of the Emancipation
Proclamation, leaving out the reference to its military necessity and in-
voking only the nobler considerations of justice and God. The drum supporting the temple carries a frieze of thirty-six female allegories representing the states of the Union during Lincoln's presidency. Below the temple,
in the middle of the main structure, is the monument's most unusual element: a sculptural cycle of African American history, featuring four
standing black male figures, one at each corner. On the base below the
black figures are four bas-reliefs illustrating events in the life and death of

Lincoln, and on the four outside corners of the monument are "mourning Victories" with trumpets reversed, which return the viewer to the theme of martyrdom highlighted by the temple at the top.

The African American cycle is made especially conspicuous by its position in the center of the monument. From the front, the viewer sees the first and last figures in the cycle as they frame the memorial structure. On the right is a seminude slave, with head downcast and wrists manacled together, "exposed for sale" as Hosmer explained; on the left is a fully clothed soldier gazing straight out and holding a bayonetted rifle, as if at picket duty. Here in effect are the two poles of masculinity, as measured on the axis of power. The first figure has been stripped of clothes and power, bound so that his hands are immobile; he drops his head in shame. The last figure, his hands freed, holds a gun and wears the uniform of national power; his gaze can now meet the world's from a position of strength. Behind these figures are the two intermediate figures in the cycle, the second being a field slave who rests on a hoe and drops his head, and the third being a "contraband" type, or, as Hosmer put, "a guide and assistant to our troops," who carries a basket of food in one arm. There are some interesting nuances in the treatment of these intermediary figures (see fig. 4.3, a second version of Hosmer's design, for a clearer view of these figures). The field slave holds the hoe in much the same way the soldier holds his gun, a compositional rhyme that serves to underscore the irony and injustice of expropriating the slave's labor. The basket of food carried by the third figure represents that historic moment when the fruits of the slave's agricultural labor are no longer expropriated but turned by him toward his own liberation.[18]

As a composition Hosmer turned the whole monument into a kind of spatial pyramid, insisting at each level on the four corners so that they made continuous lines sweeping upward and inward. Within the pyramid there was considerable freedom to interweave the themes of emancipation, martyrdom, and Union. Emancipation is represented in the uppermost inscription and the cycle in the middle, martyrdom in the dead figure of Lincoln up above and the mourning figures at the bottom, Union in the frieze of allegories below Lincoln and the eagles and shields just beneath. For clarity of outline and internal harmony Hosmer repeated the poses of her figures: all the mourning figures kneel, all the black figures stand. This decision had important consequences, for it forced an even more decisive break with the inconography of manumission. Though Lincoln is represented up above the black figures to maintain the hierarchy of heroism, he is in the horizontal position while they stand erect. His power and agency have been drained from him by death, as if to reemerge in the emancipated slaves beneath him. In Hosmer's design, Lincoln's act of emancipation is not illustrated in an invented interaction but recollected in his words, chosen to resonate in the present. The viewer is, of course, supposed to grasp the interconnections between Lincoln's acts, the Union victory, and the slave's liberation, but the decision to represent the hero in his tragic end allows the narrative of liberation to stand more forcefully on its own, in its own space, propelled by its own internal logic.

In choosing to juxtapose the figure of the slave and that of the soldier, Hosmer was embodying a trope by then quite familiar in the rhetoric of emancipation. During the war, when the Union command recognized the military advantage of arming slaves, blacks and whites immediately sensed that military service would profoundly change the social construction of black masculinity. "The black man is henceforth to assume a new *status* among us," one senator asserted in 1864.[19] To be a soldier in battle was the ultimate test of manhood, because men battled men and battled to the death. For the male slave the test was even more profound since his masculinity had been denied from the outset. "If slaves will make good soldiers," one Confederate general declared, "our whole theory of slavery is wrong."[20] As we have seen, in the representations of the dominant culture, the male slave could demonstrate his manhood only insofar as he resisted or escaped slavery. To become a Union soldier, then, was not only to acquire conventional trappings of masculinity but to resist the very institution that suppressed his masculinity in the first place. As one slave turned soldier commented in 1863: "Now we sogers are men—men de first time in our lives. Now we can look our masters in de face. They used to sell and whip us, and we did not dare say one word. Now we ain't afraid, if they meet us, to run the bayonet through them."[21] Remarkably, Hosmer's cycle seizes on many of the same elements in this juxtaposition—the alteration in the black man's gaze, the helpless exposure to violence transformed into power to return violence with violence, even the image of the bayonet as symbolic of that new power.

Wearing a uniform and carrying a gun did in fact give the former slave a sense of power and respect unimaginable under slavery. The annals of the war and its aftermath are full of anecdotes of former slaves, now soldiers, refusing to show deference to whites and sometimes even witnessing the spectacle of a former master crouching before them.[22] The "before-and-after" images that became popular during the war made the change visible on the body itself by deliberately contrasting the slovenly dress and posture of the slave (often, it seems, posed as such in a studio) with the crisp uniform and erect stance of the slave-turned-soldier (see fig. 3.3).[23] The new black man in this pair embodied the stunning optimism of his era: in one simple change of outfit, he stepped out of one entrenched tradition of popular representation—the ragged, feeble, pathetic "darky" familiar from minstrelsy and caricature—and into a brave new world of civic display.

The dramatic transformation of the slave into the soldier served as a kind of visual rebuttal to the argument, sometimes heard, that the habits of obedience and subordination inculcated under slavery actually prepared slaves for life as soldiers. The image of self-transformation completed the work that officers like Thomas Wentworth Higginson, one of the first white commanders of black troops during the war, initiated. "The more strongly we marked the difference between the slave and the soldier," he recalled later, "the better for the regiment. One half of military duty lies in obedience, the other half in self-respect. A soldier without self-respect is worthless." The image of the slave-turned-soldier made that self-respect palpable in the trappings of the body itself.[24]

In embodying this opposition of slave and soldier in a sculptural cycle, Hosmer claimed to be representing no more than "the condition of the negro as it actually existed at different periods of the President's four years of office."[25] This formulation reduces the cycle to a properly commemorative image, illustrating the history of Lincoln's era. Yet the figures could not help but read as a statement about the future, about the promise of emancipation. By the end of the cycle the black figure is not trapped in an everlasting posture of debasement, as the freed slaves are in the manumission imagery. He is erect, intact, unwounded, alert but not rigid. He has acquired manhood (the level gaze), power (the gun), and legitimacy (the uniform)—all three reinforcing and requiring one another. His "elevation" is already complete. If Ward's *Freedman* posed a question about the black man's fate, Hosmer's narrative supplies an answer by giving the black man a clear social identity, the image of the citizen-soldier keeping vigil. This was the very image that would become the accepted icon of manhood in the white soldier monuments erected over the next several decades.

The implications of Hosmer's narrative are clear enough, especially so in 1865–66 when the political struggle over the legacy of the war was turning increasingly on the definition of the rights of the freedmen. In her cycle the figure of the black man has done everything he can to make his body and his action conform to the standards of citizenship. He has labored, even without reward; helped the Union when opportunity arose; become a model soldier himself. If his emancipation remains incomplete, it is only because white culture refuses to grant it, refuses to acknowledge the "progress" defined by and in Hosmer's sculpture. Hosmer's design envisions not only a new African American man, but a new American society in which he can find acceptance.

Hosmer's decision to install this imagery at the heart of her memorial structure—the black figures occupy the center of the imaginary pyramid of space—was a radical proposal for it insisted on the centrality of the African American subject, when only a short time before that subject was,

4.3 Harriet Hosmer, design for Freedmen's Memorial to Lincoln,
in [London] *Art-Journal* 7 (January 1, 1868): 8.

sculpturally speaking, invisible. Critics who saw the model or photographs of it did not fail to appreciate the significance. Before Hosmer,
wrote the *Independent*, "sculpture [of Lincoln] remained silent, or only
feebly articulate. It has spoken at last—to a negro woman whom Lincoln
emancipated—by Harriet Hosmer, the New England artist." It was of
course the "negro" connection that gave her design voice, made it speak
for the age. The monument was "Hosmer's masterpiece" and "our greatest work of art." Critics singled out the African American statues as the
best part of the design, and *Harper's Monthly* hoped Hosmer would execute them whatever the fate of the monument.[26]

Despite the praise Hosmer tinkered with the placement of the African
American cycle, and actually made a second design in which the same
cycle occupies the outermost corners while the allegories shift inward
and become standing figures passing wreaths of victory down toward
the black men (fig. 4.3). In this design, published in the London *Art-
Journal*, Lincoln is a standing figure holding a broken chain, and the allegories therefore serve as intermediary figures linking him with the African American; we read down from his emancipatory act through the

allegories to the achievement of black liberation. The whole design returns the center of agency and responsibility to the active figure of Lincoln. Hosmer then rejected this revised design and returned to her original, except that she tried simply reversing the placement of the mourning
figures and the black figures. She was trying to solve a formal problem,
which was how to lead the eye downward through the composition. The
mourning figures, with their diagonal trumpets, created a graceful link
between top and bottom, while the emancipation cycle tended to catch
the eye and hold it there. "For point of sentiment" she preferred the black
figures in the center, but "for the general outline" she preferred the
mourning figures there.[27]

By the time Hosmer was considering these changes, the Western Sanitary Commission had come to realize that it could not muster the huge
sums needed to carry out Hosmer's project. But her design had acquired
a life of its own, and in the commissioners' minds it became more important to erect it than to preserve the original idea of the fund. Hence, in the
summer of 1868, they made the extraordinary offer of merging their resources with those of the National Lincoln Monument Association in
Springfield. There was just one condition: Hosmer's design had to be
chosen. This proposal would have further diminished the importance of
the original black donors, as their contributions would simply disappear
into the much larger fund already collected for the tomb. Ultimately the
move failed, but out of it came one extremely revealing document—a
letter written on Hosmer's behalf, with the commission's approval, by the
distinguished Henry Bellows, president of the U.S. Sanitary Commission,
the major war relief agency for the Union.[28]

Bellows's letter, an elaborate defense of Hosmer's design addressed to
the governor of Illinois, is one of the most learned essays on monuments
written in the nineteenth century, but quite apart from its general interest
it demonstrates how even such a clear program as Hosmer's could be
dissociated from the freedmen and reinterpreted to fit the demands of a
new monument and a new public. Bellows begins his exposition by arguing that the preservation of the Union was the "object" of the war, while
emancipation, however noble a result, was merely the "condition" of the
war's success. This distinction then determines how the commemorative
attention of the monument should be distributed. It is fit for the freedmen's monument to make emancipation its leading idea, but "in a *National* Monument" the theme of emancipation must remain subsidiary to
the dominant theme of Union. Implicit is the idea that emancipation—
and the shift from slave to free society it entailed—was less a shared "national" interest than the maintenance of Union. Bellows claims that Hosmer's design lays the stress on Union where it belongs—in the upper part
of the structure, the temple. As for the inscription from the Emancipation

Proclamation on the temple, which seems to undercut his argument, he points out that the word slavery does not occur in it. Slavery is represented instead on the lower level, on a platform of its own—"as if detaching Slavery and all its works from a Union, which was foreign in all its purposes and in its very spirit from that historical accident and incubus." While it should be remarked that this interpretation rests on some dubious claims—that slavery was foreign to the national spirit, that Hosmer's design reflects that foreignness—it is especially notable that the argument turns the earlier praise for Hosmer's model on its head. For the *Independent* the "negro" theme is what made the design "articulate" to the public; the critic even suggested that there should be black figures among the allegories in the Union frieze. But for Bellows blackness must be contained, made secondary, to the point that it remain outside the very structure representing nationality. In rhetorically detaching the idea of slavery from this structure, Bellows must detach the emancipated as well. He concedes that the four statues do give the idea of emancipation an appropriately conspicuous place in the monument, but emphasizes that it is a lower place, representing emancipation as "a blessing, which being *deprivative*, leaves the Union itself without any mark of its late accursed presence." Hence the emancipation cycle, in this reading, shifts from a narrative of liberation and creation, social death and rebirth, to a mere sign of negation, a reminder of the *absence* of slavery from the newly unified nation.

We cannot know whether Bellows's letter represents Hosmer's intention. It does represent one way of rewriting her design without having to change the design itself, and she may well have approved of that rewriting. But Bellows's effort came to nothing. The Springfield association had already committed itself to a design competition, and although Hosmer's design was entered it was not even among the top vote-getters in the jury's balloting. The association ended up choosing a design by Larkin Mead which minimized the issue of emancipation much further than Bellows ever could with Hosmer's design. Mead returned to the formula of a standing Lincoln holding a scroll, on which was inscribed "Emancipation." This was the only reference to the subject. The subsidiary figures were not African Americans but white soldiers disposed in four combat groups; the sculpture turned the commemorative focus to the idea of warfare.

The Springfield competition is important to us because it was the only open competition for a monument to Lincoln held in the nineteenth century.[29] In fact the competition was held to publicize the project and legitimize it as a truly national undertaking. The dozens of entries received, mostly from sculptors and architects, represent in a fragmentary way the possibilities of the collective imagination; they show the range of solutions that could be advanced even within the restrictive forum of a professional competition effectively open only to white artists who could command significant resources. What is interesting is that a substantial number of designs did propose to bring the African American body into representation, and—even more strikingly—the association looked seriously at them. Unfortunately, except for Hosmer's design and two others, the visual records of these entries have disappeared and we can imagine them only through written descriptions.[30]

Overall at least a quarter of the entries did include figures of freed men or women. The two designs submitted by sculptor Leonard Volk, for example, included statues of a freed slave and a Union soldier (presumably white) flanking the entrance to the tomb structure. One of the two designs incorporated a highly unusual allegory of emancipation: the figure of a slave woman holding a tablet bearing the Emancipation Proclamation. A few entries even tried to situate African American figures outside the conventional domains of allegory or documentary history. While Hosmer's model ostensibly recorded the past achievements of African Americans under Lincoln's administration, some designs actually took the emancipation theme out of the commemorative framework of "history" and situated it frankly in the contemporary context of debates over freedmen's rights. C. G. Volk's design included a group "representing the white and black boy building together, symbolizing the present position of the two races"; the board deciding the competition apparently discussed the design with the artist and left a note saying that it "considers past present and prospective of slavery."[31] However the design may have looked, it seemed to be a serious attempt at an interracial image, clearly departing from the commemorative norm. That it received any serious notice—and it did earn a few votes in the first balloting—indicates a surprising degree of openness to new racial representations never before seen in sculpture.

The most radical proposal came from Philadelphia sculptor A. E. Harnische; it deliberately set out to represent Lincoln's act of emancipation as "the introduction of a new era in [American] history."[32] In this multi-tiered assemblage of sculpture, with Lincoln holding the Emancipation Proclamation at the top, a cycle of conventional allegorical figures is coupled with a cycle of emancipation groups that address some of the central issues of Reconstruction. Next to last in the emancipation cycle is a figure of Power paired with a group representing education, in which male and female figures read a book; finally there is the figure of Justice to whom a freedman "with unshackled hands appeals for his rights as such." Here Harnische's design abandons the commemorative conceit entirely and becomes an open plea for the future. Lincoln's proclamation reads as the catalyst for a train of events whose final outcome is unresolved. This appeal for education, power, and justice for the former slaves—none of which had yet been realized, despite Reconstruction—must have seemed too hot to handle, and the entry received no votes.[33]

With the Springfield group's eventual decision to avoid any representation of emancipated figures, whether secondary or not, the efforts on behalf of Hosmer's proposal came to an end. At this point the Western Sanitary Commission's campaign took one final surprising turn. Still lacking sufficient funds for what it considered to be a worthy monument, the commission decided to throw its money to yet another National Lincoln Monument Association and another design. This was the proposal, sponsored by leading Republicans in Congress and the administration, for an immense national monument to Lincoln and his era, to be erected on the Capitol grounds in Washington. Although it was to be funded by private donation, it was virtually an official project of the federal government, with the funds even managed by the U.S. treasurer.[34]

Of the two National Lincoln Monument Associations, this one was certainly the more logical home for the freedmen's fund. Unlike the Springfield monument, the Washington project was driven by the rhetoric of radical Reconstruction, with its platform of universal male suffrage and equal rights. Congress initiated the project in March 1867, shortly after it had passed the first Reconstruction Act, which required states in the South to ratify the Fourteenth Amendment (equal rights) and guarantee black male suffrage. The same coalition in Congress that passed this act also passed the bill sponsoring the national monument. The bill created "the Lincoln Monument Association, for the purpose of erecting a monument in the city of Washington, commemorative of the great charter of emancipation and universal liberty in America."[35] The dominant theme of the monument was thus fixed from the outset, and it looked forward more than backward. Note how the language slips from Lincoln to emancipation to universal liberty; by the end of this sequence the commemorative program encompasses the radical Republican agenda of racial equality under the law encoded in the term *universal* liberty. Under this formulation Lincoln himself is reconstructed, no longer simply the Civil War president but the founder of a new nation-state empowered to complete the "charter" he initiated with the Emancipation Proclamation. Ostensibly authorizing a monument to Lincoln, the bill really called for a monument to a newly emergent ideal of an interracial nationality.

The original fund-raising appeal of the association published in 1867 made that ideal explicit in the very first sentence, addressing "the loyal people of the United States of all classes, without distinction as to race or color."[36] This formulation is noticeably different from the fund-raising appeals of the Springfield association, which tended to treat African Americans as a separate constituency; here the emphasis is on one people,

united across divisions of class and race. Frederick Douglass had been
appointed to the board of managers, and this first fund-raising appeal
seems to bear his imprint.[37] At the end of his acrimonious exchange two
years earlier with the "Colored People's Educational Monument Association," he had declared that he was never opposed to the idea of "mixing"
white and black contributions to build a suitable monument to Lincoln,
as long as the final result was not labeled a "colored" monument. In fact,
for Douglass an all-black project was worthy if carried out honestly, but
he preferred a mixed project, "a People's monument to Abraham Lincoln
without distinction of color." He even suggested that the Colored People's Educational Monument Association turn over its money to a common fund for a people's monument because it "would be in harmony
with our demands not for special privileges but for common rights and
common equality before the law."[38]

It was perhaps in this spirit that the board of managers approached the
Western Sanitary Commission in 1868 and began to negotiate for the
freedmen's fund. By the end of the year the managers and the commission
had worked out a deal, but the terms of the agreement betrayed the ideal
that Douglass had promoted and the managers themselves had embraced
in their first appeal for contributions. The commission agreed to transfer
its $20,000 in funds to pay for the upper portion of the monument con-
taining an effigy of Lincoln, that portion to be officially designated the
freedmen's contribution.[39] The designation was obviously meant to preserve, at least in part, the integrity of the original freedmen's fund. But at
the same time that designation dramatically altered the larger Reconstruction project: it created a monument within a monument, a color distinction built into the very fabric of the whole.

Moreover, the design that the Western Sanitary Commission bought
its way into was problematic from the beginning. Chosen without competition in early 1868, the design by the sculptor Clark Mills made Hosmer's look simple and sparse by comparison [fig. 4.4]. A densely packed
pyramid of sculpture, the model included over two dozen portrait statues
of famous men in addition to a seated Lincoln on top, posed in the act of
signing the proclamation and surrounded by allegories of justice, liberty,
and time. In addition it included, on the next to lowest tier, an elaborate
emancipation cycle, the only other besides Hosmer's that was approved
and published in an adopted design. But Mills's cycle, though it was organized around the same basic idea of a progress from slavery to freedom,
departed significantly from Hosmer's example. Here is the description
taken from the stereo photograph distributed to subscribers:

> The first . . . presents the slave in his most abject state, as when brought to
> this country. Here we behold him nude, deprived of all which tends to elate
> the heart with any spirit of pride or independence.

4.4 Clark Mills, model for National Lincoln Monument,
circa 1868, plaster (now lost).

The second represents a less abject stage. He is here partly clad, more
enlightened, and hence, realizing his bondage, startles with a love of Freedom.

The third . . . is the ransomed slave, redeemed from bondage by the blood
of Liberty, who, having struck off his shackles, holds them triumphantly
aloft. The slave is pictured gratefully bowing at her feet.[40]

We do not know whether this description came from Mills or from the
sponsors, but in either case it betrays an unshakable condescension toward the people it represents and supposedly commemorates. The African arrives abject, without self-pride or any notion of freedom or independence. These are acquired, paradoxically, by the enlightenment made
possible under slavery (an assertion very close to the proslavery arguments made before the war); only then does the slave belatedly "realize
his bondage" and feel "a love of Freedom." Of course, despite that new-
found love, the slave cannot break his own shackles but must kneel to an
allegorical Liberty, symbolic of the nation that paid his "ransom" in
blood.

The groups as they appear in photographs of the model do represent a substantial departure from Hosmer's imagery. The two groups that frame the front side of the monument are not the first and last in the cycle but the first and second, so that the image of emancipation ends up on the very rear of the monument facing away from Lincoln. All three groups pair a standing figure with a sitting or kneeling figure, and all three, even the last, adopt the conventional slave postures of abasement or obeisance. In the second group, for example, where the slave "startles" to a love for freedom, the seated pose recalls the traditional emblem for suffering (as did Brown's slave figure for the Washington pediment) and the standing recalls Michelangelo's writhing slave figures, now in the Louvre. In the final group the manumission imagery reasserts itself, made ideal by the abstract agency of the allegorical figure. Yet the slave figure is even more obeisant than in the other designs we have seen, with his head still bowed and his hands reaching up to touch the proffered arm of his savior.

When the cycle is viewed within its sculptural context, the African American figures read even less as historical persons and more as signs of the nation's moral achievement. The cycle is sandwiched between two massive tiers of portrait statuary of great men, meant to represent the organizations and forces that "stood by" Lincoln and helped him triumph. Below the slaves are the great military heroes like Sherman and Grant striding forward on horseback; above are standing figures of representative cabinet officials, relief organizers, and ministers who helped advance the cause. In a monument that sought to materialize the history of an era in a vast array of heroic men, all represented standing or astride a horse, the black figures are conspicuous in their difference. In sculptural terms, they are shut out from the realist realm of the heroic likeness. It is not simply their anonymity, but their bodily self-absorption that is responsible. Bent over themselves or writhing to break free, their bodies have not yet attained the confident address to the world that would enable them to join the ranks of heroes and thereby enter the national chronicle of achievement. Their lack of historical identity and agency turns them into emblems rather than actors: their bodies define the moral cause for which the great white men on the monument struggled and fought.

It does seem peculiar that an association ostensibly dedicated to representing the new idea of universal liberty would choose such a paternalistic design, which despite the allegories of liberty and justice on top, reinscribed subservience in the black body and reaffirmed the black man's segregation from the civic realm of the hero. It is doubly peculiar when the personal history of the artist is considered. Mills was a slaveowner and used slave labor in his bronze foundry in Maryland until nearly the end of the Civil War; in one of the supreme ironies of Lincoln's era,

Mills's slaves help cast the collosal statue of Freedom which was installed atop the Capitol dome in December 1863 and immediately hailed as an augur of emancipation.[41] Mills had begun his career as a sculptor in South Carolina and retained strong ties with the region. In fact, in the spring of 1865, Mills was accused in the *New York Post* and the *Washington Star* of being a Confederate sympathizer (a charge that was actually corroborated by an informer), and at the same time he lost his studio inside the Capitol building.[42]

Moreover, Mills had acquired an infamous reputation in the art establishment as a philistine who won public commissions by pandering to popular taste. He was in almost every respect the opposite of Hosmer as an artist. Whereas she formally studied anatomy and carefully absorbed the classical canon in Italy, choosing to practice there amid the examples of antiquity, he was a self-taught artist who ignored the canon and never stepped foot in Europe. His great feat was to build his own bronze foundry and, without training or experience, cast the first equestrian statue in the United States—the Andrew Jackson Monument erected in Washington in 1853. Flouting classical models, Mills took the pose and gesture directly from a popular print and received enormous public acclaim simply because he managed to balance the horse on its hind legs. Both critics and admirers treated Mills's work as a litmus of the popular, and indeed of the American—insofar as these two notions were so often conflated. He was either an authentic exponent of American individualism and "natural" taste, as Stephen Douglas claimed in his oration at the Jackson Monument, or the embodiment of American arrogance and tastelessness.[43]

So why would an association of radical Republicans choose the design of a sculptor with so controversial a reputation, tainted by slavery and disloyalty? And why would the sponsors of the Freedmen's Memorial throw their chips in with a design and approach to design so different from Hosmer's? We cannot know for sure, since most of the relevant papers of both the association and the artist have been lost. But we may begin to find answers in an essay published in 1870 by Hosmer's supporter Henry Bellows, who turns out to be a link between the two projects. Bellows was chosen as one of the "representative men" included on Mills's pedestal, and he used his essay to promote the grand scheme. Although the design would have "a thousand defects of detail," he wrote, "we expect a result, grand and majestic, with something of the vastness and roughness of this stage of the popular taste, but at least an honest expression of American largeness of feeling and grandeur of purpose."[44] The terms of praise for Mills's design are entirely different from those he had applied to Hosmer's. Hosmer's was above all a work of art, to be compared with the great monuments of Europe. Art as understood in the nineteenth century demanded formal unity, the subordination of details to the expression of a leading idea or ideas; as Bellows had put it in his Illinois letter, "the real test of the artist's genius" is not so much the choice of ideas but "the *management* of these ideas."[45] Hosmer had skillfully united the ideas of Union and emancipation in a harmonious whole. In defending the Mills design Bellows deliberately suspends his critical faculties. Mills's monument is not to be judged as a work of art but as an authentic expression of American character and sentiment. It is rough and defective in detail, but it is ambitious in its scope, accessible to popular taste, and honestly American.

Though both the designs by Hosmer and Mills are embedded in the mimetic tradition, centering on the imitation of the human figure, they nevertheless arrive at antithetical conceptions of the sculptural monument. For Hosmer mimesis is not an end in itself. Her model is really an allegorical monument, an exposition of ideas, with only one portrait effigy, that of the central hero. All her sculptural cycles—even the ostensibly "realistic" cycle of African Americans—are sign systems, meant to be read as the inscriptions are. They draw attention to their own act of historical interpretation, and in turn demand interpretation from the viewer. Mills is much more profoundly attached to realism. His design is above all an accumulation of effigies of great men, interspersed with some allegorical sculpture. Those effigies are not signs but likenesses, stand-ins for the real thing. They are not meant to interpret history but to duplicate it, to bring it back to life. Lincoln is not so much explained as he is surrounded by the men who helped him make history. The emancipation cycle appears anomalous amid these ranks of heroes above and below it. We can either see Mills's African American figures as "realistic," in which case they are pathetic historical specimens, or we can demote them to the secondary status of allegory. In Hosmer's design, by contrast, the emancipation cycle is central because it is vital to the monument's act of interpretation. For the critics, that self-conscious semiotic mediation was what made Hosmer an artist; Mills was "popular" or "natural" because he seemed to devalue that mediation.

If Mills's monument therefore did not conform to European models, that very disparity could be used to prove its authenticity. The association published a statement attributed to Lincoln's secretary of state, William Seward, who, having "seen the principal Monuments in Europe," asserted that "Europe could not have such a Monument for she has not such a history."[46] In this account Seward had been shown the design by Lincoln himself. According to the story Mills had actually conceived the monument while Lincoln was still alive (a claim that is indeed plausible) and had given a drawing of the design to Lincoln, who praised it but passed it on to Seward because he had traveled to Europe and was a "judge of art."[47] The story capitalizes on familiar elements of the Mills mystique: first the popular appreciation from the untutored Lincoln, then the surprise judgment of the learned critic who is won over precisely because Mills has *not* emulated the art of Europe but directly captured American history itself.

In fact, contrary to the thrust of the story, Mills did look to Europe to mediate his representation of American history. For his vast pedestal he adapted a celebrated Prussian work, the equestrian monument in Berlin to Frederick the Great by Christian Daniel Rauch, completed in 1851. In this monument a colossal equestrian statue of the king rests on a multi-tiered pedestal that serves as a kind of scaffold carrying various combinations of equestrian statues, standing figures, allegories, and bas-reliefs— representing the great men and accomplishments of the king's reign. This work inspired three huge monument proposals by Mills, the first of which was an equestrian monument to Washington proposed in the mid-1850s, the second the Lincoln monument, and the third a monument to Lincoln's adversary Robert E. Lee, entered in an 1877 competition.[48] Rauch's design gave Mills a prototype for a vast all-purpose monument, a flexible framework to accommodate all sorts of sculpture (historical portraiture, allegory, myth) in all sorts of formats (pedestrian, equestrian, bas-relief). For each monument and each ideological program, Mills reshuffled the components and filled in the iconographical blanks. He could easily shift the scheme from Union to Confederate commemoration without altering the general principle of the design. That general principle might be described in a word as conglomeration. Mills crowded as much "history" as possible onto the sculptural scaffold—history being represented primarily by an accretion of individual men, and only secondarily by allegory that suggests their collective achievement. Inscriptions or texts played no significant part.

In her monument Hosmer had tried to create a coherent movement from top to bottom, not by recourse to the unifying gesture of Lincoln himself, who was disabled within the composition, but by unfolding and interweaving key historical themes at various levels. The themes of Union and emancipation thus read as historically interconnected, converging in the martyrdom of the single hero. In Mills's design, by contrast, we confront a cacaphony of gesturing heroes, distributed on various levels that have little to do with one another. Mills made no special effort to integrate his emancipation cycle into the larger framework. It is positioned arbitrarily between two levels of white heroes; the levels could easily be reshuffled and repacked, just as they were in the other monuments of this type he designed.

Predictably Mills's design was criticized in the press as a monstrosity,[49] but remarkably the very same formal qualities that made it an aesthetic jumble proved useful to the sponsors who adopted it. The multiplicity and interchangeability of the elements in Mills's design turned out to be well suited to the strategy of the monument campaign as it evolved over time. The association, it seems, quickly abandoned the idea of raising the vast sums necessary for a major monument simply by a mass appeal to the "loyal people," without distinction as to class or race. Instead it reconceived its base of support as a patchwork of smaller, more specialized constituencies that would be willing to fund a particular element of the monument. Mills's design lent itself quite well to this strategy of fragmenting the public into interest groups. His assemblage could easily be broken down into subcomponents, each with its own target constituency and its own separate subscription fund. To begin with, the statues of the "representative men" were conceived virtually as independent monuments, chosen not by the artist but by the association itself as it tried to assemble a cross section of interests that would bring in maximum donations. There were separate funds established for Salmon Chase, General Grant, and Henry Ward Beecher among others, with the idea that their statues would be cast in bronze as soon as the fund filled up. Statues were also assigned to key supporters of the monument: Henry Bellows, as we have seen, and James Yeatman, president of the Western Sanitary Commission, who seems to have been chosen as thanks for the $20,000 in freedmen's money his group promised.[50]

For the sponsors, what Mills's design lost in coherence it gained in the malleability and reach of its representation. Figures could be added, subtracted, or replaced at will, in a relentless search for new sources of funds. This seemed to be exactly what the sponsors had in mind from the start: they adopted the design only in its "general features," and left control of the "details" to their own board of managers, "to be decided upon from time to time, as the Board may deem advisable."[51]

The point is not that the fragmentation of the design reflected some truth about the public. Rather, the sponsors used the design to fragment their public, and in the process ended up fragmenting the design even further. One of the first decisions the managers made, a few months after adopting Mills's model, was to make a critical change in the emancipation cycle. In place of the final group with the kneeling slave, the managers substituted a portrait statue of Frederick Douglass, "as the representative of the liberated race"—even though Douglass was still on the board of managers at the time! In one simple move the managers created a new subscription fund and answered two of the strongest objections to Mills's cycle. They got rid of the most blatant image of subservience and introduced a specific black historical actor, a man who had liberated himself from slavery. "Under the influence of American progressivism," the association's pamphlet explained, "[he] stands forth not only freed, but cultured."[52] This was indeed a dramatic shift from the still degraded figure of the anonymous freedman, although the statue of Douglass did not fully join the universe of heroes on the monument because it remained segregated from the white ranks above and below him. Nevertheless, the black man now seemed to enter the realm of national history as an agent in his own right. The managers' action did receive notice and praise in a national convention of "the colored men of America" held in Washington in January 1869: a resolution was offered thanking the association for "the unmistakeable recognition of our citizenship, and the patriotism of our race, in the present struggle for national unity."[53] Also sometime during this early period in the campaign the managers seem to have replaced the allegorical figure of time with a figure of equality, a bold reference to the central policy goal of Reconstruction championed by Douglass and other radical Republicans. But this change is difficult to determine with certainty because there are contradictory descriptions of the monument. One of the consequences of the managers' design strategy is that no one could agree on what the design was at any given moment.[54]

These changes may well have helped paved the way for the Western Sanitary Commission to join its funds to the campaign. The most decisive factor, though, was probably the organizational structure of the campaign and the monument itself. Unlike the Springfield association, the Washington managers had no trouble slicing off a portion of the monument and designating it as the contribution of the freedmen. This was simply the further fracturing of a project already conceived as fractured. Moreover, the freedmen's portion was the pinnacle of the monument, containing the statue of Lincoln. The sponsors of the freedmen's fund could therefore persuade themselves that they were applying the money in the interests of the original subscribers, by giving them a statue of Lincoln and a visible sign of their civic act on the structure of the monument.

When the managers were negotiating with the Western Sanitary Commission's president, James Yeatman, they made another dramatic change to Mills's emancipation cycle. They eliminated the remaining two groups and substituted two works altogether different in theme: a female figure of "America caring for her disabled soldiers," meant to represent the work of woman; and the figure of a common soldier.[55] Their logic was straightforward. Where only one constituency, the freed slaves, had originally been represented (and pitifully at that), there were now three constituencies—freedmen, women, and veterans. The impulse for the change apparently came from a request in December 1868 by the women of the Ladies' Union Aid Society of St. Louis, who, on hearing that their colleague Yeatman was to be included on the monument, asserted that the monument would be "incomplete" without representing the work of female relief agencies. They were right, in a sense, since the logic of "representativeness" was by now intrinsic to the design. The women's organization wanted three statues of specific women—Dorothea Dix, Clara Barton, and Mary Bickerdyke—but the board of managers refused to grant them any such historical legitimacy and reduced them to the more traditionally female role of allegory, the maternal figure of America nursing the wounded.[56] The addition of the common soldier seems to have been the managers' own idea for expanding the monument's reference.

Substituting three separate sculptures in place of the one cycle fit the operative principle of both the design and the campaign, which was to maximize representational reach. Moreover, the managers could feel satisfied that they had enhanced the dignity of the African American representation even though they had reduced its presence. Nevertheless, this final change to the emancipation imagery confirmed the increasing distance between the operative principle of the campaign and its original mission. Without the allegory of racial freedom and "progress," however compromised that was, there was no substantial representation of a common moral purpose unifying the vast cross section of heroes the managers had assembled. The figure of Lincoln on top, quill in hand, could not rescue the pedestal below from its collapse into a representational hodge-podge of disparate and ever changing elements. Writing to Yeatman from Italy, Western Sanitary Commission founder William Greenleaf Eliot complained that it was "a stupendous pot-pourri, in honor of everybody and therefore nobody."[57] Eliot put his finger right on the problem: in the rush to expand its historical representation, it had lost whatever historical meaning it once had.

Despite the sponsors' radical ideal of a monument embodying a new interracial unity, they still saw the nation as fractured into separate and racially segregated interest groups, which needed their own particular incentives to cooperate in the collective enterprise. The original vision of a public united in the general interest of universal liberty gave way to a pork-barrel model of multiple constituencies acting in self-interest. Mills's design facilitated this fracturing of the public. The populist sculptor provided the structure through which the sponsors could channel their old-fashioned patronage, dispensing representational plums to those constituencies willing to pay for them.

Ultimately the strategy failed. The managers collected nowhere near the funds necessary, and the modest sums they did collect were bizarrely managed out of the U.S. treasurer's office. Mills received at least $10,000 from the fund for models he made of the "representative men," and other expenditures bordered on embezzlement, including, as the New York Times reported, almost $1,500 to replace fur coats stolen at the 1868 presidential inaugural ball (because it took place in the Treasury Building!).[58] There were several attempts to revive the project into the 1880s, and two of the figures were actually cast in bronze, one by Mills himself in 1880 and one posthumously.[59] But the grandiose scheme by this time had no real prospects.

While it is impossible to know with certainty why one monument campaign succeeds and another fails, the record here suggests that this monument to "national unity, based on universal liberty," failed because it could not overcome the contradictions embedded within it. These were not merely the contradictions in Mills himself, egregious as they were, but in the very politics of Reconstruction, which animated the whole project. The radical Republicans who conceived the monument as their signpost proclaimed a new era of racial equality in law without building the psychological and social structures that could support equality. Without those structures their political program was doomed. By the early 1870s the nation was clearly retreating from the Reconstruction agenda of equal rights, and, increasingly, whites who had championed the cause of the freed slaves were now accusing blacks of abusing their new civic privileges. The original rhetoric of the monument's sponsors must have seemed outdated within three or four years; indeed, Bellows's 1870 article betrays none of the initial enthusiasm for universal liberty. Yet to reduce the monument's failure to politics is a little like putting the cart before the horse. The demise of Reconstruction was a failure of the culture as a whole, not just a failure to write better legislation or send more troops. Reconstruction failed because it could not (or would not) reconstruct the cultural structures underlying slavery: the idea of race and the idea of a nation built on racial opposition. The same failure was enacted in the design of the monument and of the monument's campaign, well before the political momentum of Reconstruction waned. The sponsors proclaimed a monument to national unity and universal liberty without knowing how to build those ideals into their own project. Even within the relatively narrow compass of a work of sculpture and a fund-raising strategy to get it built, they could not install an imaginary conception of the public that corresponded to what they claimed the new nation was already becoming. How could they hope to establish interracial unity when they could not give it credible form in their own work? The nation's most ambitious proposal for a monument to emancipation collapsed, we can argue, because it was dedicated to a new order that it did not comprehend and could not visualize.

To this point, every attempt to introduce the emancipated body into national sculpture had failed. With the collapse of the campaigns behind Mills's and Hosmer's designs, the grand emancipation cycles vanished altogether, never to reappear.[60] The Freedmen's Memorial itself came close

to extinction, before being rescued and redirected to a design far more
more modest in scale.

The sponsors of the Freedmen's Memorial regretted their decision to
join the National Lincoln Monument Association almost as soon as they
had made it. Eliot's letter to James Yeatman of November 1869, complaining bitterly of the "Washington Folly," offered an alternative should
the occasion ever arise. This was Thomas Ball's model of Lincoln and
the kneeling slave, which Eliot had just seen and liked in Ball's Florence
studio. Eliot did not give any extended analysis but merely remarked that
"the African type is well maintained without over-doing" and that "the
likeness of Lincoln is softened, but perfectly correct."[61] Eliot, who evidently fancied himself something of a critic, was impressed with how Ball
tempered the nonclassical features of both Lincoln and the African American in order to make them more conventionally sculptural.

Sometime after 1871 the Western Sanitary Commission withdrew
from the moribund Washington project and commissioned Ball to execute a monument based on the group Eliot had seen. (The commission
also fought off one last spirited effort to grab the freedmen's fund by the
association in Springfield, which claimed to have more direct insight into
the wishes of "the colored people.")[62] The U.S. Congress agreed to pay
for the pedestal and to set aside a site in a residential square on the eastern
edge of Capitol Hill, at that time bordering on fields. The site was quite
literally marginal, but it was directly on axis with the Capitol itself and
did not suffer from the problems of the Mall, which was then a swampy
overgrown mess. The monument was unveiled on the eleventh anniversary of Lincoln's death, April 14, 1876, with the president, Congress,
and the Supreme Court all in attendance and with an oration by none
other than Frederick Douglass.[63] It was a first in more than one respect.
As Douglass remarked, it was the first time his "race" had ever erected a
monument to a great American. It was also, as Douglass did not remark
(for reasons that will become clearer), the first time his "race" had ever
appeared in a national monument.

As finally executed the figure of the black man differed in a few respects
from Ball's original. The commissioners saw the original figure (fig. 3.11)
as both passive and idealized. Despite Eliot's original reaction that the
"African type" was not overdone, they asked Ball for a more "representative form of a negro," without the liberty cap, and in a pose "helping to
break the chain that had bound him."[64] As Yeatman later explained, this
would "bring the presentation nearer to the historical fact, by making the
emancipated slave an agent in his own deliverance."[65] It is interesting that
the sponsors noted some of the basic defects of the manumission iconography, notably the way it deprived the freed slave of any agency in his
own emancipation. The solution, as they saw it, was to transform the
slave from the ideal figure sporting the liberty cap into a realistic portrait

4.5 Thomas Ball, model for Freedmen's Memorial to
Lincoln, circa 1874, plaster (now lost).

figure, and to change his pose. The commissioners sent Ball photographs
of a former slave named Archer Alexander, who was harbored by Eliot in
1863 while on the run from slavery and who then became his servant.
Ball remodeled the facial features after the photos, and he made one slight
change to the pose: he straightened the figure's bent right arm and made
it culminate in a clenched fist (fig. 4.5). Yeatman asserted at the dedication that "the ideal group is thus converted into the literal truth of history
without losing anything of its artistic conception or effect."[66]

From our vantage point Ball's composition became an even stranger
hybrid of allegory and realism. The new historical specificity of the black
figure, insofar as it was recognizable at all, made the narrative conceit of
Lincoln and the slave much more difficult to sustain. Putting the face of a
real man on the allegorical slave not only made the figure's nudity nonsensical but also changed the dynamics of the piece entirely. It now became a group portrait of two historical figures who had never actually
met, much less under the circumstances Ball's design suggests. Read as the
"literal truth of history," the monument was bound to have troubling
implications.

It is worth looking for a moment at the historical figure of Archer Alexander whose likeness was supposed to help guarantee that literal truth, especially since Eliot and the commission took every opportunity to emphasize Alexander's presence on the monument itself. Eliot published a narrative of the monument and its unknown hero some twenty years later.[67] This little volume is the best document we have of the mentality of the monument's sponsors, and it is a fascinating revelation of the ironies that pervaded the whole project. There is the irony that Alexander was Eliot's servant, and so the inevitably subservient relationship of the former slave to the monument's sponsor was in a sense reencoded in the design of the monument. But this is a rather superficial observation and does not begin to capture the complexities of Eliot's account. The book is largely the story of Alexander's escape in 1863 from a Confederate-sympathizing slaveholder in Missouri, and his subsequent travails as a fugitive in this border state where slavery was still legal but the institution was eroding under the pressure of military rule. Eliot's narrative confronted a basic problem from the start: since Alexander was owned in Missouri, he was not even indirectly freed by Lincoln's proclamation, which did not apply in the border states. If anything, the choice of Alexander underscored the real historical limitations of Lincoln's act. Eliot's book reveals that he was no strong fan of Lincoln's. Eliot had supported Frémont, the initial military commander in Missouri, who was fired by Lincoln because he issued a proclamation freeing all slaves of disloyal masters. (In fact, it was Frémont who authorized the foundation of the Western Sanitary Commission.) Lincoln, in Eliot's words, "unfortunately and unwisely revoked" Fremont's proclamation, so instead of declaring Alexander free Lincoln had actually declared him still a slave![68]

Alexander owed his freedom to his own escape and to the sympathetic policies of the military authorities in Missouri in early 1863, who were then allied with antislavery unionists. He found his way to Eliot's property on the outskirts of St. Louis in February, and Eliot obtained a military order giving protection to Alexander. Alexander was then kidnapped by bounty hunters, only to be recaptured dramatically by the military authorities and returned to Eliot's home. What Eliot does not report is that if Alexander had escaped a few months later his fate might have been different because Lincoln, under pressure from proslavery unionists, once again removed the military commander responsible for the liberal protection of fugitive slaves. Shortly after Alexander's rescue, Lincoln replaced both the Union commander and the provost marshal who had signed Alexander's protection papers.[69] As Eliot knew well but only suggested between the lines, Lincoln was really a hindrance to freedom in this particular narrative. Eliot's defense of the "truth" of the monument, at the end of the narrative, therefore rings hollow: "His freedom came directly from the hand of President Lincoln, by provost-marshal authority, and his own hands had helped to break the chains that bound him."[70] Lincoln was only nominally in charge of the "provost-marshal authority" and he did his level best to prevent that authority from assisting the policy of emancipation.

Eliot concluded his narrative with an anecdote about Alexander's reaction to seeing himself represented on the freedmen's monument. Eliot writes that Alexander began to laugh and then, "he presently sobered down and exclaimed, 'Now I'se a white man! Now I'se free!'"[71] The anecdote, as constructed by Eliot, is peculiarly double-edged. It is supposed to explain and indeed celebrate Alexander's inclusion in an honorific medium devoted to white men, while at the same time it points with a kind of paternal wink at Alexander's naiveté. The story cancels its own message; it confirms the distance between the high-cultural enterprise of sculpture and the low-cultural subject of the black man, the man whose dialect marks his blackness even as he asserts his whiteness ("Now I'se a white man"). So too does the monument cancel its own presumed message: it permits a space for the black man in national sculpture only by witholding the promise of a common masculinity, by insisting instead on the overarching opposition of whiteness and blackness.

The racial integration of monumental sculpture gestured toward what Frederick Douglass had demanded in 1865—the black man's "incorporation into the American body politic." With its three-dimensional presence, its attention to the human body in space, sculpture was ideally suited to realizing that corporeal metaphor of civic participation. As Eliot's anecdote presupposes, public sculpture was a promised land of sorts, offering not only representation in the symbolic space of nationality but "elevation" into the inner sanctum of white culture. Yet the logic of the medium betrayed its message of uplift, for it fixed its white and black figures in an immutable relationship. In bronze, Archer Alexander can never rise and stand, never come to consciousness of his own power. The narrative remains frozen in place, the monument perpetuating its image of racial difference for eternity.

It is no wonder, then, that Douglass in his oration did not draw attention to Alexander and his unprecedented appearance in the medium of public sculpture. According to the historian John Cromwell, who heard the speech at close range, Douglass referred to the black figure only once, in an ad-libbed aside which did not appear in the published version. As Cromwell later paraphrased it, Douglass objected to the monument's design because "it showed the negro on his knee when a more manly attitude would have been indicative of freedom."[72] The concern here with "manliness" is consistent with Douglass's lifelong understanding of masculinity as the structural opposite of slavery, an understanding that inevitably gendered emancipation as well. In the same oration Douglass claimed that under Lincoln's rule "we saw ourselves gradually lifted from the depths of slavery to the heights of liberty and manhood."[73] For Douglass entry into civic life meant that racial difference was subordinated to the common mantle of masculinity; as he argued in 1865, "the fact of my being a negro is far less important in determining my duty than the fact that I am a 'man,' and linked to all mankind as a man and a brother."[74] Emancipation, whether figured as the acquisition of whiteness or of masculinity, implied a rise to a position of dominance. Ball's black man was still mired in the depths of the dominated—neither white nor manly nor free.

The monument's sponsors would have us believe that Ball's changes had corrected this deficiency. It all hinged on the new right arm supposedly breaking the chains, and its ability to convey self-determination. Yet that tensed arm, with its clenched fist, is simply attached to the rest of the body, which in all essential respects retains the original pose. It seems that Ball tried to combine two incompatible narratives in one body's movement. The original narrative was one of recognition, that very first moment of emancipation when the slave realizes that his chains have somehow been broken and lifts his head in response. The second narrative is one of resistance, and it renders the first narrative nonsensical.[75] How can the slave just come to recognize his broken chains when he ˈ ˈmself has been doing the breaking? It could happen only in an infantile sense, as when a baby comes to recognize something she or he has inadvertently accomplished. Resistance, the deliberate defiance of an external authority, really cannot be embodied in Ball's self-contained figure. His figure is all about coming to consciousness, the first internal awakening of a human being prostrated by oppression. Resistance belongs to a later (or earlier) stage in this figure's story. The narrative becomes even more contradictory when the second figure in the group is taken into account. Why is the slave straining against his chains when his deliverer hovers over him? It made some sense to join the two figures in this way when the conceit was that Lincoln had bestowed freedom on the unknowing slave, but now that the slave participates knowingly in his own liberation Lincoln must hover as a sort of anxious parent watching over the child trying to do for himself. The contradictions multiply simply because Ball did not rethink the slave's body as a whole. To do so would have required a drastic change in the relationship of the two figures—in effect, a new monument.

The changes the sponsors requested could not be accommodated meaningfully within the basic framework of Ball's design. Their request was, fundamentally, absurd, and Ball responded understandably by making the least change possible. For Douglass these minor revisions made little difference. Whether his arm was bent or straight, whether he was Archer Alexander or not, the black man still kneeled, and so he forfeited his manhood. The pamphlet recording the dedication tried to gloss the pose by claiming that he was "represented as just rising from the earth," and indeed an approving notice published in the black journal from Hampton, *Southern Workman,* echoed this more optimistic description. There was enough ambiguity in the pose to permit many different narrative interpretations, from Lincoln "blessing" the slave to his "beckoning the slave to rise," but most contemporary viewers who wrote about the group followed Douglass and recognized that the slave was in the act of crouching, not rising. Aptly, the *New York Evening Post* just before the dedication described the slave figure as "almost prostrate."[76]

Ball's design was a failure to imagine emancipation at the most fundamental level, in the language of the human body and its interaction with other bodies. This was the very language in which sculpture dealt, and in which the concept of race originated. That is why the outcome of this long monument campaign was so significant. The abstract goal of political equality, enshrined in the politics of Reconstruction, could not be achieved without a more profound rethinking of what equality meant in the experience and understanding of the body. At this basic level the Freedmen's Memorial offered a stark lesson. Instead of representing a new order, it reasserted the old racial structure and power relations of slavery. And insofar as it equated masculinity with power and domination, it held no future promise of emancipation for the black man at all. For in a masculine universe ruled by this logic of domination, not everyone can dominate. Some men must sink to their knees if others are to stand up and assume power. In Ball's world—which in many respects is still our world—equality is not simply a long way off; it remains outside even the imagination.

DOUGLASS made one more extraordinary assertion in his oration at the monument, cutting against the celebratory grain of the event. He argued that Lincoln "was preeminently the white man's President, entirely devoted to the welfare of white men," and therefore the duty of commemorating him really belonged to those white men, not to the former slaves who were never "the special objects of his consideration." (How well the story of Archer Alexander would support his argument!) Nevertheless the freedmen had a right to build their monument and it would serve a purpose: it would defend black citizens against the "slander" of ingratitude. When "it is attempted to scourge us beyond the range of human brotherhood," Douglass concluded, "we may calmly point to the monument we have this day erected to the memory of Abraham Lincoln."[77] Douglass at once swept aside the paternalist argument that his race owed Lincoln a special debt of patronage, as a manumitted slave would an old master, and reframed the monumental enterprise as a way of joining in a truly shared national memory. It was not the color-blind enterprise—the "people's" monument—he had advocated in 1865 and later worked for, but it was a contribution to a common commemorative cause.

For Douglass this was above all a monument to Lincoln, which would take its place alongside other monuments to Lincoln in a shared civic space. But this is not what the monument became, in part because the design Douglass so disliked would not allow it. With its kneeling slave setting the work apart from all other monuments to Lincoln in America, the monument soon acquired special status as the definitive sculptural treatment of emancipation. First the nomenclature changed: the "Freedmen's Memorial Monument to Abraham Lincoln," as it was called in its dedicatory pamphlet, became known as the Emancipation Monument. A replica was erected in Boston in 1879 as "the emancipation group" (fig. 4.6), paid for not by freedmen but by the wealthy benefactor and abolitionist Moses Kimball; the inscription left no doubt of its purpose by declaring in the first line, "A Race Set Free."[78] From then on the name seems to have stuck, appearing for example in an African American textbook of 1882 on emancipation.[79] By 1916 Freeman Murray acknowledged that the group had become the single most commonly reproduced image of emancipation, the very "exemplification" of the concept. Dismayed by its black figure, he made a spirited case for unfastening the work from this referent. As a monument to Lincoln, he had fewer objections to it (though he would prefer the figure of the slave removed altogether); as a monument to emancipation, he found it perverse, more the image of "a man who has perhaps escaped extreme punishment by commutation of sentence, than a man who feels that he is one of those who, as the Declaration of Independence expresses it, 'are, and of right ought to be free.'"[80] This is the sharpest critical analysis we have of the narrative energy of the slave figure—one who is responding to salvation bestowed unexpectedly from above, rather than feeling the impulse for freedom from within—but it did not succeed in dislodging the canonical status of the work. The monument was reproduced on a three-cent stamp commemorating emancipation in 1940, and black historian Benjamin Quarles devoted the first chapter of his *Lincoln and the Negro* to its history ("Charlotte Scott's Mite"). As late as the 1960s the monument was still prominently featured in magazine articles about African American landmarks, despite its popular epithet "Shine, sir?"[81]

Here is a rare case of a public sculpture creating a potent image that enters the culture at large. As that image travels from monument to book illustration to postage stamp, the honorific power and ideal status of the original medium drain away, and the image comes to seem natural, con-

4.6 Thomas Ball, *Emancipation Group*, 1879, Park Square, Boston.

densing as it does a whole historical mythology of emancipation. The fact that the emancipated themselves "erected" it—their total lack of participation in the design process glossed over by this conventional rhetoric—then serves as further confirmation of the image's authenticity. As the image is reproduced and recirculated, ever more distant from the original context of its production, it becomes archetypal, lodged in the collective consciousness even of those who despised it.[82]

With the idea of emancipation affixed indelibly to this one image, the monumental Lincolns of the future no longer needed to represent it. Once Lincoln had his kneeling slave, the slave could then disappear from the commemorative stage. Emancipation had become marginal: a black debt, a black theme, a black monument. The pressures of external events certainly played their part, helping to reinforce the internal logic of commemoration. Reconstruction officially ended the same year the Freedmen's Memorial was dedicated, and with it the old dreams of political equality were finally extinguished. The whole idea that emancipation might change the nation itself—and the very nature of freedom for both white and black—could now be forgotten. From here on out the Lincoln of commemoration could become the "white man's President," as Douglass had asserted, and emancipation could become the black man's gift. Lincoln could reemerge as the mystical "preserver" of Union, rather than the creator of a new nation.[83]

Ironically, then, Ball's monument paved the way for a new "white" image of Lincoln, which the sculptor Augustus Saint-Gaudens provided in his celebrated work of 1887, the only monument to Lincoln erected in the decade following the Freedmen's Memorial (fig. 4.7, 4.8). Saint-Gaudens boldly dispensed with the conventional scroll and all other references to the Emancipation Proclamation. The sculptor was committed to a "realism" that eschewed artificial sculptural devices like the scroll which Lincoln would not actually have held or used. Saint-Gaudens's problem was to make the ideal Lincoln (the soul, the moral stature) emerge from within the physical Lincoln, represented truthfully with the clothes and props of his own time.[84] This was the old chestnut of portrait statuary but Saint-Gaudens took it more seriously than any other sculptor before him (with the possible exception of Ward), thinking the problem through down to the smallest particulars of pose and the most subtle folds of drapery. Theatrical narrative conceits like Ball's had no place in this rigorous project.

After experimenting with many different poses, seated and standing, arms crossed in thought or holding forth a document, Saint-Gaudens devised a brilliant synthesis.[85] He posed Lincoln standing before a chair of state, as if he has just risen to address an audience gathered before him; he tilts his head down in thought, while he rests his left hand on his coat lapel and holds his right hand in a fist behind his back. Here the narrative conceit of the monument meshes seamlessly with the physical act of viewing: we become Lincoln's audience. The idea of associating a standing figure with an empty seat was entirely novel in public sculpture, and it served to amplify the combination of traits Saint-Gaudens sought to register in the figure itself. This was the man of decision and the man of reflection brought together in one body and one moment. Though paused in thought, the body projects vigorously in space, not simply in the advanced left foot but in the huge forward arc created by the swelling chest and the coat draping off of it. The perfectly still left hand we see from the front is counterbalanced by the repressed energy of the right, tensed behind his back; the continuous lines of the coat and the trouser seam are disrupted by the watch chain tumbling haphazardly down the vest. The modeling of the tousled hair and the creased clothing maintains this subtle equilibrium of superficial disorder and underlying structure, energy, and calm.

4.7–8 Augustus Saint-Gaudens and Stanford White, Lincoln Monument (*Standing Lincoln*), 1887, Lincoln Park, Chicago. *Below*: Detail of statue.

Although Saint-Gaudens toyed with the idea of putting a document in Lincoln's hand, perhaps a reference to the proclamation, in the end he decided to remove all referents to external achievements and, radically, to internalize the figure both in its composition and significance. Lincoln stands before an audience but concentrates on his own thoughts, gazing in on himself; we too gaze in on him and divine his character, not his accomplishments. We bring our knowledge of his act of emancipation to the figure, but in the process the specific historical act becomes transfigured into an eternal moral quality intrinsic to Lincoln's "ideal" self. For all Saint-Gaudens's fidelity to contemporary details, the figure stands apart from history and its messy irresolutions and becomes a pure embodiment of moral perfection. Whatever contribution Lincoln made to the destruction of slavery is thereby elided, absorbed instead into Lincoln's inner "essence."

With the omission of any sort of political iconography in the sculpture, a heavy burden fell on the inscriptions to situate Lincoln as a historical figure. These consist of quotable aphorisms on the exedra behind the statue, and two documents inscribed on small bronze globes that frame the steps in front: the Gettysburg Address and the so-called Greeley letter, in which Lincoln clearly explained that his paramount objective was to save the Union, with or without slavery. This was the very same document often used by apologists of the Confederacy to prove that the war had nothing to do with slavery. The inscription is easily overlooked since the sculpture is the overwhelming center of attention, but the message of retreat from the cause of emancipation is still unmistakable and surely deliberate (though the documents do not tell us who was responsible for choosing the texts).[86]

Saint-Gaudens was invited to design the monument by a committee that did not have to raise any funds, the money having been given by the bequest of a wealthy Chicago benefactor. The committee actually corresponded initially with Thomas Ball, but eventually decided to go in a new direction, choosing Saint-Gaudens without even seeing a preliminary design from him. Both sponsor and artist had a free hand and did not need to strive for popular consent.[87] Nevertheless, the final work became the most popular monument to Lincoln in America, achieving a reputation as the definitive portrayal.[88] The favorable criticism of the work, multiplying in the 1890s, tended to argue that Saint-Gaudens had made a "loftier" Lincoln by removing the historical onus of emancipation; the same critics applauded the choice of the Greeley letter (which they attributed to the artist) precisely because it put Lincoln in his "true" historical perspective. "Journey to Chicago and kneel before the bronze statue by Augustus Saint-Gaudens," wrote Charles Henry Hart, unwittingly recollecting the pose of Ball's slave, and you will discover that "it is not Abraham Lincoln the liberator of slaves, but Abraham Lincoln the Saviour of the Union."[89] The most grandiloquent summation of its effect came from Lorado Taft, perhaps the most influential critic ever of American sculpture, who declared in 1896, "One stands before it and feels himself in the very presence of America's greatest soul."[90] Divorced from any specific history, Saint-Gaudens's Lincoln came to personify those qualities of moral order and decisive action essential to the postwar conception of America itself.[91]

Saint-Gaudens, in effect, emancipated Lincoln from emancipation, and thereby emancipated white viewers from its historical burden. However confused and degrading Ball's figure of the slave was, it did draw attention to the issue of the freed slaves' continuing presence in society. It was an interracial monument, making African Americans visible in a medium that had insisted on their invisibility, their imperviousness to sculptural representation. Faced with this slight opening, Saint-Gaudens decisively closed the door. By supplanting the Freedmen's Memorial with a newly definitive Lincoln, he helped to dissociate Ball's monument from the national memory of Lincoln and to consolidate that monument's hold on the now marginal theme of emancipation. By creating a "white" Lincoln purged of responsibility for the millions of emancipated, he helped make Ball's Lincoln the patron saint of an increasingly subcollective "black" memory.

At the same time that Saint-Gaudens solved the political problem posed by the commemoration of Lincoln, he solved the aesthetic problem that Lincoln seemed to typify. As critics like Marianna van Rensellaer argued, Saint-Gaudens's Lincoln revivified the standard portrait monument, turning the most unpromising of contemporary figures into eloquent sculpture. Here was the "ideal" Lincoln embedded in the prosaic likeness, without any theatrical props or artificial narrative conceits.[92] In effect Saint-Gaudens had finally realized, in a mainstream monument, the sculptural promise that some critics had seen years earlier in Ward's figure of the *Freedman*—a synthesis of the real and the ideal. But Saint-Gaudens managed this achievement without recourse to the black body, without its liberating indeterminacy. He achieved his synthesis by erasing the black body and instead devising a new sort of sculptural decorum for the contemporary white hero. Whereas the example of the *Freedman* ultimately could not be repeated, Saint-Gaudens's ideal could be and was. The new era of sculpture once promised by the *Freedman* was opened in his absence.

We can bring this story fittingly to a close by taking a brief look at the final efforts of Harriet Hosmer in the 1890s to carry out her lifelong dream of a monument to Lincoln and emancipation. Still active in her sixties, she pursued the commission for yet another monument to Lincoln in Chicago, this also funded by a citizen's bequest. Hosmer was well aware of Saint-Gaudens's now celebrated statue, and she proposed a design intended not to "clash" with the work but to be its "complement."[93] Where his was a single figure, hers would be a group; where his was "realistic," hers would be frankly ideal; where his abandoned the representation of emancipation, hers would embrace it. She spent several years making and revising a model, and for awhile she seemed to have the inside track for the commission. But the sponsors, after paying her for the model, eventually became fed up with her endless reworkings of it and decided to give the commission instead to Saint-Gaudens.[94]

Hosmer's basic scheme for the monument survives in descriptions published in contemporary newspapers. Again it was an ambitious pyramid of sculpture, but without the "realistic" central cycle of African American history that had defined the earlier monument's program. On top was a seated figure of Lincoln in meditation, poised above the inscription "God sent me a vision." That vision was represented on the level underneath, in the form of a seated "African Sibyl," dressed in a tiger skin, who twists up toward Lincoln while grasping an open book inscribed with Lincoln's words, "If slavery is not wrong, nothing is wrong." Clinging to the huge lower leg of this Michaelangelesque allegory of Africa is a nude black child with broken chains, who looks up toward the sibyl and Lincoln. (One drawing of this group does survive in a photograph [fig. 4.9].) Balancing the group on the other side of the monument was a female mourning victory of classical Greek features, meant to counterpoise the idea of Greek beauty and civilization to the idea of the primitive embodied in the African group.[95]

It should be obvious by now how thoroughly Hosmer departed from her earlier representation of emancipation. The new design aggrandized the figure of Lincoln at the expense of the material and historical weight of the emancipated slaves. Lincoln here becomes not merely the agent but the prophet of emancipation, acting out of nothing less than divine inspiration. The African American representation now is entirely subsumed within the narrative of Lincoln's moral grandeur. Where the earlier representation had been an independent cycle, culminating in an image of martial manhood, the new group shrinks the emancipated body to one black putto, representative of a race in its infancy, still cleaving to its African origins. That allegory of Africa, while majestic and mysterious, functions at the same time as a sign of the primitive, contrasting with the civilized norm of the Grecian allegory on the right. The idea of racial backwardness is clearly encoded in the African group, leaving no room for reading African American agency into the historical process of emancipation or its aftermath.

4.9 Harriet Hosmer, *African Sibyl*, design for portion of Lincoln Monument, circa 1890 (now lost).

Hosmer proudly announced that she had come up with a bold design that would revitalize the old neoclassical school of ideal sculpture, long since supplanted by the realism of Ward and Saint-Gaudens among others. She told the newspapers, "This I consider the triumph of my desire to incorporate classic beauty of outline and grace with a modern subject in a manner that will, at a glance, tell its own story. It is a foundation on which to erect the new school, which has been my constant dream."[96] She thought she had fashioned an ideal narrative on a preeminently modern subject; it was simple and unified, told allegorically but without the old neoclassical resort to piles of abstruse signifiers based on ancient mythology. Its poetic impact, she reported, was confirmed by no less than Browning and Tennyson. She also thought that political circumstances were now right for such a design. She had been working on it at least since the early 1870s, and now its time had apparently come. "Now that sectional prejudices have died away between what was the North and South, I believe it will be received in the spirit in which it was designed and executed—merely a work of modern art. A few years since it would not have been."[97]

The problem was that Hosmer's monument was no longer modern at all. The new artistic "school" she hoped to exemplify had already been pioneered, in much different form, by Saint-Gaudens, who had shown convincingly how to represent the ideal within the prosaic outer forms of contemporary man and contemporary life. The poetic mode favored by Hosmer and her British luminaries belonged to a different world, of expatriates living in the glow of antiquity, not of businessmen in New York and Chicago whose money and influence were becoming the driving force behind public sculpture. It must have been an especially bitter ending for her when, in 1897, the commission for the second Lincoln in Chicago went once again to Saint-Gaudens. The majestic seated figure he produced—which anticipated by several years Daniel Chester French's much better known effigy for the Lincoln Memorial in Washington—even further distanced the historical figure of Lincoln from the travails of emancipation, but neither he nor Hosmer lived to see the monument erected.[98]

THE great contrast between Hosmer's original model for a Lincoln monument, designed for the Western Sanitary Commission in the summer of 1866, and her final design presented in the early 1890s tells us much about the historical distance traveled in between. When Hosmer devised her slave-to-soldier cycle, black men were serving as federal soldiers in the Reconstruction South. Emancipation was still in progress: the possibilities seemed bright, or at least open-ended. Hosmer's model did not so much commemorate emancipation as bring a vision of it to life. By the 1890s, however, emancipation was over. It now belonged to history, and it already had its definitive commemorative image in Thomas Ball's monument to Lincoln. Accordingly Hosmer's final work "remembers" emancipation as if across a vast stretch of historical time. The subject enters the realm of myth: Lincoln becomes prophet, Africa becomes sibyl, slaves regress to a mythical infancy.

Hosmer's temporal retreat—from the contemporary world of the soldier to the mythological realm of the sibyl—coincided with a broad political retreat from the goals of Reconstruction. By the turn of the century, the last remnants of the political gains created by Reconstruction had been overturned by the U.S. Supreme Court, which sanctioned the Jim Crow regime of "separate but equal." In this climate, a monument to emancipation was hopelessly old-fashioned. Hosmer's only choice was to push memory backward, into a past even more remote from the present. Had her monument been erected, it might have seemed passé to many critics but its retreat from the living struggle of emancipation probably would not have troubled them. The optimistic fervor of the 1860s lay dormant, never entirely forgotten but no longer acknowledged publicly. Many decades would pass before its memory could be effectively revived.

CHAPTER FIVE

SLAVERY'S
MEMORIAL

THE FREEDMEN'S MEMORIAL became the nation's monument to emancipation even though the design might have better commemorated slavery. If one changed the white hero from Lincoln to say, John C. Calhoun, and took away the chains and the whipping post, the work would have functioned rather well as an illustration of the old proslavery argument: a benevolent master gradually uplifting the primitive African into Christian civilization through the secure shelter of slavery. Both the narrative and the image of Ball's group were still that deeply embedded in the relations of paternalistic domination and racial subordination fundamental to the American slave system.

Yet monuments openly sympathetic to slavery simply did not exist. After the Civil War, slavery fell in the trashheap of history, and even its most ardent advocates before the war were now forsaking it. Within a remarkably short period of time, white Southerners were not only repudiating the institution that had been central to their society but writing it out of their history of the war. The Confederacy was not formed to protect slavery, they claimed, but to protect states' rights; the war was not fought over slavery but over the abstract issue of sovereignty. A massive and deliberate process of collective forgetting took place, which has still not been reversed. Only recently have historians seriously challenged the erasure of slavery from the Confederate consciousness, despite overwhelming evidence that proslavery ideology became even more central to white Southern identity during the war than before. "Leaders of the secession movement across the South cited slavery as the most compelling reason for southern independence," Drew Gilpin Faust has written, and the same reasoning was repeated in press, pulpit, and school alike until virtually the end of the war. "Negro slavery is the South," wrote one Georgia editor in 1862, "and the South is negro slavery."[1]

The business of Confederate commemoration after the war was to smash this equation. This involved a vertiginous shift in consciousness. Articles of faith that had been widely inculcated suddenly had to be disavowed. Personal and institutional memories had to be thoroughly revised and resorted. In short, the South had to be reconstructed, though not along the lines contemplated by the Northern victors.

In this process of reconstruction slavery disappeared but, in a peculiar way, remained central. It was the invisible or unspeakable core that structured what could be made visible or utterable. A nation formed expressly to protect slaveholding, no longer a nation and no longer slaveholding, sought to redefine itself as an abstract moral cause. If the grand emancipation designs of the 1860s were monuments to a new order that never came to be, the Confederate monuments erected after the war commemorated an old order that never existed in the first place—a slave society without the moral impediment of slavery. Contradictions were inherent in both these Northern and Southern projects of reconstruction. Yet the contradictions fatally undermined the former while the latter held together in surprising equilibrium.

As the radical Northern campaign of commemoration fizzled, white Southerners began to adapt their commemorative project to the changing conditions of postwar society. The centerpiece of their effort was the former capital of the Confederacy, Richmond, Virginia. Richmond was an industrial and financial center that was steeped in the complex historical associations of the Old South. Its heritage encompassed the highest of high culture—Jefferson's neo-Roman Capitol, with Houdon's great statue of Washington inside—as well as the second largest slave market in the antebellum South. At the same time, modern Richmond strived to be a showcase of business enterprise and urban progress. Richmond was the center of the "Lost Cause," as the Confederacy came to be known, but it was by no means backward-looking. The commemoration of the Lost Cause sought to span the old and the new, to integrate history and progress—which is precisely why slavery had no legitimate place in the commemorative order. The key figure in the cult of the Lost Cause was Robert E. Lee, the Confederate commander whose death in 1870 spurred a host of ambitious memorial schemes. The key monument was the huge equestrian statue erected on the suburban outskirts of Richmond in 1890, after a very long and sometimes bitter campaign. The history of that campaign and its outcome offers ample evidence of the white South's erasure of slavery from its official past. But if the same evidence is read a little against the grain, it soon reveals slavery's hidden cultural work as a controlling absence, with a subtle but nevertheless crucial impact on the sculptural configuration of Southern white heroism.

While Lincoln was the indisputable embodiment of the Union and its moral cause, Lee was the embodiment of the Confederacy. He had served as commander of the Army of Northern Virginia, the most successful of the Confederate armies, whose list of battles included most of the celebrated engagements of the war. That a political leader would represent the Union and a military leader would come to represent the Confederacy deserves some examination. Jefferson Davis, Lincoln's actual counterpart as president of the Confederacy, was put in the unpopular position of prosecuting a national war effort among states that were in theory independent. So, of course, was Lincoln, whose own popularity during his lifetime suffered as a result. Yet Davis did not end the war a martyr, as Lincoln did. He was captured while allegedly trying to escape disguised in women's clothing; the incident became a cause célèbre and a major affront to Southern white "manhood." Lee, on the other hand, was an extraordinarily respected figure, always represented as the South's exemplar of manhood.[2]

However significant, these facts do not get to the root of the matter. The fundamental effect of installing Lee as the South's premier representative was that it depoliticized the Confederacy after the fact. With Lee as the major historical actor, the story of the Lost Cause became a glorious military record rather than a political struggle to secure a slaveholding nation. The white South's urgent need to dissociate the Confederacy from slavery after the war dictated this strategy of depoliticization. Davis was a plantation owner and large-scale slaveholder from the Deep South, whose own interests, like the Confederacy's, were obviously intertwined with the institution of slavery. Lee, on the other hand, was a professional military man from Virginia who owned few slaves before the war, and who claimed after the war to have "always been in favor of emancipation—gradual emancipation."[3] Although Lee's own statements on slavery recorded in several letters from 1856 to 1865 hardly support this retrospective claim, what matters is that he was less vitally attached to the institution than the typical Southern planter and he could more credibly claim afterward that he had not fought to defend it. In the late 1860s he was a living example of the white South's collective reversal on slavery. His historical role as a leader of soldiers—not a maker of policy—complemented and enhanced that personal example. In some ways he fit the classical mold of the reluctant leader, as George Washington had, and like Washington—the fellow Virginian with whom Lee was often compared—he was thought to be above politics. For all these reasons he was the obvious man to personify a newly revised, newly remembered Confederacy—a Confederacy that pretended to have fought a heroic struggle not for slavery but for liberty, defined as the right of states to self-determination.[4]

As he became the white South's answer to Lincoln, Lee compared favorably in one obvious and important way. He was "perfection" in his physical appearance. No artist, one writer claimed, could improve on the "grand original."[5] Where Lincoln was thought to embody "the sculpturally impossible," to use Marianna Griswold van Rensselaer's pithy phrase,[6] Southern writers described Lee as if his person were already a work of art, embodying the very qualities thought essential to sculpture: repose, beauty, strength.[7] If Lincoln was a sculptural problem, then, Lee was a readymade specimen.

With the equation of canonical whiteness and moral virtue so deeply embedded in the consciousness of race, Lee's outward appearance was easily read as a reflection of inner superiority. This equation reappears frequently in descriptions by men and women alike, as in this gushing account written by a Maryland woman: "The man who stood before us, the embodiment of a Lost Cause, was the realized King Arthur. The soul that looked out of his eyes was as honest and fearless as when it first looked on life. One saw the character, as clear as crystal . . . and the heart, as tender as that of ideal womanhood."[8] These kinds of juxtapositions—King Arthur and ideal womanhood—were commonly invoked to suggest the visible range of virtues synthesized in the single figure of Lee, a range that could bridge even the customary gap between the sexes. While Lee's image thus benefited from the association of qualities normally sorted by gender, this synthesis serves to underscore the image's racial exclusivity. Lee may have been man and woman, but he was not white and black. He functioned much more readily than Lincoln ever could as a racial icon.

Lee offered white Southerners a hero in their own image, an instrument with which they could prod white Northerners to realign their sympathies along proper racial lines. The war had disrupted traditional patterns of cultural difference by allying white with black and pitting white against white. To ardent Unionists Lee was nothing less than a traitor, while the black men who fought against him were heroes. But white Southerners worked hard to reverse these sentiments. Lee was hardly a traitor, they argued, but instead was a courageous Christian gentleman who loved the Union and returned to it wholeheartedly after his defeat. As time passed, white Northerners increasingly accepted the argument. The legitimation of Lee after the war helped to reestablish old lines of racial sympathy. The losers in this process of reconciliation were of course African Americans, who could not possibly accept Lee as their hero. If Lee was no longer traitor, no longer "other," otherness was left to reside in the emancipated slaves and their descendants who did not forget that the Confederacy with Lee at its head had fought to keep them in bondage.

Lee's canonical whiteness was essential to his postwar rehabilitation. It forced white Northerners to confront their own racial loyalties and it gave white Southerners a racial model with which to justify both the Confederacy and their postwar politics of white supremacy. Lincoln was never a comparable racial model: he did not have the right looks or the military bearing. The irony is that sculptors were inspired to turn the

noncanonical Lincoln into a manumitting master, but a master nevertheless, whereas Lee's mastership had to be displaced, or represented by very
subtle means. For Lee an imagery of mastery and indeed domination did
emerge, but not in the obvious territory of race relations. It emerged
rather in the relationship of the hero to his animal servant, the horse
Traveller.[9]

The equestrian image, of course, was the standard formula for the representation of military heroes, precisely because it did encode the idea of
command in the apparently natural dominance of man over animal. Yet
in reality there is something unnatural about that dominance: horses are
bigger and stronger than their human riders. They are controlled by a
combination of cultural authority—the whole structure of confinement
and reward/punishment—and the personal authority of the rider, who
communicates and reinforces in subtle (or not so subtle) physical signals
the structure of authority behind him. If the relationship is properly
tuned, the self-control of the rider becomes indistinguishable from control over the horse. The ideal of decorum thus seems to merge in a natural
way with the idea of dominance. This made the equestrian image the
historically preferred image for leadership in general, and the equestrian
statue the most prestigious form of public sculpture. It was the standard
solution for military commanders because the idea of command defined
them; the relationship of man to horse could easily be read as the relationship of officer to troops.

All this took on a special—one is tempted to say obsessive—character
in the commemoration of Robert E. Lee. For no other American hero of
the nineteenth century did the relationship of horse and rider assume such
acute significance. It was as if the commemorative fortunes of the hero,
the Confederacy, and the white South all rested on correctly defining and
representing that subtle, if commonplace, union of man and animal
(fig. 5.1). Consider one simple anecdote published in 1886 in the heat of
the campaign to finish the equestrian monument to Lee in Richmond, a
story about Traveller and an unlucky "negro boy" who tried to mount
him. Like much of the lore about Lee and Traveller, it described a perfect
sympathy between them. But this particular tale had an interesting twist.
It aimed to prove that the horse, who "partook of the repose of his master
when General Lee was on him, . . . was by no means the 'amiable' animal
some have described." The story undoubtedly came from the Richmond-
based sculptor Edward Valentine, who asked to see Traveller ridden so
that he could study the action of the horse. This was in 1871, a year after
Lee's death. One of Lee's daughters "ordered a negro boy to mount," and
though Traveller was fourteen years old and looking very meek he thrust
his forefeet in the air and "positively refused to allow the mount." Only
after a "young Texan," a college student from Washington and Lee,

5.1 A. Hoen and Co., *Genl. Lee on Traveler*, 1876, lithograph.

brought a new saddle and mounted the animal himself could the demonstration take place. The story is far-fetched in its racism. Would Traveller's owners have never before had a "negro boy" mount him for
exercise? The story is constructed to show how Traveller instinctively
understood the white supremacist system that elevated Lee to its pinnacle.
He refused to allow blacks to ride him and responded only to legitimate
white authority, in this case the college-educated Texan. Ultimately only
Lee could entirely tame the horse's high spirits and make him seem calm,
because Lee had so mastered the practice of "absolute control."[10]

The anecdote was published in the main Richmond newspaper as part
of its campaign to promote Valentine's model for an equestrian monument. What the public wanted in an equestrian statue of Lee, according to
the paper, was not necessarily an exact likeness of Traveller (who was
smaller and scrawnier than the typical Virginia thoroughbred) but an
image that captured the underlying significance of Lee's relationship to
the horse. This the paper summarized as "power in repose."[11] Lee's
power over the stronger, wilder animal was so complete that it did not
need to be exercised. Lee did not have to spur or whip or strangle with the
reins; his moral authority achieved what mere physical domination could
accomplish only imperfectly. As Jabez Curry observed, Lee's attitude on

his horse was "not that of an Equestrian, making a display of his skill or strength, but that of a well-trained officer, perfectly at ease and consciously master of an inferior animal."[12]

The equestrian relationship was thus an overripe metaphor, referring ultimately to the nature of power in society. The image of Lee on his horse worked beautifully as a model of leadership for a white supremacist society trying to legitimate its own authority. Reconstruction had ended sooner and less violently in Virginia than in states further south, in part because the white leadership realized that it could extend some political privileges to the black population without undermining the fundamental premise of white rule.[13] In this pre–Jim Crow era, before the outright exclusion of African Americans from the civic realm, the white supremacist system relied on symbolic expressions of a racial harmony achieved under the firm but patient hand of a white-dominated government. White authority was (mis)represented as moral rather than physical force, a natural relation of superior to inferior race. Hence, in the Traveller story, the Negro boy's inability to subdue the stronger animal signifies a failure of moral force, of natural leadership, whereas Lee has so much of it that the horse calms under him without any sign of physical coercion whatsoever. The equestrian Lee is at once a retrospective image of the benevolent master, good to his inferiors, and a prospective image of a postwar white government claiming to know what is best for its own black population. The great power of this equestrian image was that it could bridge the old regime of slavery and the new regime of white rule without explicitly representing either; it helped legitimate the continuity between the two even as it disguised the physical and institutional forces that propped up both of them.

Since the equestrian image of Lee stood for nothing less than the moral authority of the Confederacy and of white power in general, the campaign to erect an equestrian monument was an extraordinarily high-stakes affair. Getting the image just right proved exceptionally difficult and divisive. Three different groups representing major divisions within the white Virginia elite strove to control the monument campaign and mold it in their own image. One was a group of veteran officers from Lee's Army of Northern Virginia, headed by the notorious "irreconcilable" Jubal Early who wanted to perpetuate the policy and imagery of Southern defiance. Another was a "ladies' committee" of women from pedigreed Virginia families who wanted a monument of artistic distinction. The third group was an official body headed by the governor of Virginia, which saw in the monument campaign an opportunity for political accommodation between North and South. All three groups shared the presuppositions of white supremacy and shared the same basic image of Lee as "power in repose." Yet a long process of conflict and compromise was necessary to mold their competing visions into a single monument.[14]

One key set of differences involved the ritual of the monument campaign, namely who would be asked to contribute and how they would be approached. The ritual of fund raising was crucial because on it turned the whole question of what public the monument stood for, whose collective memory was represented there. Though all three groups were centered in Virginia they envisioned a public subscription that would be national, or at least regional, in scope. But Jubal Early's group sought contributions only from the veterans who had actually fought under Lee's command; the monument was to be a kind of votive offering from the troops to their departed leader. The group issued an appeal in 1871 "To the Survivors of the Army of Northern Virginia" for their "spontaneous offerings." However the language of the appeal did not assume spontaneous support and ended by leaning heavily on images of military obedience: contributing was both a soldier's duty and a test of his devotion to his dead commander. Moreover, agents who would press the appeal personally were to "collect" (i.e., solicit) the contributions, on commission.[15] Early had grave misgivings about employing salaried agents because for him the enterprise was not a business proposition; it was supposed to be a ritual of voluntary participation. Early eventually fired all his agents, but all the various organizations involved in fund raising for the Lee Monument at one time or another had recourse to paid agents. The ladies' committee employed them early on with notable success, and later the governor's association sent agents throughout the South as far away as Texas.[16] The governor's secretary explained that only direct, personal solicitation would get results and that the preferred agent was "a crippled, maimed Confederate," smooth of speech and "apt to interest the women."[17] In other words, the techniques of persuasion, pity, and even romance were not only admissible but seen as necessary.

These techniques were made necessary by the widespread refusal to accept the basic premise of the public subscription—that donations measured allegiance to the hero's memory. The agents wanted to make the question of contributing a ritual test of each person's devotion to the hero: if you believed in Lee, ran their logic, you would contribute to this monument. But in case after case individuals pleaded extenuating circumstances: crop failure, yellow fever, poverty. Or, more defiantly, many people made clear that, despite their admiration of Lee, they had other priorities for their money, notably other monuments proposed at the local or state level. Texans, for example, told the governor's agent that they would not contribute toward a monument in Virginia until they had done their commemorative duty for Sam Houston or the heroes of the Alamo.[18]

Given the enormous difficulties involved in soliciting contributions for a monument, even one to a man as admired as Lee, the self-imposed limitations of the veterans' group were bound to be fatal. In 1875, when a Confederate veteran was elected governor of Virginia, Early gave up and handed his meager funds over to the monument association then being organized by the new governor, James Kemper, and his specially appointed secretary, Samuel Bassett French. Kemper's association widened the scope of the fund-raising campaign not only to get more money but to construct a powerful image of popular unity. This was to be a people's monument to their greatest hero, not a demonstration of soldiers' loyalty to authority. For this reason certain kinds of contributions assumed an importance far beyond their cash value. The association brought its campaign to the public schools, for example, and many responded enthusiastically though with little means—like the Custis School whose subscriptions totaled forty-seven cents, mostly from children donating a penny each. The image of schoolchildren contributing their precious pennies buoyed the standing of the enterprise and seemed to confirm that the memory of Lee still had a force in popular culture, if only the monument could tap it.[19]

One kind of contribution particularly gratified Governor Kemper's board because it seemed to belie the racial exclusivity inherent in the whole project: a contribution from African Americans. The one documented example, probably unique, occurred in the town of Terry, Mississippi, where the white and black populations both donated to the campaign. This extraordinary event came to the attention of Kemper and the board, who saw in it justification for their view that "the interests of the white and coloured races of the South are so intermixed, that to promote them, there must be a cordial unity of purpose."[20] The black man responsible for organizing his community in the effort, William Bingham, received a special letter of commendation from Secretary French, which concluded:

> Under Providence the white and black man of the South have had their lots cast in the same place, and true wisdom determines that they should be friends not enemies: and every evidence of the breaking down of the partition wall between them, raised by bad men, for personal ends, will be hailed by all good men as an omen of better days in the future, to be encouraged in every suitable way.[21]

The apparent sincerity of the letter makes it all the more ironic. The board in reality made no effort to solicit contributions from African American communities and was careful not to make appeals in towns under "Radical" (i.e., Republican or black) rule. Everyone understood why a monument to Lee would not represent the "interests" of the "coloured race," why it was not an instrument of racial harmony. A few years earlier, for example, a much-publicized dispute had erupted when white legislators in Virginia proposed to purchase an official portrait of Lee for the State Capitol. Black legislators opposed the idea because "General Lee had fought to keep [them] in slavery," and the *Richmond Dispatch* reported that "nobody was surprised" at their response.[22] It was obvious that the commemoration of Lee provoked racial discord. Yet according to French this was the fault of the "bad men" (meaning the Radicals), who were dividing the races; "good men" like William Bingham realized that their best interests lay with the white race and not against it.

In the 1870s Kemper's administration represented the moderate wing of the ruling white party, keen to foster a symbolic front of racial harmony. Unlike such "irreconcilables" as Jubal Early who did not want any blacks participating in civic life and ritual, except as servants, the moderates could accept a greater social and political role for blacks as long as blacks accepted the general terms of white supremacy.[23] Thus Bingham's activity was particularly welcome: it represented that "cordial unity" of the races that came with the acceptance of white domination. Blacks had a place in the commemorative ritual. They could enter into this construction of "collective" memory, created by and for whites, and in so doing become visible within the collective, though visibility came at an enormous price—that of relinquishing the claim to a countermemory more in line with their own hopes for liberation. This tension between visibility and self-definition would become even sharper in the more conspicuous ritual events organized later in the campaign.

For the governor the Lee monument project was part of a larger political campaign to legitimate Southern white supremacy in the national consciousness. The commemorative project paralleled Kemper's public policy, which was a series of delicate negotiations with Northern racial policy calculated at once to defend white rule at home and encourage Northern aid and cooperation. Kemper was a pragmatist, steering a middle course in between the "irreconcilables," who scorned Northern whites and their Southern black allies, and the "scalawags," who appealed to the black vote.[24] He deliberately took the monument campaign out of the hands of the irreconcilables and delegated it instead to the politically moderate French, a crony of the notorious political boss William Mahone, Confederate general turned railroad entrepreneur whose politics of accommodation made him a traitor to traditionalists like Early.[25] By giving the monument campaign to a Mahone ally, Kemper was not only dispensing patronage to a powerful supporter who had helped him get elected but forging the kind of coalition he felt the future demanded. Kemper and French conducted the monument campaign in this spirit of coalition building. They were happy to take contributions from anyone, and were especially gratified when money came from Union supporters. On these few occasions French would stress that Lee was not merely a Confederate but "a great American soldier" and that the board looked forward to the day when the sections were reconciled and "peace and brotherly love shall everywhere prevail."[26] Lee was offered as a hero for all, not just for those of unimpeachable loyalty to the Confederate cause but for Northern whites and even for Southern blacks willing to embrace him. The commemoration of Lee thus provided a symbolic field in which to build a new image of popular unity and reconciliation under traditional white rule.

The handful of women who comprised the ladies' committee probably approved of these goals, though their views are harder to read. Unlike their male counterparts, they were not public figures and preferred to keep out of the public eye. Yet they too conceived of their project as a broad-based monument, "designed to go down to posterity as an exponent of the nation's devotion and admiration for our immortal Lee."[27] Their differences with the governor's association revolved not around the ritual of the campaign but around the question of how the monument would take concrete form. The women wanted above all a work of art, and they were fully prepared to go outside the South and even outside the country to get it. For the governor's board, however, art had little if any importance. The board approached the design process in the same spirit it approached the fund-raising process, as an opportunity for coalition building. When the board decided to hold a design competition in 1877, French assembled a jury of several dozen Southerners who constituted a cross section of white leadership in local and national politics, religion, and society; the idea was to create a powerful coalition that would support the design, give it broad respectability, and get it built. Though French gave the jury specific instructions in how to evaluate the designs, the process of evaluation appeared to be an elaborate charade intended primarily to identify the candidate with the most political support.[28]

The women's committee repudiated this process and the whole political arena in which it took place. The committee gave voice to conventionally feminine concerns in a century that made women the primary guardians of "culture," understood as the domain of gentility, social refinement, and aesthetic grace. As women from some of the most elite families in Virginia, they were perfectly positioned to play their cultural role. " 'Art is long' though 'time is fleeting,' " argued Sarah Nicholas Randolph, head of the committee, and "the work whose execution we are directing will stand long after our generation is lost in oblivion."[29] In this long view of the case, the immediate political tasks of coalition building carried little weight. The women seemed to feel confident that Lee would thrive in Southern memory; what mattered to them was that his image ascend into the realm of culture, that it be wrapped in and refined by the medium of art. They wanted a monument that would ultimately transcend the South, its local politics and tastes. Art was the vehicle. It was art that would secure Lee's position in the national pantheon of great men; art that would enable him to take his rightful place in the universal narrative of human progress, which it was the mission of culture to relate.[30]

The issue of art was so pivotal for the women's committee that it led to a painful public breach between the women and the governor's association. They refused to accept the results of the governor's 1877 design competition, held on to the money they had promised to the official association, and several years later sponsored a design competition of their own organized along radically different lines. Comparing these two design competitions is a fascinating exercise, for it demonstrates vividly the stakes of representation. Even people who shared the same basic image of Lee could approach the problem of his representation in fundamentally different ways.

The two design competitions were based on opposing methods of viewing and evaluating sculpture. To begin with, the two juries had divergent expectations of what the sculptor's model was supposed to show. The competition sponsored by the women's committee was juried by professional artists who were accustomed to judging competition models as sketches, exercises in composition rather than finished detail. But the governor's jury of 1877 viewed the models not as sketches but as miniature versions of the final design. They showed little interest in the aesthetic values that the sketch was meant to demonstrate—the harmony of lines and forms, the beauty or originality of the controlling idea. This is because the heart of the design problem, as they saw it, was the hero's likeness. "A *man on a horse* will not suffice," French told a potential competitor, "General Lee's effigy alone will satisfy the public."[31] The board told its judges to attend to "portraiture, skill in workmanship, and true conceptions of the hero and the cause he represented."[32] This group of requirements deliberately spoke to the demands of "truth" rather than "art"; and in fact the two categories were often framed as opposing, even irreconcilable, terms. For most of the judges the evaluation of truth boiled down to assessing likeness and pose. The "conception of the cause" had become so grounded in ideas about Lee's physical appearance and demeanor that the representational problem was drastically simplified in this way.[33]

This did not mean that creating a faithful likeness and an apt pose was a simple job. So much rested on the notion of Lee as a specimen of physical and moral perfection that he became an almost impossible standard of representation. He embodied a synthesis of virtues—strength and repose, forcefulness and modesty, manliness and grace—which, it is true, seemed to make him an eminently fit subject for sculpture, inasmuch as standard academic doctrine stressed a similar equipoise of discipline and energy and a similar faith in the equation of physical and moral beauty. But negotiating such a synthesis in practice—particularly in a portrait statue rather than an ideal subject—was a highly problematic task. To complicate it, many of the judges had extremely precise visual memories of Lee and his horsemanship, which gave them extraordinary critical confidence and rigor, even as they apologized for not being judges of "art." The judges tended to measure the horse and rider, point by point, against a fixed, a priori image of Lee on horseback. Even judges who had not known Lee personally used the same procedure, probably based on their familiarity with prints like *Lee on Traveller* (fig. 5.1) (which the governor's association had published as a fund-raising device). One such judge explained that he had to "create for myself a standard of what an equestrian statue of General Lee ought to be, and then determine which of the models inspected by me approached nearest to that conception."[34] In this mode of objective comparison, judges studied Lee's mount in the saddle, the position of his bridle arm, the rigidity of his legs, and diverse points of human and equine anatomy with an eye to detail that very few of the models withstood. One can appreciate the acuteness of this criticism by testing it against the only plaster model still in existence, the entry of Edward Valentine (fig. 5.2). His model received mixed reviews but several negative observations cropped up repeatedly—for example, the defectiveness of the horse's neck. One judge noted that "from the throat latch to his breast is almost a perpendicular," which, he argued, suggests a horse in motion, except that this one is supposed to be at rest, four feet on the ground. "The horse," he concluded, "presents very much the appearance of a Christmas toy," an image another judge echoed when he wrote disparagingly that the model was "very pretty as an ornament."[35]

Throughout this criticism there is a notable absence of the kind of narrative reading one might expect from "untrained" critics. If judges did visualize a narrative, it was almost always to show how the sculptor had gone wrong. Thus descriptions like "an old granger going to church on his waggon horse" or "a farmer drowsily wending his way across his broad acres" used narrative terms to satirize particular compositions.[36] Almost all the judges favored a still pose, as if Lee and his horse were in front of a camera (which they were in the print of *Lee on Traveller*, made from a photograph). A pose that suggested a more elaborate narrative quickly took the sculptor into dangerous territory. The entry of Moses Ezekiel (fig. 5.3), an expatriate Virginian working in Rome, seemed to be

5.2 Edward Valentine, model for Lee monument,
circa 1877, plaster.

the worst transgressor in this respect; one judge could only make sense of
the horse's pose if its rider were in the act of lassoing a wild animal. To
represent Lee's mastery as an overt display of restraining force, along the
lines of this model, was a fatal error.[37] Any narrative but the most minimal seemed to contaminate the canonical relationship between the horse
and the rider. In particular, the narrative of domination had to be suppressed, hidden within a more static image of latent power.

It is harder to specify exactly how the judges operated in the women's
competition because the documents (if there were any) do not survive. But
we can draw some good inferences based on the composition of the jury.
The women deliberately chose a small jury of one architect and two sculptors, all Northerners and all respected "professional" monument makers.
The architect was federal official Edward Clark, and the sculptors were
two famous men we have already encountered for their important role in
Union commemoration: John Quincy Adams Ward and Augustus Saint-
Gaudens. These three men no doubt ignored the details examined so

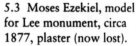
5.3 Moses Ezekiel, model
for Lee monument, circa
1877, plaster (now lost).

closely in the earlier competition and looked at the models instead as
mere sketches, intended, as Saint-Gaudens later said, "to indicate only the
general treatment of the proposed work."[38] This way of looking was
above all academic, geared toward evaluating how the theme was rendered in the main lines and formal relationships of the composition. One
gets a sense of what the judges were looking for by studying Charles
Niehaus's prizewinning model, which survives in a studio photograph
dated August 11, 1885 (fig. 5.4). Unlike *Lee on Traveller*, posed still before a camera, horse and rider here are in movement. The design features
a strong leading diagonal connecting the angle of the horse's lowered
head with the right front leg planted beneath. Contrasting with this
powerful leaning pull of the horse is the fixed upright position of the
rider, as stable as a carousel pole. In narrative terms, Lee maintains perfect balance as he restrains the animal's bursting internal energy. In
compositional terms, Lee's vertical body anchors the group in place while
the horse's forward-pointing diagonal breaks the design's symmetry and

5.4 Charles Niehaus, model for Lee monument, circa 1886,
plaster (now lost).

puts the whole in motion. Niehaus, it seems, negotiated a proper balance
between compositional values of dynamism and stability, and between
representational values of force and sobriety. The judges overlooked a
detail of Niehaus's model that drew intense criticism from Virginians
monitoring the competition results: the bobtail on Lee's horse. This was
a representational gaffe that would have disqualified Niehaus from serious consideration in the men's competition. The bobtail simply did not
belong on a Virginia gentleman's horse. It carried suggestions of effemi-
nacy, as the Richmond *Whig* implied when it said that Lee might as well
have had "his hair banged."[39] Jubal Early went so far as to write the
governor and tell him that if the design were ever erected he would "feel
like collecting the survivors of the 2nd Corps, and going to Richmond to
blow up the thing with dynamite."[40]

There were bitter differences, then, between the two approaches to
sculpture represented in these design competitions. They had become po-

larized around what were seen as two conflicting values: artistry and objectivity. For the most part the Virginia press came down on the side of
objectivity, and kept arguing that all the public really wanted was "Lee as
he actually was," not a figure smothered by the "tricks" and "adulteries"
of art.[41] The *Norfolk Landmark* argued that the sponsors of the monument should listen to the veterans, and that the veterans "call with one
voice for the subordination of Art to Nature."[42] This was a familiar sort
of dispute, repeated many times in the history of nineteenth-century
American public sculpture. Without a set of academic institutions to establish standards of production and channel patronage, as in France,
American sculptural practice in the mid-nineteenth century still had two
extreme flanks—one intent on professionalizing sculpture by mastering
the Western European tradition, and the other intent on marketing an
image of "natural" American genius in tune with popular taste. Harriet
Hosmer and Clark Mills, as we have seen, were representative of these
opposing flanks in the 1860s, but the rhetorical dispute between "art"
on the one side and "nature" and "the people" on the other would continue for decades to mark discussions of public art, especially military
monuments.

The governor and his board aligned themselves with the popular flank
and effectively rigged their competition against European artists.[43] Not
suprisingly, the jury ended up supporting a popular sculptor in the self-
taught mold. The surprise was that their choice was neither a man nor a
Southerner. She was Vinnie Ream, the former protégé of Clark Mills,
most famous for her likeness of Lincoln in the federal Capitol. Ream was
an extremely complex figure who grew up in the West, in and out of the
border states, and who managed to use this experience to play an ambiguous political role herself, moving successfully between radical Republicans and ex-Confederates.[44] She won the 1877 competition by producing
an exacting likeness of Lee (the model does not survive) and by mobilizing
a network of Southern congressmen to lobby on her behalf.[45]

The results of the competition, however, were never made public because the women's committee refused to accept them. Ream's gender was
not enough to satisfy the women and may in fact have hurt her standing
with them. Her lobbying practices had given her a notorious reputation,
created largely by female critics in the Northern press. She also represented the very sort of popular sculptural practice the women's committee was trying to transcend; in their published letter refusing to sanction
the competition, Sarah Randolph declared that "we have only one aim in
view, which is to secure that which, being the noblest and most beautiful,
will be the most appropriate."[46] Governor Kemper's failure to rally the
women's committee behind his jury's choice effectively put an end to his

association's fund-raising hopes and left an opening for the women to advance their own competition, organized specifically to encourage European entries.

Ironically, though, the winner of this competition—Charles Niehaus—was not a European artist but a young, unknown German American sculptor from Ohio. The entrant with the greatest international standing, French sculptor Antonin Mercié, did not even receive honorable mention.[47] If Ezekiel's model was the standard of folly in the first competition, Mercié's performed the same role in the second. Written descriptions of the model indicate that Lee was depicted on a rearing horse, riding over "the shrieking and prostrate victims of a battle-field"—though Mercié later explained that the dying soldiers were meant to be Lee's own men, "stretching for a last affectionate glance of their leader."[48] This Napoleonic conception managed to violate the Lee cult's proscription on narrative display, the professional judges' notion of sculptural decorum, and the ladies' sense of gentility. Saint-Gaudens himself is said to have condemned the model as "an utter misconception of General Lee's character."[49] The common reaction to Mercié's entry from both the artist-judges and the popular press shows that there was some common ground between them, however polarized their positions. Both the professional and the popular schools of criticism condemned energetic narrative treatments because they threatened to confuse or even cancel the image of benign leadership the monument was supposed to project.

Nevertheless, the commission for the Lee Monument eventually went to this same Mercié, even though he had so completely botched the job in his competition entry. The prizewinner Niehaus was an untried sculptor, Mercié a known quantity. In fact, Saint-Gaudens knew him personally. Both had trained at the Ecole des Beaux-Arts in Paris, and Mercié was a model of the sort of academic professionalism Saint-Gaudens believed American sculpture needed.[50] For reasons that will never be clear—perhaps stemming from the amazing bobtail controversy—Niehaus's prizewinning design was rejected, and Saint-Gaudens persuaded the women's committee to give Mercié another chance by submitting a revised model. By this time, in the spring of 1886, the ladies' committee was finally in the process of officially merging with the governor's association, now headed by Governor Fitzhugh Lee, nephew of the hero himself. It appears that the women cut a deal with the governor: he could pick the site for the monument if they could choose the artist. Working together, they instructed Mercié to send a second model, and to represent the horse with all four feet on the ground. This simple instruction was enough to bring Mercié's new composition approximately into line with the prevailing image of Lee; that and a good deal of application to the fine points of likeness and costume (closely monitored by Governor Lee) finally led to

5.5 Antonin Mercié and Paul Pujol, Lee Monument,
1890, Monument Avenue, Richmond.

a contract with the artist.[51] Mercié's final design appropriately emphasized sobriety and stability (fig. 5.5). He showed Lee exerting only the
slighest pressure on the reins; he spread the legs of the horse to the edges
of the supporting plinth, and spread the legs of the rider to echo the slope
of the pedestal (which was designed by Beaux-Arts-trained architect Paul
Pujol). Seen from any side, therefore, the outlines of the monument form
a graceful but stable pyramid, the equestrian group extending and fulfill-
ing the directional flow of the pedestal.

Four feet on the ground and a good likeness: after all the controversy
it turned out to be fairly straightforward to reconcile the demands of
"truth" and the demands of "art," to satisfy both popular and professional tastes. After a concerted effort in the Virginia press to overturn the
selection of Mercié, the artist's revised design calmed the fears of veterans
and others with a stake in the Lee cult. "The soldiers will know him,"
trumpeted one Richmond headline; the article went on to relate how one
Confederate veteran who saw the statue in the foundry "experienced all
his old-time emotions, and his heart told him, 'That's Marse Robert!'"[52]

Still, Mercié had had to lobby hard for even the most minor departure from the canonical image of Lee on Traveller. The sculptor insisted, for example, on representing Lee bareheaded and with one side of his collar upturned to break the hard lines of the uniform. As long as he could argue that these innovations enhanced Lee's natural physical beauty, he remained on safe ground.[53] The ladies for their part succeeded in obtaining a work of impeccable craftsmanship elevated and transfigured by its elegant pedestal, as if the aesthetic values that were deliberately submerged in the hero's likeness could flourish in the nonrepresentational base, with its sensuous play of convex and concave surfaces. Here was an artistic achievement that could draw the admiration of someone like Henry James, who compared the monument to "some precious pearl of ocean washed up on a rude bare strand."[54]

James was here referring to the monument's barren site on the outskirts of the city, surely the most bizarre location ever chosen for a Beaux-Arts-designed monument. In a bold move Governor Lee had decided not to build the monument on the grounds of the State Capitol, where the original governor's association had planned to build and where every major public sculpture in the city had previously gone. Instead he chose to locate the monument in a plot of empty farmland owned by a local capitalist, who planned to transform the property into an elegant residential subdivision; the Lee Monument in this plan was to be the crowning feature of a new boulevard named Monument Avenue, which would serve as the suburban frontier of the city's western expansion. In the internal debate over the monument's site, Sarah Randolph of the ladies' committee had urged a serene park setting on the grounds of its "eternal fitness"; in other words she wanted the monument's surroundings to remain fixed in unchanging "nature," not in city neighborhoods that tended to rise and fall in economic cycles.[55] Certainly she did not want her project associated with a real estate venture that speculated blatantly on the prestige value of Lee and his monument.

But that is exactly what the governor's scheme was, "a plain business proposition" in his own words, and it soon paid off handsomely.[56] After a couple of decades in which the city formally annexed the property and actively promoted its development, Monument Avenue filled in and became the most fashionable address in town. The avenue became home to the city's elite—the "New South" elite of merchants, lawyers, and other professionals who had subsumed and displaced the old planter class. At the same time the avenue also became home to a whole series of major public monuments to Confederate leaders, which were placed on axis with the original monument to Lee; monuments to Jefferson Davis and J.E.B. Stuart erected in 1907 cemented the boulevard's new reputation. The decision to shift the Lee site away from the state Capitol and into the

5.6 Photograph of Monument Avenue, circa 1907, in Richmond Chamber of
Commerce, *Richmond, Virginia, 1907*, n.p.

city's suburbs—ironically, made by a state governor—thus sparked a critical change in the monumental layout of the city. From now on the most
important Confederate figures were memorialized in an entirely separate
zone, a city-sponsored precinct fully integrated into the modern civic fabric and clearly intended to showcase civic progress. The development of
this new Confederate boulevard in the interest of progress even swept
away the remnants of earthworks left from the Confederate defense of
Richmond, which had been preserved as important markers of the past.[57]
Early promotional photographs of the avenue highlight this full-fledged
embrace of modernity. In one image published in 1907 (fig. 5.6), the
equestrian of Lee appears on the horizon, just off center, circumscribed
within a linear network of residential amenities that are the real focus of
the composition: the trees freshly planted in the grassy median and the
adjoining strips of asphalt converge in perfect orthogonals on the distant
monument; the telephone pole anchored in the foreground, dead center,
towers beside the monument and holds a wire that skims just above the
statue's head—all this framed in a filigreed oval. Such imagery made Lee's
universe—and the institution of slavery which had been central to it—an
ever more distant memory.

Unexpectedly, then, the once unpromising location of the Lee Monument turned out to have great symbolic value. It further cemented the
depoliticization of Lee by moving him away from the old precinct of
the Confederate Capitol and quite literally into the city of the future—a
residential neighborhood not yet even built. Once the boulevard began to

fill in around the monument, it effectively asserted the continuity between old and new regimes, between the Confederate past and a modern South now oriented to the mainstream national values of business and progress. "We are all hunting for dollars," wrote the *New York Herald* at the monument's dedication, summing up its lesson of national reconciliation in strikingly unsentimental terms. The statement, reprinted approvingly in the Richmond papers, was corroborated by their various reports on the healthy prices commanded by the subdivided lots surrounding the monument.[58]

The monument in its suburban site thus managed to heal a number of divisions that had opened up in the course of the monument campaign. These were divisions between truth and art, between business and gentility, indeed between male and female elites. The gendering of the dispute had been particularly embarrassing to the white leadership, and the successful merger of the men's and women's efforts provided the symbolic closure necessary to complete the ritual of commemoration. The combination of masculine and feminine principles proved irresistible, both working in the service of a politics of white supremacy. The ladies' committee contributed a normative notion of culture in which art and virtue supposedly coincided. The governor contributed a "plain business proposition" with its vision of civic progress and private profit. Circumscribing and embellishing the equestrian likeness of Lee, these principles of culture and capitalist progress served to refine the statue's already subtle narrative of power. Just as the rider's brute mastery of the animal was disguised as a narrative of self-mastery—a relation of power transformed into a revelation of self—so the brute fact of white domination embodied in slavery was disguised as a lesson in the white man's own capacity for valor and achievement. Occasionally the disguise might be stripped off. After the cornerstone-laying ceremony in 1887, the *Richmond Dispatch* argued that the example of Lee vindicated the Old South and its slaveholding class: "Was there ever on this planet a nobler class of men?" The editorial went on to resurrect some of the standard planks of the proslavery argument familiar from antebellum times.[59] But by the time the monument was completed, the ritual steered clear of such overt defenses; ceremony and commentary were orchestrated to support the monument's assertion of mainstream values. The monument in its final incarnation thus clothed white power in an image of civilization—a civilization that presupposed whiteness as a kind of moral prerequisite.

"A people carves its own image in the monuments of its great men." Thus began Archer Anderson's oration at the dedication of the monument in May 1890.[60] The dedication ceremony was a huge ritual affair designed to construct an image of this collective, this "people," who had supposedly erected the monument. The ceremony deliberately rallied whites of all classes together, papering over class divisions that had erupted earlier in the campaign and had threatened for a while to disrupt the image of white solidarity advanced by the sponsors. A labor party had taken control of the Richmond city council in the late 1880s, and its coalition of blacks and working-class whites actually refused to vote subsidies for the monument in its suburban location because it would "benefit only a certain class of people."[61] But this alliance across racial lines was short-lived, and when the council changed hands it fell back into line, as did the white organizations representing farmers and laborers. By the time of the monument's dedication, populist and conservative groups, laborers and elites, veterans and women, all came together to pay homage to the hero's statue in a much-trumpeted ceremony of popular harmony. Anderson, in his oration, made the unity seem natural, an inevitable consequence of Lee's great moral character:

> It is, besides and above all, the unique combination in him of moral strength with moral beauty, of all that is great in heroic action with all that is good in common life, that will make of this pile of stone a sacred shrine, dear throughout coming ages, not to soldiers only, but to all "helpers and friends of mankind."[62]

The only division that refused to be healed—even superficially or symbolically—was the racial division central to the very subject and imagery of the monument. The "cordial unity of the races" imagined by Governor Kemper's board did not materialize, as African Americans for the most part refused to have anything to do with the ceremonies surrounding the completion of the monument. The only African American participants reported in the white newspapers were the faithful body servants of old Confederate veterans, who, speaking in dialect, provided a sentimental spectacle for white readers.[63] While orators trumpeted the monument's popularity, John Mitchell, the defiant editor of the *Richmond Planet*, the local black newspaper, hammered away at the monument's pretenses. "The people of the South had to grunt and groan to raise a few thousand dollars for the Lee monument," he wrote just before its dedication.[64] In an aside calculated to provoke, he claimed that "the men who talk most about the valor of Lee, and the blood of the brave Confederate dead are those who never smelt powder or engaged in a battle. Most of them were at table, either on top or under it, when the war was going on."[65] After the dedication ceremony, in an extraordinary paragraph, Mitchell reported this reaction: "An old colored man after seeing the mammoth parade of the ex-Confederates on May 29th and gazing at the rebel flags, exclaimed, 'The Southern white folks is on top—the Southern white folks is on top!'"[66] Here was a stunningly clear statement of the case, which stripped the civilizing clothing off the monument and the ritual surrounding it, to lay bare its simple message of white domination. The anecdote concludes on a rather different note, however: "After thinking for a moment a smile lit up his countenance as he chuckled with evident satisfaction, 'But we've got the government! We've got the government!'"[67] The man consoled himself with the reminder that, even though white Southerners had local control of the ritual, "we" were part of a group—the Republican Party—that had control of the national government (Benjamin Harrison had defeated Democratic incumbent Grover Cleveland in the last presidential election). This perspective seemed to deflate the pretensions of the "mammoth parade" and to upset the order ("white folks on top") figured in its ritual.

Yet the paragraph is really a poignant moment of wishful thinking, for the confident assertion "we've got the government" gave no hint of the problematic relationship between African Americans and the national entity that supposedly represented them. Both party and nation had turned their backs on the Reconstruction agenda of civil rights and were coming to embrace the spirit of Confederate commemoration. Much of the Northern press, in fact, responded favorably to the Lee Monument and treated it as a legitimate national monument. The *New York Times* argued that Lee's "memory is . . . a possession of the American people, and the monument that recalls it is itself a national possession."[68] The *Times* was merely echoing the argument put forth in the opening paragraph of Archer Anderson's oration, which asserted that "all who bear the American name may proudly consent that posterity shall judge them by the structure, which we are here to dedicate."[69] In their alienation from the monument and all it represented, African Americans were now losing even their entitlement to "the American name."

African Americans had to respond, then, from an ever more marginal position. Mitchell himself used the forum of the *Planet* and his position on the Richmond city council, where he was one of three remaining black council members; this was before the full implementation of Jim Crow, which eliminated all elected black officials. These three were the only council members who refused to vote for a city appropriation of $7,500 for the monument's dedication ceremonies. Mitchell argued that those who wore the "clinking chains of slavery" should be allowed to "keep silent" and refrain from voting.[70] Public silence, rather than active protest, was in reality their only feasible, nonsuicidal option. This was the dilemma the monument posed: to maintain the integrity of their countermemory, a memory centered around the historical experience of slavery, blacks had to witness their own silence or disappearance within the larger collective, the "people." Yet they they were not entirely invisible, as Mitchell constantly reminded his readers. He commented with fine irony on a disjunction characteristic of Southern society: though blacks were

5.7 Photograph after hoisting of the Lee statue, May 29, 1890.

absent from the ritual labor of erecting the monument—the cornerstone laying and the ceremonial hauling of the statue and finally the unveiling—they were heavily engaged in the actual physical work that made the rituals possible.

> The Negro was in the Northern processions on Decoration Day [Memorial Day] and in the Southern ones, if only to carry buckets of ice-water. He put up the Lee Monument, and should the time come, will be there to take it down. He's black and sometimes greasy, but who could do with out the Negro.[71]

Mitchell's point is documented in a remarkable photograph of the monument taken just after the statue was hoisted up top to the pedestal (fig. 5.7). Still draped in white to prepare for the ceremonial unveiling, the statue looks a ghostly counterimage of itself. Four black laborers appear in the lower register of the photograph, standing presumably on a scaffold just below the plinth. Three white men and a barefoot boy—innocent representatives of the common people who share the statue as their "posssession"—take privileged places at camera level on the plinth itself and touch the legs of the bronze horse with proprietary nonchalance. The four black men seem to float beneath, their heads caught poking out in the odd intervals between bronze, pants, and wires. In a classic "return of the repressed," they materialize here as a kind of subtext to the monument's text. They are the memory of the "clinking chains" of slavery. The Confederacy was founded on their backs. They are the labor that built the South's wealth and that dug its defenses when the wealth was threatened. They are the bottom rail without which a top rail cannot exist. They are the hero's anti-image, without which the hero himself could not exist. They are, as Mitchell pointed out, indispensable—the unspoken reference of every claim the monument makes.

For the most part, of course, white observers did not read the imagery this way. They did not choose to see how white and black worlds might interlock and clash within the concrete reality of the monument. One notable exception, worth exploring in some detail, is Henry James, who saw the monument while on an American tour shortly after the turn of the century. In the essay on Richmond which he published in the *American Scene*, James claimed, astonishingly, that the whole town reeked of slavery despite itself. It was not by any obvious or intentional references, James argued, but by the very lack of genuine historical references to the past. He had come to Richmond expecting to find "vivid images," the "haunted scene" of the war's great tragedy. What he found instead was a place "that looked to me simply blank and void . . . a poor Northern city." His disappointment was intense until he realized that this very blankness was in itself significant: it was the consequence of the old fallacy of slavery. In "the large, sad poorness" of Richmond, James found himself "tasting, mystically, of the very essence of the old Southern idea—the hugest fallacy, as it hovered there to one's backward, one's ranging vision, for which hundreds of thousands of men had ever lain down their lives."[72] The intellectual and cultural absurdity of trying to maintain slavery in the modern world had so blighted the South that it was left with no visible cultural past, a void where its heart should have been. James ended his essay with the Lee Monument, which, stranded in its absurdly empty modern surroundings, seemed emblemmatic of the South's condition. Leaving the monument, and leaving Richmond, James imagined the statue "communing, at its altitude, which represents thus some prodigious exemplary perched position, some everlasting high stool of penitence, with the very heaven of futility."[73]

In one crucial respect, though, for James there was a concrete material legacy of the old institution of slavery, and this was "the intimate presence of the negro." The "negro's" unavoidable proximity was the essential burden of the South, he argued. "One saw them [meaning white Southerners] not much less imprisoned in it and overdarkened by it today than they had been in the time of their so fallacious presumption." Throughout his discussion the African American appears not as a legitimate element of the Southern scene—the implied South is always white—

but as a kind of virus preying upon it. James himself felt profoundly "discomposed," even "threatened," by the sight of "tattermalion darkies" who "lounged and sunned themselves within range" at the Washington train station, or by the black teamsters in Richmond "who now emphasized for me with every degree of violence the already-apprehended note of the negro really at home." Here was "the Southern black as we knew him not, and had not within the memory of man known him, at the North"—that is to say, still dark, still "African," posing the "formidable question, which rose suddenly like some beast that had sprung from the jungle."[74] Doubtless the laborers in the hoisting photograph would pose the same question for James, the question posed by the inescapability of the "Southern black." Yet there is an insight to be drawn from James's paranoid ruminations on the black other. If the Lee Monument was a brilliant effort to re-present white mastery in the postwar world, then James's reading of the Richmond scene suggests that it rested on a precarious foundation. The black men in the picture duly mark and confirm the hierarchical order of the white supremacist society, but by their very presence they threaten to destabilize that order. James's sympathies are entirely with the white half of the equation, which he feels he understands; their past and their present, he thinks, are both linked tragically to a strange and unknowable race. That such an ardent anitslavery Northerner would feel this way suggests why the Lee Monument in particular and the Lost Cause in general could so easily enter the mainstream of national memory.[75]

IN James's text, the social relation of white and black is tragically vexed, forever linked to the originating tragedy of slavery. This was a quintessential (though not universal) Northern view, and there was a white Southern answer to it. That answer revolved around the mythology of the "faithful slave." Under slavery, some white Southerners maintained, "the intimate presence of the negro" was not a problem but actually a source of social comfort and joy. Whites and blacks had once known, respected, and loved one another, they argued, in a way Northerners could not understand. Emancipation had all but destroyed this intimacy, they lamented, but it survived at least in memory.

Six years after the dedication of the Lee Monument, in the rural South Carolina town of Fort Mill, these sentiments found explicit expression in a modest monument erected on the town green, near the Confederate soldier monument (fig. 5.8). Financed by Captain Samuel White, Confederate veteran and owner of the local cotton mills, it was inscribed and "dedicated to the faithful slaves who, loyal to a sacred trust, toiled for the support of the army, with matchless devotion; and with sterling fidelity guarded our defenseless homes, women and children, during the struggle

5.8–10 Monument to
faithful slaves, 1896, Fort
Mill, South Carolina.
Below: relief panels.

for the principles of our 'Confederate States of America.'" The monument is a small marble obelisk with two relief panels, now heavily eroded, the work of an anonymous carver—probably an artisan employed by a cemetery-monument supplier. One panel depicts a mammy with a child in her arms seated on the steps of the master's house (fig. 5.9), and the other a field laborer sitting on a log, a sickle leaning against his shoulder (fig. 5.10). As the local newspapers described them, the panels showed "an old colored woman nursing a pretty little white child" and "an old colored man . . . taking an honest rest."[76] This little monument, modest as it was, shared something in common with Henry Kirke Brown's massive antebellum project for the South Carolina State House: both meant to bring the labor of slaves out of visual purgatory and into the purview of public sculpture. The Fort Mill monument was the first and only representation of the "faithful slave" in a postbellum monument. It was a monument generated from a former slaveholder's perspective, designed not to celebrate slavery's demise but to muse nostalgically over its passing.

Before this little monument appeared, all the energies of Confederate commemoration had gone in an entirely different direction, propelled by the urgent need after the war to dissociate the Southern cause from slavery. The Lee Monument was a high point in this campaign to restructure the historical memory of Southern society. With striking success the monument helped refashion an image of white rule freed from the brutal footing of slavery, even as that image depended upon and perpetuated the structure of racial domination instituted under slavery. Once this purified image had been consolidated and accepted even by important elements of Northern public opinion, there was some room for white Southerners to return to the problem of slavery and its role in their consciousness. They had defended and maintained the institution for most of their history, after all; it could not be simply expurgated from memory. The sentiments that inspired the Fort Mill monument remained common enough, kept alive in family lore and even sometimes in cemetery monuments erected by families to their domestic servants.[77] The same sentiments were increasingly entering into Southern literature about the old plantation South, exemplified in Thomas Nelson Page's dialect stories of "Marse Chan" appearing in the early 1880s in the national magazine *Century*.[78] The question was how these sentiments could enter the field of commemoration, so obsessed as it was with constructing an image of white valor purged of the moral incubus of slavery.

With the passage of time, some white Southerners came to see slavery as peculiarly suited to commemoration, a kind of golden age of race relations, built on intimate bonds between blacks and whites: the bond of mammy and child, of young master and his black playmates, of soldier and body servant. The memory of these familial relationships, and of the system that fostered them, they argued, had to be preserved in public form before the last of the old slaves and masters took their personal stories to the grave. As the century came to a close, recreations of slave life began to be staged in public performances, for example at the Atlanta Cotton States exposition of 1895. At the same time a few plaques and shafts began to appear in public places to commemorate slaves. On at least one Confederate soldier monument, that in Columbia, North Carolina (1912), one of the inscriptions included a statement "in appreciation of our faithful slaves." In the early twentieth century several attempts were made to augment these localized efforts with a regional or even national monument to the "faithful old slaves." The United Daughters of the Confederacy took up the question in 1904 and promoted the idea in the *Confederate Veteran*, and in the 1910s renewed efforts to erect monuments to loyal slaves in every Southern state. In the 1920s some Southern white women worked to erect a monument in honor of the "black mammy" in Washington.[79] But the more ambitious schemes never materialized. The only Southern monument comparable in any way to the Fort Mill experiment is the notorious full-length statue of an aged, bent black man doffing his hat, erected in 1927 in Natchitoches, Louisiana, and inscribed "in grateful recognition of the arduous and faithful service of the good darkies of Louisiana." Like the aged hero of Stephen Foster's song *My Old Kentucky Home* ("The head must bow, and the back will have to bend, wherever the darkey may go"), this figure is best understood as a former slave—one who has survived emancipation but who retains the appropriate posture and attitude of servility, of "faithfulness."[80]

The Fort Mill monument remains unique as a representation of slavery, one that is deliberately comprehensive, including both house slavery and field slavery, female and male labor. Naturally that labor is sentimentalized. It is relegated to the domain of the elderly, and in both images work is either suspended or disguised. The field hand rests, the bundles of wheat in the background testifying to his labor without him having to engage in it. The woman's work is negated more radically: it is transformed into maternal love, as she returns the child's embrace and their two heads touch. The mammy scene received special attention in the local accounts of the monument, precisely because it represented the relationship of master to slave not as one of domination but of mutual affection. "Love itself" could be read in the features of her face, according to one account (written before those features were lost to erosion).[81] Captain White himself had loved his "old negro mammy," the papers explained, "who crooned him to sleep when a babe," and his monument was meant "to teach generations yet unborn that though black in skin, and servile in station, there existed between the negro and the master a bond of love broken only by death."[82] An obituary for White published in 1911 said that "often the slave women would love the children of their owners more than they did their own offspring"—a remarkable claim showing the depths of self-delusion and outright dishonesty involved in the mythology of the mammy—and "this affection, which Northern philanthropy sought to destroy, Capt. White determined to commemorate, and hence erected the slave monument to silently, but constantly proclaim its truth."[83] The relationship of slave women to the young masters they cared for and helped rear was undoubtedly fraught with tragic psychological complexity for both parties. The monument condenses that relationship—and the whole structure of forced labor involved in it—to the simple love of a mother for her child.

The slave monument was one of four monuments sponsored by White and located on the Fort Mill town green. The first was a standard Confederate soldier monument, erected in 1891, with its generic image of a white infantryman. The three others were far more unusual and gave this little monumental precinct a unique status in the Southern landscape. They were monuments to Confederate women, to faithful slaves, and to local Catawba Indians who fought for the Confederacy. One might be tempted to label this commemorative program an essay in "diversity," shattering the usual commemorative exclusions of race and gender, but of course it was a representation of diversity within the paternalistic framework of a powerful white man. Captain White was the wealthiest man, the biggest property owner, and the major employer in the area. From a family of cotton planters, he built a pair of cotton mills after the war and thereby transformed Fort Mill from a tiny agricultural village into a small maufacturing town of 2,000. He was unquestionably the local boss. Each of the monuments he sponsored recognized those individuals who did credit to their race or gender by doing their social duty as he understood and helped define it. All the monuments inscribed names of actual people he had known. On the slave monument the names chosen "among the many faithful" have an especially personal connection: eight of the ten are named White. They were his own, or his family's, slaves. The other two are Springs and Spratt, both names of leading families in town who became part of the cotton mill business White had founded.[84]

The faithful-slave monument became rather widely known despite its modest size, its artistic anonymity, and its marginal location. The dedication in May 1896 was well publicized and, according to the newspapers, was attended by "thousands," many of them from outside the area. For the main attraction, the oration, White succeeded in booking Polk Miller, a nationally recognized white performer of "plantation negro" music and "negro sketches" in dialect, who had two years earlier appeared on stage with Mark Twain at Madison Square Garden. Miller's stage act professed to give "the general public a true and faithful reproduction of

Plantation Life and Scenes before the War," but unlike the old minstrel performers he did not appear in blackface and instead posed as a "delineator" of the "Folk Lore" and music of the slave South.[85] Miller had grown up the son of a slaveowner on a southern Virginia plantation and had (like White) fought for the Confederacy. He began his recital career in Southern cities in the early 1890s but rather soon found sympathetic audiences in the North as well. He claimed to be correcting the misconstructions of black dialect and character found in minstrel shows and published stories. His recital was "not a *burlesque*," according to his publicity brochure, but a representation of "the *real* negro." At the same time he made clear that this "real negro" was not "the young negro of today," whom he despised, but the "old issue darky" of his boyhood. Miller laced his performances with social commentary satirizing emancipation and black efforts at self-improvement, much of this rhetoric taken directly from the old proslavery argument:

> As long as there is left in the South an honest, truthful, old-time "howdy, Marster," negro of the good old days gone-by, he'll tell you that the accomplishment of the freedom of the negro, for which Horace Greeley and Wendell Phillips labored so hard and so long, took out of his life those rays of sunshine which made him not only the happiest creature on earth, but the subject of story and song which delight the people of the South who knew him, loved him, and whose like the world will never, never see again. Will the young negro of to-day ever have a book written about him?[86]

In some ways Miller's material was territory that African Americans themselves had already begun to stake out, with the Fisk Jubilee Singers' performances of spirituals and the explorations of folklore in the *Southern Workman* and the fiction of Charles Chesnutt.[87] It is evident that a profound contest was underway over the proper stewardship and significance of this cultural legacy of slavery, and Miller was right in the middle of it. He played to white audiences but occasionally received protests from the black press or from African Americans who happened to see his show, as they did at Chatauqua in 1895; for them, Miller's show was indeed burlesque, presenting only "that grotesque and illiterate side of the negro."[88] Miller eventually added a black vocal quartet to his act and thereby competed directly with the Fisk Singers, whom he mocked in his ad as white men "parading in a dark skin"; his own singers, the ad declared, were "genuine negroes . . . taken from the Tobacco Factories in Richmond" who "act and sing like the real Southern Darkey in his 'workin' clothes." W.E.B. DuBois no doubt had Miller's group in mind when he wrote, in *The Souls of Black Folk* (1903), that the Fisk Singers "have been imitated—sometimes well, by the singers of Hampton and Atlanta, and sometimes ill, by straggling quartettes."[89]

Miller did not have his quartet at the time of the Fort Mill dedication, but he did capitalize on the presence of "genuine negroes"—the many former slaves who were reported to be in attendance. Unlike the Lee Monument ceremonies, this ceremony demanded their participation, their symbolic assent to its claims. Ex-slaves pulled the cord to unveil the shaft, spoke in gratitude to Captain White, and sang an "old plantation song." According to the white newspapers, "the hearts of the plantation negroes were won" by Miller's speech, and "they nodded their assent when he struck a sympathetic chord and told of the love between the slaves and their masters and mistresses."[90] It would have been interesting to hear the reaction of someone like DuBois to this white-orchestrated performance designed to reveal the authentic emotional life of slavery. Reception of the monument in the black press unfortunately has proved elusive, but the monument was actually noted with approval twenty years later in Freeman Murray's study on emancipation in American sculpture. He wrote that "there is no gainsaying the praiseworthy motives which prompted its erection and the very laudatory character of the tribute inscribed on it."[91] By this time the imagery of blacks in popular culture had become increasingly vicious, with the stereotype of the docile slave being edged out by the figure of the predatory black male rapist and murderer exemplified in D. W. Griffith's film *Birth of a Nation* (1915). In this climate the figure of the faithful slave could be read as a "positive" type, no matter how much it misrepresented the nature of the relationships fostered by slavery. And in this climate, not even Miller's "old issue" black quartet could survive, as the hostility to black performers on "white" stages eventually forced him to disband the group.[92]

White's monument is one of those rare public monuments that gives voice and form to sentiments that could not be represented in the commemorative mainstream. Indeed the whole work is really about sentiment, not slavery. The monument transforms this extreme institution of domination into the nostalgic fiction of a lost love. Dear as this fiction was to many white Southerners, it had to be banished from their more official program of memory because the institution of slavery, unlike the figure of Lee or even the idea of the Lost Cause, was no longer "American." Even sentimentalized, slavery did not have a legitimate place in the modern nation's self-image. And however much white Southerners might scorn the North and "Northern philanthropy," they still craved legitimacy in the nation the North had conquered and redefined. The final chapter of the book takes up this issue by examining how local publics, from both North and South, sought national legitimacy in the new form of the common-soldier monument.

CHAPTER SIX

COMMON SOLDIERS

SAMUEL WHITE'S modest monument to the "faithful slaves" of Fort Mill, South Carolina, with its little list of names meant to lift the former chattel out of historical oblivion, alerts us to one final, but decisive, shift in the history of nineteenth-century public monuments. This was the great enlargement of the commemorative sphere to include not only monuments to celebrated leaders like Lincoln and Lee but monuments to common men and women unknown to the public at large. The common soldier, in particular, emerged in the last third of the century as the most prolific figure in public sculpture, appearing not just in urban areas, where public sculpture traditionally belonged, but even in tiny hamlets that had never before seen a single public statue. The war memorial as we know it today took form here at this time, decades before similar memorials became common in Europe.

The earliest such memorials were simple shafts often erected in town cemeteries and dedicated to soldiers who had died in the war. They were funereal, and for good reason. The sheer extent of death was astounding, far beyond anything ever experienced in American history; almost no community was left untouched. The early monuments attested to this terrible simplicity, condensing the war's meaning into lists of names recorded in stone. But in the late 1860s the sculptural figure of the common soldier began to emerge on these monuments, and the monuments themselves increasingly were integrated into the towns' public space—in village greens, courthouse grounds, public parks. The monuments, in other words, were coming to honor not only the dead but the living veteran, who saw himself represented in the public statue of the soldier. Often it was the veterans themselves, or their loved ones, who mobilized to erect this new form of war memorial.[1]

The soldier figure was supposed to be universal in its reference, a generic representative of the rank and file. Yet the figure was particularized in certain crucial respects, most fundamentally in its facial typing. The generic physiognomy was meant to condense the polyglot faces of the nation into a standard "American" type. What it meant for a face to be "American" was not easy to define, but whiteness was a prerequisite—so obvious to most that it needed no comment. John Quincy Adams Ward's

6.1 Richard Morris Hunt and John Quincy Adams Ward,
7th Regiment Memorial, 1869–74, Central Park, New York City.

figure for the 7th Regiment Memorial in New York (fig. 6.1), an early and well-known example, was described in characteristic fashion as "a national head, a true American face, not to be mistaken for one of any other nation; and it is also frank, noble, brave, and good—not that of the mere routine soldier of a regular army, but the citizen soldier of the best type."[2] To be "American" in this case meant being a "citizen" or volunteer soldier rather than a "regular" soldier; in the United States the regular army was still tainted in many ways, not least by the immigrant and lower-class origins of many of the men in its ranks. While this particular regiment and its monument were more snobbish than most, even much less elite common-soldier monuments shared the model of the American citizen-soldier as a superior native, white "type" of manhood.

The other particularity of the common-soldier figure was its pose and format. Typically a lone infantryman, the figure usually stood at the top of a pedestal or column holding a rifle upright. Ward's soldier turns his head to the right and stands in a relaxed contrapposto pose, as if on guard duty; later versions overwhelmingly favored some variant of this basic "parade rest" type. Only occasionally does the common soldier appear as a combatant, and even more rarely does the soldier's figure carry any of the marks of war's calamity—rents in the uniform or physical abrasions to the body or even signs of fatigue.[3] Never, of course, does death obtrude in the sculptural program, even though the soldier's corpse had become a commonplace motif in other media, particularly in the war photography pioneered at this time.

Authentic in its recreation of period uniforms, ideal in its representation of the intact and vigorous white male body, the standing-soldier monument spread from town to town, village to village, throughout the North and South (fig. 6.2). More elaborate war memorials with bigger sculptural programs were sometimes erected in larger cities, but even these often just multiplied the basic formula—replacing the single infantryman with four generic figures to represent the four separate branches of the armed services. Union and Confederate monuments followed the same pattern: once separate and opposing nations, the two sides became indistinguishable in their war memorials except in small details of uniform, insignia, and inscriptions.[4] A monument industry developed to meet the demand, packaging the services of granite companies, marble quarries, and metal foundries directly to the monument consumers, the local associations of men and women who volunteered to organize campaigns. With dealers and catalogs of readymade soldier figures, the industry could supply soldier monuments cheaply and quickly to local communities without them even having to approach a sculptor.[5]

Writing in 1866, on the eve of this great new era of the public monument, William Dean Howells was still able to argue for a different sort of war memorial. In his "Question of Monuments," published in the *Atlantic*, Howells voiced the antimilitarist sentiments common to his Boston intellectual circle.[6] For him it was a blessing that the martial spirit of the war had not yet translated itself into public monuments. "We are not a military people," he insisted, and indeed by some measures he was right. Of all the Western powers, the United States had by far the smallest standing army; to fight all its wars the country had had to depend on the patriotic spirit of volunteers who took up arms only temporarily (and often reluctantly).[7] Barely a year after Appomatox, Howells could actually claim that "the pride which we felt in our army as a body, and in the men merely as soldiers, was an exultation which has already in great part subsided." Instead of "a standing army in bronze and marble," then, he looked forward to another sort of sculptural monument. Howells wanted society to forget what the soldiers did in the war; it was simply

6.2 Confederate Soldier Monument, 1909, Livingston, Alabama.

too terrible to contemplate—as the war photographs attested, even if only in a limited way. Instead, Howells argued, the monuments of the war should remember what the soldiers' terrible deeds finally achieved, for this was the only way that he and many like him could make sense of the incomprehensible carnage of the war. And what that carnage achieved seemed to be nothing less than a sweeping moral transformation of society—a "change which has come upon races, ethics, and ideas in this new world." The question, ultimately, was how to represent such an epochal transformation. The problem was that there were few, if any, sculptural models up to the task. Howells did not want public sculpture to resort to the "dreary means of conventional allegory," those "scantily-draped, improper figures, happily called Liberties." He could point only to the example of Ward's *Freedman*, an essentially ephemeral piece, as we have seen, that did not readily lend itself to commemorative use.

Nevertheless, for Howells, it was "the full expression of one idea that should be commemorated, and would better celebrate the great deeds of our soldiers than bass-reliefs of battles, and statues of captains, and groups of privates."

Accustomed as we are to the modern soldier monument, enshrining the customs of remembering the fallen and honoring the veteran, Howells's suggestion seems wildly naive. To imagine war memorials of nude black men erected across the Union in "the busy hearts of towns," where Howells hoped such memorials would go, is to imagine a radically different nation. But to account for the utter failure of Howells's vision, and for the emergence of a new brand of common-soldier commemoration in its stead, we must first recognize that in 1866 the possibilities were still wide open. War memorials as such barely existed before the Civil War. Browsing through Benson Lossing's exhaustive field guide to Revolutionary sites, published in 1850, one finds numerous small shafts erected in cemeteries over the remains of officers and individual heroes, some of them financed by public sources.[8] But there were few collective memorials of any kind: a handful of shafts marking the site of a battle and sometimes inscribing the names of the fallen and, most rare of all, a couple of allegorical monuments commemorating dead officers or soldiers. Howells would certainly have known the great obelisk at Bunker Hill (1843) or the much more modest shafts at Lexington (1799) and Concord (1836); only the Lexington shaft inscribed names of fallen soldiers.[9] He would also have seen Washington, D.C.'s only war memorial, the Tripoli Memorial, an allegorical monument to naval officers slain in the Mediterranean, located until 1860 at the west front of the Capitol.[10] Where he might have seen "groups of privates" is harder to say for they did not yet exist, though the standing-soldier monument that would become the predominant type probably first appeared as early as 1865.[11]

How then do we explain the subsequent popularization of the common-soldier monument, well before the type took hold in Europe, in a society ostensibly far less militarized? The simple, and seemingly reasonable, answer points to the sheer magnitude of the war's tragedy. This was the nation's first experience of mass warfare, with slaughter on a scale unimaginable before then; the number of casualties in the single battle of Gettysburg, for example, nearly doubled total battle casualties for all previous American wars *combined*. But to argue for the common-soldier monument as a simple expression of grief for the fallen—a natural response to collective trauma—ends up accounting for very little about the form or pattern of subsequent commemoration. Most of the soldier monuments were built decades after the war, reaching peak levels thirty to fifty years later, long after the shock of the experience had faded.[12] And virtually absent from this phenomenon was the black soldier—a figure who had occupied so much attention during the war and immediately afterward. Though blacks and whites united as soldiers in a common ordeal, the common-soldier monument, ironically, ended up dividing them. These facts point to other forces at work beyond the therapeutic needs of the survivors.

In this chapter I will argue that the modern soldier monument arose to perform a more complex cultural task, not merely to assuage the collective grief of a nation but to rehabilitate and modernize the seminal figure of the citizen-soldier. Central to the founding mythology of the American nation, the citizen-soldier could not and did not survive the trauma of the Civil War intact. The new realities of mass warfare—not the least of which was the introduction of nearly 200,000 black men into the Union army—forced a profound reappraisal of what it meant to be a soldier and a man. On the one hand, to be a soldier was to test one's manhood, which is why so many men volunteered for the war and then stayed to die. On the other hand, to be a soldier was to become a virtual slave, to forfeit the very sense of personal responsibility and agency supposed to define manhood. The war memorials of the late nineteenth century negotiated this paradox of masculinity and in the process created a new model of the citizen-soldier for the nation. In these new monuments, built around the idea of duty and its standard performance by ordinary soldiers, the moral achievements that Howells had sought to extract from war's violence became strictly secondary. The figure of the black soldier, inextricably linked to the memory of slavery, became unrepresentable. The whole idea of a "new world" created by the war lapsed in favor of the advancement in civic space of a normative white soldier and citizen. It is this lapse of memory, I will argue, that is the key to understanding the distinctiveness of the American war memorial tradition and the peculiar racial formation it constructed and enforced.

THE citizen-soldier has occupied a pivotal position in the history of American nationalism. For a long time most Americans thought that a regular army—a "standing army"—was unnecessary because the citizens themselves would spring to their nation's defense, as they seemed to do with such success in the Revolution and the War of 1812.[13] George Washington, the first citizen-soldier, was mythologized as the model, a modern version of the ancient Roman Cincinnatus who dropped his plow to lead the defense of the republic. Later Jefferson, Jackson, and others would continue to dismiss the standing army and to promote the ideal of an armed male populace that could defend itself.[14] Observers from Europe in the mid-nineteenth century noted that some American men did seem to have a mania for arms and martial display, in the volunteer companies which they organized and drilled on civic occasions;[15] these volunteer companies would later supply much of the manpower (and the casualties) for the Civil War. The myth of the citizen-soldier accorded well with the republican ideology of self-government, with its antistatist bias and its distrust specifically of federal power.

Why then were there so few monuments, before the Civil War, to this mythical hero, and none that actually embodied him in figurative sculpture? Before the Civil War the apparatus of commemoration overwhelmingly favored the officer or the singular hero. The lack of commemorative enterprise on behalf of the ordinary citizen-soldier points, I think, to important cracks in the rhetorical edifice supporting him. The fact was that before the Civil War the United States had never mobilized a mass army of citizen-soldiers. The Revolutionary army was a pitiful affair, reluctantly recruited, barely a few thousand strong at the time of Washington's victory. Washington himself yearned for a regular army of trained soldiers, comparable with the British force, because the volunteer enlistments at his disposal were so few and unreliable, the troops undisciplined and prone to desertion. Ironically Washington won the war by avoiding fighting whenever possible; battle as it was conceived up until the Civil War required coordinated masses of drilled soldiers who could maintain strict formations under enemy fire—precisely the sort of army Washington did not have.[16] After the Revolution the federal government did manage to establish a small regular army, mainly for the defense of the frontier against Indians, and a professional academy for training officers at West Point, unique in the Western world; this nucleus of trained soldiers would prove crucial in all the wars the nation fought and won, even though the soldiers themselves suffered the reputation of being the scum and refuse of American society.[17]

All this points to a profound duality in the image of the American warrior. On the one hand, there was the patriotic citizen who took up arms at times of crisis and won glory in the field of battle; on the other hand, there was the everyday soldier whose life was circumscribed by subordination to authority and regimentation of routine. These represented two extremes of masculinity, one the hero and the other the slave. The mythology of the citizen-soldier of course played up the heroic dimension. It represented the soldier's experience as the ultimate test of personal agency, where the individual man was enabled to make his mark upon history itself. The terrible reputation of the regular soldier revealed the dark underbelly of this mythical construction. For if the citizen-soldier was thought somehow to escape the oppressive power relations of the military—to operate as a free individual on the terrain of history—the regular soldier was indelibly marked by the military institution and his powerlessness within it.

It is remarkable how much the imagery and the practices of military life paralleled those of slavery. The root word of infantry is of course infant, and both the soldier and the slave were systematically subjected to infantilization. "Unconditional submission is the only footing upon which slavery should be placed," wrote one slaveholder in 1860; "it is precisely similar to the attitude of a minor to his parent, or a soldier to his general." Apologists for slavery sometimes even compared their system favorably with the oppression of soldiers or sailors.[18] Nowhere but in slavery was the individual's personal freedom and responsibility curtailed so dramatically, life so routinized by external authority, as in the military. There are many stories about volunteers demoralized by the regimentation and discipline of soldier life. Camp life drained the recruit of his sense of independence, as one soldier explained: "Soldiering is a lazy life and I think it is the next thing to slavery. A man becomes dependent and looks for his officers to provide for him and bid him to do this and that."[19] For James Garfield this life at the whim of officers was a steady lesson in "the power of tyranny," which he thought might give the rank and file a sympathy for the plight of slaves.[20] For Confederate soldiers the experience was particularly galling because they were extremely conscious of their status in relation to slaves; required to carry passes to leave camp, for example, they were humiliated by this archetypal image of black slavery.[21] Some slaveowners specifically recommended the use of army regulations as a code of discipline for slaves, and flogging—the classic instrument of discipline in slavery—was until 1861 also a basic punishment for soldiers. (Washington, a plantation slaveholder, was particularly keen on its use in the army.)[22] For slaveholder and general alike, maintaining authority was the essential problem: how to control a large crowd of people greatly outnumbering the authorities and shape it into a working or a fighting force that would lay its bodies on the line.[23]

The lack of freedom and independence, the poor food and living conditions, and the separation from civilized society were all more reminiscent of the liminal world of slavery than of ordinary civil life. Regular army soldiers often described themselves this way, as "outcasts" from society.[24] Volunteers too, describing their plight, sometimes used the same language of brutalization applied to slaves: "nasty as hogs, and half starved," one Union soldier lamented.[25] The marginal position of soldier and slave led to an uncanny convergence in their negative stereotypes. They were either infantilized by excessive control on the one hand, or licentious, without self-control, on the other. "Unless a man can drink, lie, steal, and swear," one old soldier explained, toting up a list of vices commonly attributed to slaves, "he is not fit for a soldier." This image of the army as "a school of iniquity" was even more widespread outside the army.[26]

The Civil War represented the first time in American history that a mass army of volunteers had to endure the reality of prolonged life as soldiers. A staggering number of men went through the experience: somewhere between one-third and one-half of the able-bodied male population of the country ended up serving in the war.[27] The volunteers discovered soon enough, as Garfield did, that they could not entirely escape the metaphor of enslavement that operated within the regular army. They also found that the myth of individual heroism that animated their whole enterprise had little to do with the conditions of real combat, whether they were in the "unspectacular duty of standing to be shot at" (to use John Keegan's pithy description of the infantryman's role) or sitting huddled in the trenches in the drawn-out battles of the war's end.[28] Whether in combat or in camp, the typical common soldier shared with the slave a drastic curtailing of personal agency and a concomitant loss of "manhood."

The entry of ex-slaves into the Union forces beginning in late 1862 added a final twist. Now some people could actually suggest that slavery was excellent preparation for soldiering. Henry T. Johns, for example, wrote during the war that "[the slaves'] docility, their habits of unquestioning obedience, pre-eminently fit them for soldiers."[29] Even Massachusetts abolitionist Thomas Wentworth Higginson, commander of a regiment of former slaves, in letters written in 1862 emphasized his recruits' childlike character and argued that "to learn the drill . . . the more childlike these pupils are the better." Thus he concluded that his slaves turned soldiers had a special "aptitude for drill and discipline." Though Higginson later disavowed the common idea that "plantation discipline" was good preparation for the life of a soldier, his own descriptions of his troops lent support to that notion.[30] And while supporters of black troops could make such arguments, opponents could complain that the arming of former slaves meant that free white men lacked the manhood to get the job done themselves. Either way, for white soldiers the figure of the slave-turned-soldier complicated their already tenuous hold on masculinity.[31] Even Confederate soldiers at the end of the war faced these issues as their government voted to raise slave regiments (recruited too late, however, to go into action).[32]

To begin to appreciate the depth of this manifold assault on the citizen-soldier's personal agency, we can take a look at an extraordinary image of warfare painted by Winslow Homer in 1864 at the time of the siege of Petersburg (fig. 6.3).[33] Homer's painting is not a spectacular image of armies arrayed against one another in full dress and regalia, the sort of battle image Americans were accustomed to seeing and which seemed to represent war as a wonderful extension of the civic parade-ground drills they saw at home.[34] Instead it is a subtle representation of the new and

6.3 Winslow Homer, *Defiance: Inviting a Shot before Petersburg*, 1864, oil on panel.

frightful war of attrition the conflict had become. One is struck first by the figure of the individual soldier who stands in profile high above the horizon, as if on a pedestal, against a bright backdrop of sky and clouds. Here is the picture's center: its hero, or antihero. He is the sole figure who mediates between the dark world of the earthworks below—where we as viewers of the scene are situated—and the heavenly realm of glory above. The pictorial monotony of repeated tree stumps beneath him attests to the surreal environment of trench warfare, which Homer had himself witnessed as a sketch artist for an illustrated newspaper; the natural world has been leveled to create an empty "no-man's land" between opposing earthworks. The men huddle behind the rampart in a long retreating serpentine line, their faces blank and their bayonets propped up uselessly. Indeed this basic weapon of hand-to-hand combat is the symbol of everything trench warfare has negated: here the armies do not confront one another man to man but sit hidden and idle, passively enduring the anonymous, long-range fire of sharpshooters' rifles and artillery.

Within this bizarre landscape of stalemate, devoid of the traditional narrative of battle, Homer creates a solitary event. A single soldier has jumped up on the rampart carrying no weapon and confronting the inhuman landscape before him. With his bare hands, clenched fists, and boxer's stance, he looks less like a soldier than a man spoiling for a fistfight. His act of defiance is directed not so much at the enemy, it seems,

6.4 Photograph of dead Confederate at Petersburg, circa 1864.

as at the whole impersonal logic of modern battle. He is trying to create
a stage for individual action, a moral space where he can be recognized,
and for this one moment he has succeeded. Yet in this ephemeral moment
lies the irony of the picture. Homer appears to elevate the hero and im-
mortalize his act, but in the far distance the painter has inserted the pictorial cues that signal the hero's undoing—a flame and a puff of smoke from
the sharpshooters' rifles trained on him. Read from right to left, Homer's
picture reveals the soldier's gesture as quixotic. We know that his attempt
to rewrite his own story into some recognizable narrative of male honor
will fail; he will be shot down, swallowed up by the hellish terrain below,
and forgotten (fig. 6.4).

   This account has deliberately overlooked one crucial element, the figure of the black banjo player who stares up at the defiant soldier. In one
sense this figure serves simply to locate us in the Confederate trench, and
by doing so reinforces various myths about the North and the South—the
notion of the Confederate as rebel, for instance, and the idea of the North
as more captive to technology. And the caricatured features of the banjo
player's face, lifted directly from the popular type of the darky, recall
myths about plantation slavery on which Stephen Foster and others
traded. Yet his appearance here, and his pivotal position in the narrative,

are not without irony too. He is the only figure connected by gaze to the rebel, and the only other figure besides him whose face rises above the rampart. Insofar as the white man on the rampart is the sign of the rebellion and the black man is the sign of slavery, the two are directly linked. It requires only a little stretch of the imagination to see the rebel as dancing to the darky's tune—and dying for it.[35]

What Homer's painting so powerfully evokes is the intersection of two huge social forces reshaping the moral logic of battle and the individual soldier's place within it: technology and ideology. The individual soldier's ability to prove himself as Homer's protagonist wanted to—in a "fair fight," face to face, between equals—had been steadily declining since the introduction of firearms centuries earlier. Increasingly the line soldier was expected to perform not as a fighter but as a machine, efficiently dispensing and withstanding ammunition of death.[36] Nevertheless it was still reasonable for the early nineteenth-century soldier to think of his army itself as a fighting body, engaged in head-to-head combat. The experience of the Civil War made even this illusion increasingly untenable as the new technology of long-range warfare, propelled by the rifle and the Minié bullet, rendered the Napoleonic style of decisive battle obsolete. Highly effective long-range weaponry led instead to the kind of defensive stalemate Homer depicted; this prolonged the war enormously and multiplied the scale and severity of casualties beyond anything Americans had ever conceived. It also transformed war by totalizing it, so that armies could no longer rely on fighting one another in brief, ostensibly glorious episodes of battle but had to endure long, constant periods of terror and violence while the civilian infrastructure of transportation, industry, and agriculture became as critical a target as the soldiers themselves. All of these developments, in turn, intensified the ideological character of the war. Keegan has called the armies of the Union and the Confederacy "the first truly ideological armies of history," meaning that they were not fighting simply for a leader or against a foreign invader. This is highly debatable, given that most white soldiers, initially at least, seemed to have little investment in any definition of the cause beyond the customary defense of flag or home or comrade.[37] Yet the totalization of the conflict changed even that, forcing the fundamental issues of slavery and emancipation more into the forefront. For the Northern army black emancipation came to make sense as a military strategy to increase its own armed force and to destroy the South's infrastructure. Union soldiers found themselves, willy-nilly, waging an abolitionist war against slavery, and Confederates found themselves fighting to ward off the unknown terrors of emancipation. Forces far beyond the control of the individual soldier converged on him and sapped him of the myth of personal agency. Battling for causes he never intended, by rules he never imagined and could barely understand, the typical soldier in the Civil War experienced a kind of alienation without parallel in Europe until the large-scale trench warfare of World War I.

So after this devastating experience, the rise of the common-soldier monument seems to present a paradox. The Civil War represented the culmination of long-standing historical developments that served to strip the common soldier of his individual initiative and his sense of personal agency, while at this very moment the soldier monument emerged and began to lend a new honor and presence to the figure of the ordinary soldier he had never before known in the civic realm. Yet this apparent paradox does not tell the whole story. Like most of the literature on the common soldier, it is geared to the experience of the white soldier. Nearly the opposite held true for black soldiers, particularly those who had escaped from slavery. For them soldiering represented an immediate infusion of power and recognition as men. However compromised the role of the individual soldier, and however much their military virtues could be dismissed as mere extensions of slave habits, for the most part their own sense of personal agency expanded enormously: they were now allowed to carry arms and to use them to defend themselves and liberate their fellow slaves. Higginson, who was used to comparing white and black troops, wrote years later, "They [black soldiers] felt it a step upward to enter military life, with its routine and discipline; whereas to white soldiers these were wholly a sacrifice, accepted only for the sake of their country."[38] For white men, soldiering took them away from society and out of their given identities as free men; for black men soldiering was a way into society and legitimate social identity. Of course soldiers who came from free black communities in the North—unlike Higginson's Southerners—already had some social position, and for them the discrimination and unequal pay they faced within the military certainly tempered the emancipatory potential of the experience.[39] But for slaves the transformation in status was extraordinary. As we have seen, this transformation from slave to soldier was enacted ritualistically in the burning of old slave outfits and the production of before-and-after photographs. The transformation penetrated even to the very body language they were expected to practice. They were asked to stand upright and look straight ahead, not to bow and scrape and doff their hat.[40]

Taking account of the slave turned soldier forces us to restate the paradox of the common-soldier monument. While the loss of agency for white men translated itself later into commemorative gain, the gain of agency for black men translated itself into commemorative loss. Almost as soon as their military service seemed to confer manhood and citizenship on them, black men were erased from the civic realm, absented from the new type of war memorial created to honor the common soldier. Even though black soldiers continued to serve in the federal army after the war, they

6.5 Thomas Nast, *Patience on a Monument*, in
Harper's Weekly (October 10, 1868): 648.

became increasingly invisible in the war's commemoration. Black soldier
monuments remained figments of the imagination, as in Thomas Nast's
devastating print, *Patience on a Monument* (1868) (fig. 6.5). Set within
the context of the white South's violent campaign to reverse Reconstruction, Nast's print for *Harper's* uses the image of a black soldier monument to create several layers of irony. Here the soldier is seated rather
than standing, downcast rather than vigilant. While his war service has
apparently elevated him atop the pedestal of civic recognition, the honor
has been turned against itself: his elevation comes at the cost of his new-
found manhood. Perched on this height, his gun rendered useless, he is
subjected to the taunts of his white enemies and he remains powerless to
defend his family below from murderous assault.

Unless we take account of this dimension of racial difference, dramatized so luridly by Nast, we misrepresent the whole phenomenon of the common-soldier monument and misunderstand its transformation of the figure of the citizen-soldier. For that transformation took place over the sculptural terrain of the male body, a terrain already profoundly racialized. The early soldier monuments consisting of simple shafts, sometimes inscribed with individual names, erased difference in death. Nothing in the names themselves denoted racial identity, except to those who knew the men behind the names. But as soon as the common soldier emerged from the inscriptions and entered the field of public sculpture, the figure entered a racially contested terrain.

When this happened, it sparked an important shift in the idea of the public monument. The great-man monuments had supposedly represented the cream of civil society, and they were set up as models for the great mass of ordinary citizens to emulate. But at the same time that men like Washington were represented as "examples," few, if any, of the great mass could ever hope to equal them and thereby enter their monumental galaxy. The great men were always white, of course, and hence embodied racial ideals and prejudices, but their difference from the common man prevailed over the sameness of their race. Sculpture marked off their exceptional status by antique costume or gesture, or by other conventional signifiers of heroic command and aura. These were the very signifiers that constituted the sculptural body and defined the province of the public sculptor's art. The entry of the common soldier into public sculpture created a profoundly different kind of sculptural body, a generic body. This was the body every citizen—every true man—was expected to inhabit. As the orator Henry Stebbins remarked of Ward's soldier figure, "it represents no knightly or warrior class, but the heroic manhood that can one day build cities or railways . . . [and the next be] the citizen soldier."[41] The body represented the ordinary man who simply did his duty for the nation. It was not a body marked off for its aura but for its conformity to a common pattern.

While the experience of the war had undermined the soldier's very integrity as an individual, the standing-soldier monument restored the individual body to center stage. Always intact, upright, vigilant, the figure was standard and anonymous but still an integral individual, set apart from his unit and thereby rescued from the undifferentiated, synchronized mass of a modern army. The sculptural body of this generic individual navigated between the two poles of heroism and slavery. Neither marked as transcendent and commanding, on the one hand, nor as bound and immobilized, on the other, the typical standing soldier offered an image of quiet self-discipline. It has often been observed that the "parade rest" pose was by far the most common, but no one to my knowledge has asked why; alternatives were, after all, available. Clearly the pose was compact, cheap, and easy to reproduce. It emphasized preparedness rather than militance, crucial for the myth of the citizen-soldier, which was always a myth of self-defense rather than conquest. It also seems—and here we come to the heart of the sculptural matter—that the pose offered an appropriate compromise between regimentation and independence. It was a standard military posture prescribed by army regulations, but one that allowed the soldier freedom to relax, to shift his weight onto one leg and lean slightly into his gun (fig. 6.1). The pose therefore retains something of the classically sculptural, the idea of the body in repose, in contrapposto, while at the same time it signifies conformity to modern army routine. The deadliness of that routine is, of course, deliberately obscured: even the gun is relaxed. We get no sense whatsoever that the soldier has surrendered his body to a military system that disciplines him to destroy other bodies and to face destruction himself. Instead, the body at parade rest suggests a body shaped by army discipline but not confined or damaged by it, a body obedient to command but still also master of itself.

We can now see how this figure of the standing soldier could successfully overcome the duality of hero and slave which had heretofore marked the image of the American soldier. By its standardization the figure could credibly represent a mass army of volunteers who had actually experienced and knew firsthand the rigors of military regimentation. At the same time it appeared to stem their loss of personal agency and their descent into metaphorical enslavement by carving out a limited sphere of individual independence. It did so in two ways: first, by insisting on representing the individual soldier, by himself and not in a group; and, second, by encoding personal agency within the subtle language of the body itself. The notion of manhood, battered as it was by the experience of the war, was reaffirmed here in a new way. It was no longer the myth of the hero who could transcend all social constraint and make his unique presence felt in battle and in history, but the myth of the commonplace soldier who could retain his individuality within the necessary bonds of discipline and loyalty to the group.

The introduction of this figure into public sculpture in the very center of the community served to reintegrate the soldier who had been cast off from society back into the social mainstream and to reconstitute military duty as a model of civic virtue as well. The process did not happen overnight. Indeed, although there was certainly a significant number of standing-soldier monuments erected in the first fifteen years after the war, particularly in New England, there were many more erected in the 1880s and beyond. Scholars have argued that both local communities and veterans in the immediate postwar years preferred to put the trauma of the war behind them. But after 1880 membership in veterans' organizations increased enormously, and communities began to draw much more attention to the role of the soldier in civic life.[42] The common-soldier monument stood at the forefront of this cultural shift; it effectively militarized the landscape of civic patriotism. There were many ways communities had participated in the war: paying increased taxes, tending to the wounded, sending food and clothing to the front. But there was one ultimate test of a community's patriotism, and that was the willingness of its men to die or risk death. The volunteers a local community sent off to war constituted its most concrete human link with the abstract entity of the nation. The soldier monument made that human link more emphatically and permanently visible than ever before. Even after the monument was erected and the enthusiasm of the monument campaign inevitably seemed to drain away, the monument still did its work simply by occupying a central place in the symbolic economy of civic space. In many places this was the only public statue in existence. Thus elevated into a local icon, the generic figure of the soldier served as a constant recognition of those ordinary men who had fought and as a model for those who would fight in the future. The generic figure represented the local population in a way the great-man monument never could. Instead of pinning the community's civic loyalty on its appreciation of great leaders, the soldier monuments celebrated the local people's continuing sacrifice of their own men for the nation. The soldier's duty was their duty, his integrity their integrity.

But why did they do their duty? What moral imperative drove them to risk their own lives? This was not a question that the simple figure of a soldier, standing at parade rest, was meant to answer. The reason the same form could work so well for both Confederate and Union monuments was that it deliberately avoided the question of moral imperative, or, rather, it elevated the concept of duty to a moral imperative of its own. "O if to fight for king and commonweal / Were piety in thine, it is in these": so the captured queen in Shakespeare's *Titus Andronicus* argued when she pleaded for the lives of her warrior sons. It was hard to challenge the logic of this argument: no one could claim that the defeated Confederates were any less dutiful soldiers than their conquerors.[43] The generic figure of the soldier performing his duty could represent anyone— a slaveholder, or an abolitionist, or simply a man looking out for his comrades. So it was left to the inscriptions, then, to elaborate on this simple and neutral image of duty. Yet the inscriptions tend to reinforce that image. They almost always make the soldier's sacrifice for the nation paramount; only secondarily do they speak to the justice of the nation's cause, if they speak of it at all. Sometimes Union inscriptions will refer to "liberty" or "freedom" (extracts from the Gettysburg Address appear on several), or occasionally to the abolition of slavery; Confederate inscrip-

6.6 George H. Mitchell and Lorado Taft, Union Soldiers' and Sailors' Monument, 1891, Yonkers, New York.

tions even more rarely will refer to something like "Constitutional government" or "state sovereignty."[44] But even here these key words are not the burden of the text but ornaments to it, which do not in any way challenge a far more more deep-seated assertion of loyalty to the nation. The soldier's duty, then, is not to an idea but to a collective that transcends the ideas of any particular moment or era, which is one reason why white Northerners and Southerners could accept each other's monuments and why the monuments could be erected so long after the event. Emphasizing the appeal of a cause would actually reverse the priorities of the soldier monument and undermine the notion of duty that its standardized figure projects.

An interesting example is the Soldiers' and Sailors' Monument erected in Yonkers, New York, in 1891 (fig. 6.6).[45] This is a more elaborate monument than the run of the mill, with five figures of servicemen and a complicated program of inscriptions—three bands, of four texts each, set on various levels of the pedestal. The central and most prominent level, the die, carries a series of remarks on the preeminence of the Union (e.g., Lincoln's statement, "My paramount object is to save the Union"); this clearly gives priority to the idea of duty to nation. Above and below the die are two smaller, contrapuntal bands, the top devoted to the personal qualities demonstrated by the servicemen, the bottom to the accomplishments realized by the war, from the stirring "slavery abolished" to the sober "credit maintained." In this context the reference to abolition does not signal the monument's commitment to any politics of racial liberation. Yonkers was in fact a stronghold of the Democratic Party during Lincoln's administration and hardly sympathetic to the cause of abolitionism. The orator who dedicated the monument twenty-five years later continued this tradition with an apologia for Southern slaveholders: their economic concerns were valid, he argued, but secession was the wrong means of redress.[46] Nevertheless the town could claim abolition as a blessing because the entire nation did; not even the Confederate monuments contested this.

There were a very few soldier monuments in the North that departed from this model of political neutrality and brought the issue of emancipation into sculptural imagery. Monuments in Providence (1871), Detroit (1881), Buffalo (1884), Brattleboro, Vermont (1887), Cleveland (1894), and Indianapolis (1899) included subsidiary images of emancipation, most of them organized conventionally around Lincoln or a kneeling black male or both.[47] The most unusual and most pointedly political, however, was the elaborate monument designed by George Bissell and erected in Waterbury, Connecticut, in 1884. It includes an emancipation group that features a seated allegorical figure and a white schoolboy gesturing to an African American boy below, who holds a hoe in one hand and with the other begins to pry open a large book in the woman's lap. According to the dedication volume, the white boy was meant to represent the North "appealing to the government to extend to the African race and to the entire South" the advantages of education, while the black boy "illustrates by his position and action the eager desire of his race to secure the education and enlightenment which they know to be necessary to success in a free republic."[48] The ragged clothes and seated posture of the African American boy contrast sharply with the neat dress and erect pose of the white boy; like the emancipation designs of the mid 1860s, which paired a standing Lincoln and a kneeling slave, this group looks forward to an uplift of the race that remains unrealized and uncertain.

WE are now in a position to begin to see how the figure of the black soldier threatened to undo the cultural work performed by the normative white image of the common soldier. The figure of the black soldier could not merely stand for a soldier. Inevitably it also signified the Union cause,

or what the Union cause came to be. The black body was already identified with slavery, and the black soldier specifically came to be identified
with emancipation—hence the motif of the black soldier on some of the
early designs for emancipation monuments. Ironically, the strength of
the black soldier's commitment to the cause effectively disqualified him
from the standard soldier monument: how could a black soldier monument avoid implying that he fought for his race rather than the nation or,
even more problematic, that the nation fought for him rather than itself?
The figure of the black soldier upset the priority of duty over cause established by the standard war memorial.

Not only would the figure of the black soldier introduce a problematic
moral dimension to the monuments, but it would alter the standard construction of the white soldier advanced in them. The typical white volunteer entered the war already possessing a basic right of citizenship and a
more or less secure social identity. If, as I have argued, he suffered a traumatic loss of agency and identity in the war, the soldier monument sought
to repair and restore him. The black soldier, whether originally free or
slave, started out instead from a position of relative social oblivion and he
brought with him, in his color and physiognomy, indelible associations
with the institution of slavery. To represent the common soldier as black
would go a long way toward erasing this stigma and symbolically confer-
ring moral agency and citizenship on him. But this was the problem: his
hold on these social prerogatives was so tenuous to begin with. This was
the major reason the figure of the black soldier never succeeded in appearing on any emancipation monuments. But to represent the black soldier
in the new genre of the common-soldier monument would not only challenge prevailing stereotypes of black masculinity but would challenge the
monuments' emerging construction of white masculinity as well. To
bring the black soldier into this sculptural terrain might easily expose the
precariousness of the *white* soldier's new hold on manhood. If the black
soldier's self-discipline could be misrepresented as a habit inculcated in
slavery, if the uniform could become the sign of unquestioning obedience
and subservience, the white soldier could fall with him back into the imagery of degradation. To erase the stigma of slavery from soldiering, it
was all too easy to erase the memory of slavery as well.

To understand how the common-soldier monument succeeded in constructing this racial formation we need to examine its phenomenal proliferation in the American landscape. The innovation of the soldier monument was not just that it created a new kind of sculptural body but that
the body was reproduced and spread in a new kind of way, creating what
might be called a new demographic of whiteness in public sculpture. The
traditional idea of the public monument was that it was unique, because
it commemorated a unique hero or event. In practice many monuments

looked alike since they shared common forms like the obelisk. But to the extent that monuments employed sculpture, the sculpture distinguished them by bringing their singular content into the language of human form. The standing-soldier monument changed all that by deliberately reproducing a generic form, with minimal variations, from monument to monument, place to place. The figure of the soldier, as we have seen, did usually appear singly, as an individual. But soon enough it became connected, by the standardization of the form, to a host of other single figures being erected in villages and towns near and far. In this way the individual figure on any given monument was reconstituted as one member of a much larger group, the very collective Howells had feared: a standing army in stone and bronze. This standing army, a repetition of ordinary soldiers in ordinary towns, was uniformly white; yet the army it ostensibly represented was not uniformly white, but marked by a historically signicant racial division. The repetition of the white citizen-soldier monument in hundreds of communities across the country thus worked to solidify the association between the white body and the moral duty of citizenship.

How did this happen? Many observers at the time ascribed the standardization of soldier monuments to an overaggressive monument industry; granite and metal companies were able to market their "stock" monuments through retail cemetery-monument dealers who operated in virtually every local community, thus creating—so the critics thought—a kind of lock on the monument consumer.[49] The implication of this argument is that local communities were merely passive customers, that they were little more than dupes of a sophisticated and centralized marketing machine. Similar arguments are often leveled at popular phenomena, and their one-sidedness is theoretically suspect. In our case, the evidence strongly suggests instead that the monument industry grew and developed to meet popular demand. The industry expanded enormously in the late nineteenth century, with many new firms created and many old firms changing their business to gear themselves to soldier monuments. The industry did not invent this new type of monument, but it did work hard to make soldier monuments cheap and easy to buy once the type was established.[50]

Some critics have simply assumed that consumers lacked the money or the taste to demand anything better, to commission monuments with more obvious and unique artistic value. These critics take it for granted that "trained" or "intelligent" consumers would always prefer artistry to standardization. As the architectural critic Henry Van Brunt wrote in 1885, monument committees "have either not possessed intelligence enough . . . or have preferred to depend upon their own uninstructed notions of the manner in which the emergency should be met. Trained intelligences have had but little opportunity to study and develop the difficult problem of a soldier's monument."[51] Yet there is a great deal to suggest that monument consumers simply did not share the critics' values. Consumers seemed to find ample room for artistry in the stonework and the overall proportions of the monument, and in the local accounts these were often described in great detail.[52] But for most consumers, it seems, the representation of the soldier was a matter of authenticity, not a field for artistic invention; pose, uniform, equipment were prescribed by military convention. There are even some cases in which local communities renounced more obviously "artistic" war memorials when the standing-soldier type became predominant. In the early 1870s, before the type was firmly established, some allegorical monuments were erected that were later replaced or supplemented with standing-soldier monuments. As one of the early compilers of Civil War monuments wrote in 1910, referring to the allegorical monument erected in Lynn, Massachusetts, in 1873, "there are many who would prefer designs and figures more indicative of the times they were made to commemorate."[53] In one case in the 1890s a local veterans' group actually sued the local monument committee when it chose an allegorical design and charged that the figure was not sufficiently "commemorative."[54]

Standardization was not therefore a weakness but a sign of commemorative authenticity, for the soldiers were themselves standardized, supplied (whenever possible) with standard-issue uniforms and weapons and taught to hold their bodies in standard poses. The very familiarity of the form was its strength, its source of larger—more national—significance. Monument committees could still assert some measure of local distinctiveness in the inscriptions and in the subtle details of the architectural embellishment, the uniform, sometimes the pose. But the important thing was to erect a soldier monument that conformed to a clear pattern; by doing so they connected their local efforts to a much larger popular program of commemoration. As the monument proclaimed the local soldier's allegiance to the nation, so the form declared local adherence to a national trend.[55]

At the same time, however, that the soldier monuments framed the efforts of local communities in national terms, they also reframed the national enterprise in local terms. Local memorials reduced the abstract concept of the nation and the national mission to a more immediate and more graspable cause. To fight for the Union was to fight for the hometown, for one's family, neighbors, business associates. This is entirely consistent with the whole strategy of the soldier monument, which, as we have seen, was fundamentally reductive. It simplified the difficult ideological struggle of the war to a question of mere allegiance, and reduced modern warfare's vast technological and logistical apparatus to a single soldier's body, a human face. While warfare had become increasingly estranged from ordinary experience, the monuments represented the war in deliberately ordinary, imaginable terms. They transformed the alien and abstract into the familiar and concrete—which is why the pressure for "authentic" realism and against "artistic" allegory was so intense.

Ironically, all this was propelled by the rise of modern nationalism. The Civil War had challenged the very integrity of the federal state, and the federal government responded with an unprecedented exercise of force affecting the life of virtually every community. The Union victory reaffirmed the legitimacy of the center and thereby cemented the nation into a now indissoluble unity. It was a striking triumph of the national over the local, just as it was a triumph of the collective over the individual. Yet the soldier monuments reasssert the irreducible integrity of the local community and the individual. They reframe the newly dominant national state not as an abstract power but as an extension of smaller, more familiar human institutions. At the end of the nineteenth century, as the soldier monument craze was coming to its peak, Americans still clung to the myth of war as a hometown fight.[56] The relationship between the local soldier monument and the nation-state was therefore fraught with ambiguity and tension. The monuments resisted national domination even as they proclaimed their loyalty to that higher authority.

Many observers in the nineteenth century recognized the powerful hold that the common-soldier monument had in local communities. Even a critic as harsh as Van Brunt conceded that there was something "distinctively American" about this new monumental trend. For him it seemed to contain the seeds of "a true indigenous art": here was a genuinely vernacular form that had evolved locally, apparently in response to authentic popular desires. Van Brunt's problem was how to tame and civilize the popular form, transform it into what he would consider art. Our problem is rather different. We must examine, in a more fundamental way, the limits of its popularity. Those limits become immediately apparent as soon as we consider the near total absence of the black soldier from the field of local war memorials. The peculiar evolution of the local monuments did not respond to the situation of the black soldier. His allegiance was much more to the nation—the federal state—than it was to the locality from which he came. He lived either as a visibly distinct "minority" in Northern communities or as a disfranchised majority in Southern communities. Either way, he was not given the same stake in local affairs as his white comrades. The very monuments that reduced the national cause to a local one thus worked to alienate the black soldier, for it was the black soldier above all who was identified with and invested in the national cause. The federal state allowed him to be recruited into military service—and placed him in "colored" regiments rather than lo-

6.7 Sandusky County Soldiers'
Monument, 1885, Fremont,
Ohio, illustration in *Proceedings
at the Unveiling of the Soldiers'
Monument on the Site of Fort
Stephenson, Fremont, Ohio,*
frontispiece.

cally organized and named regiments—and the federal state legally guaranteed his emancipation. National, not local, power was the black soldier's only possible ticket to civil rights, and it was the very failure of the nation to enforce these rights in local arenas that ultimately demonstrated the limits of national power.

Another way to frame the issue is through local demographics. Local soldier monuments clung to the traditional boundaries of municipal jurisdictions—be it the county, the city, the township. With these jurisdictions then condensed into the single figure of a soldier, that figure was virtually guaranteed to be white. Local soldier monuments, in other words, could not help but replicate the dynamics of local power. In the North, where most local Union monuments were located, the "representative" soldier, like the representative legislator, always took the image of the white majority. Theoretically blacks were represented by those majority figures. Take the case of Sandusky County, Ohio, for example, with its typical figure of a white soldier at parade rest located in the central park of the county seat of Fremont (fig. 6.7). As the orator of the occasion explained, at the 1885 dedication ceremonies, the men of the county had served in over a hundred different regiments in the Union army. With exceptional thoroughness he listed them all, and they included the 2nd and 44th "U.S. Colored Troops."[57] This explicit recognition of the black volunteer, however slight and fleeting, was extremely unusual. Yet one is left wondering to what extent the black veteran saw himself represented in the sculptural figure standing for the local community.

Fragmentary evidence suggests that African Americans tended to see themselves excluded by these monuments, but there was room for debate on the question within black communities. In 1894, when a group in Rochester, New York, started a drive to erect a monument to "Afro-American soldiers and sailors who had fallen in the Civil War," some in the local black community objected on the grounds that the soldier monument already erected represented everyone. Like the Yonkers monument this one had four figures representing the different branches of the armed service. But the chairman of the subscription drive, John Thompson, argued that the facial features on these figures represented whites, and he even claimed to be able to see an Irishman and German among them.[58] This was an extraordinary claim, perhaps the only public record of a viewer imagining ethnic origin in a generic soldier figure. Usually soldier figures were described more generally as "American," a term whose effect was to erase or mask distinctions of ethnicity and class. The uniform, after all, was supposed to nationalize the soldier-citizen by subsuming individual differences of origin and background. But by drawing attention to the possibility of seeing ethnic differences, Thompson was trying to show just how far difference could *not* go. The figure might be Irish American but was definitely not "Afro-American." Although the generic soldier figure might encompass diverse white ethnicities, since these were difficult if not impossible to tell apart anyway, the figure could not bridge the profound racial divide between white and black. Theoretically, a sculptural figure could bridge that gap simply by representing a racial mixture; there were millions of such Americans to study as models of physiognomic blending. But the American racial system destroyed this theoretical possibility by assuming all mixtures of white and black to be black, or "colored," to use the period term that made this assumption clear. To be white meant not to be "colored," that is to have no tint or trace of black African features. Thus, in practice, a sculptural figure could not encompass the two "races" of white and black because in the very act of doing so it would lose its claim on whiteness. To represent white America, the generic soldier had to expunge the signs of blackness.[59]

Viewing these monuments from across a century, one might question whether people paid enough attention to the soldier figures to register their racial composition. In their own era, the answer was clear. For all their banality, the figures were meant to be regarded carefully. They claimed to be scrupulously authentic renderings of the soldier as he appeared in wartime, and as such they were subject to careful inspection of minute details of uniform, equipment, and weaponry. The veteran who compared these aspects of the figure with his own would surely invest the facial features with a literal reality as well. Sometimes the faces on the soldier figure were said to be likenesses of particular individuals, but in most cases they claimed simply to be "representative." A newspaper account of the Pittsfield, Massachusetts, standing-soldier monument in 1872 asserted that while the face represented no particular hero or company, "there are thousands throughout these United States who [would] lead themselves to believe that the statue was intended for son, brother or lover. Physiognomists tell us that no two faces are alike, yet here is a face that will answer for hundreds of young men who went forth to die in defense of their country's flag."[60] Thus it was assumed that the face, even when generalized, should "answer for" actual servicemen, that they should be able to recognize themselves in it.

The only recognizably black standing-soldier monument I know of is located in the South, in Norfolk, Virginia. The South had a quite different demography from the North—here African Americans did sometimes constitute local majorities. But even where they might have had enough local numbers to erect a soldier monument, they avoided taking the extraordinary risk of erecting Union monuments in formerly Confederate territory. Norfolk was exceptional because it was recaptured early in the war by Union forces, and its important army fort guaranteed a large federal presence in town even after the demise of Reconstruction. The soldier monument grew out of efforts made in the 1880s by a black veteran named James Fuller, formerly a slave, to set aside a section of a local cemetery for black veterans; this section was—and still is—outside the main wall of the cemetery proper. By 1906 Fuller had raised enough money to erect a modest pedestal there for a soldier monument, which he designated an "altar" and had inscribed to the memory of the soldiers and sailors buried nearby. Not until 1920, after Fuller's death, was the figure of the soldier installed. By this time new inscriptions were added to have the figure refer to veterans of World War I as well, although the figure itself represented a Union soldier at parade rest, made to look African American by details of hair and physiognomy.[61]

The Norfolk soldier was erected relatively late, in a marginal location, and seemed to be virtually unknown outside its immediate community. Its very marginality serves to emphasize the racial character of the mainstream soldier monument. The whiteness of the standard soldier figure, though visible from the start in the individual physiognomies, was reinforced—made ever more insistent—by its repetition over time. Soldier monuments as a group took on a racial character they would not necessarily have had if seen individually, in isolation from one another. By the 1880s, when the standing-soldier monument had become commonplace, some African Americans were beginning to describe this soldier monument as a pattern of commemoration engineered and executed by white communities for white soldiers. Thus in 1888 veteran and historian George Washington Williams wrote in his *History of the Negro Troops in the War of the Rebellion* that "hamlets and villages, towns and cities, counties and states, have erected monuments and cenotaphs to commemorate the valor of their citizens. The ineffable, mute eloquence of these soldier-monuments is invaluable to the cause of National Unity. . . . The deathless deeds of the white soldier's valor are not only embalmed in song and story, but are carved in marble and bronze. But nowhere in all this free land is there a monument to brave Negro soldiers, 36,847 of whom gave up their lives in the struggle for national existence."[62] Already then the standing-soldier type could be read as a majority white monument working to exclude minority black representation. Williams saw the soldier monument phenomenon in the context of other efforts to exclude black veterans from the mainstream apparatus of Civil War commemoration, for example, by excluding blacks from national soldier cemeteries and by racially segregating the posts of the Grand Army of the Republic, the major Union veteran organization.[63]

The pattern of exclusion becomes even clearer if we compare the racial formation of the soldier monument with its gendering. Because the figure of the citizen-soldier is male, it embodied a double exclusion of women in the civil sphere: they were neither soldiers nor citizens. And yet women were prominent participants in the monument campaigns, in the overall ritual of monument construction. In many cases women formed their own memorial associations and actually sponsored the monument campaigns; this was customary procedure in the South but was also common in the North. In other cases where male veterans or "leading citizens" sponsored the campaigns, women were often credited for their fundraising work, even on the pedestal.[64] It seems that the participation of women was crucial in confirming and embracing the norm of masculinity projected by the soldier monuments. The outright exclusion of women from the sculptural form was counterbalanced by a critical role for women in the ritual surrounding the form. But African American men, who were soldiers and who were supposed to be citizens, experienced oblivion in both the form and the ritual. If they contributed to monument campaigns, their contributions were not stressed; certainly they had no organizational role comparable with that of white women.

In response to a growing recognition of the racial construction of mainstream commemoration, several serious attempts were made beginning in the late 1880s to insert the figure of the black soldier into the new monumental framework. Almost all of these attempts, not surprisingly, were for national rather than local monuments. The proposal that gathered the most support came from Williams himself, who succeeded in getting a bill passed by the U.S. Senate in late 1887 for a national monument outside Howard University in Washington, D.C.[65] As Williams envisaged it, the monument would include a parade-rest figure on top and other black-soldier figures arrayed around the base—much like the multifigured soldier monuments erected in Yonkers and Rochester and elsewhere. Inscriptions would specify the actions of the black troops, with lists of battles and exact statistics of recruits and losses.[66] It is worth quoting at length Williams's rationale for the project, published in his *History of the Negro Troops*:

> Looking back over the centuries, there would be little else to record of the poor, patient Negro save his sufferings and degradation were it not for the luminous flashes of his martial glory, which cast a light upon the background of an otherwise sombre picture. But a monument such as is here proposed would surely and safely elevate the Negro to a proud place in the history of the nation. There are hundreds of thousands of ignorant people in the streets of Paris, but the great French nation can never lack patriotic defenders so long as its multitudinous monuments teach the unerring and inspiring lessons of its history. No people can be dangerously ignorant if their government build monuments.
>
> The masses of Negroes in the United States are ignorant; but from their loins will spring only a race of patriots so long as a monument records the magnificent military achievements of the Negro soldier.[67]

Williams was alluding to two "ignorant" populations in this passage: whites who did not learn the history of black martial glory because it was considered marginal, and blacks who could not learn it because they were unschooled. His project, then, had a dual pedagogical mission. On the one hand, he hoped to alter the white-dominated representation or "picture" of history, where blacks were lost in a "sombre" background, by casting a more effective light on their military achievements. This required a shift from the metaphorical illumination of the picture to the actual illumination of a three-dimensional monument that would make the African American story visible in the full daylight of public space. On the other hand, he wanted to teach members of his own race the facts surrounding their participation in the war, to make them identify patriotically with the nation. The monument would supplement the folk memory of black combat engagements—which, he recognized obliquely, did exist—with statistically documented public knowledge. It is probably for these reasons that his suggested design followed the conventional formal vocabulary of soldier monuments. The point was not to imagine an entirely new type of monument, thereby remarginalizing its contents, but to insert his history into the standard white framework of commemoration, to use the most universally accepted signifiers of public memory.

This strategy intended not only to display certain historical facts but to guarantee their status as officially remembered knowledge. Adopting the conventional form of the soldier's monument would identify the African American experience with the white majority's experience and put the two in the same commemorative plane. But in making such a proposition, Williams was also exposing the racial bias of the typical soldier's monument: that it represented white people rather than all people. Using "Negro" models for generic soldier figures would—by violating the genre—draw attention to its implicit code of whiteness, always assumed but never recognized as such. This is the subtext of Williams's monument: beyond the story to tell about black soldiers, it carried an implied critique of their exclusion from public memory. The proposal was, in this respect, a history lesson in the social construction of memory.

The bill for its erection never made it to the House floor, however, and the project died. One of the objections Williams apparently faced was that there should be no "separate" monument for black soldiers.[68] This implied of course that the standard soldier monuments already represented them; hence an additional monument specifically honoring black soldiers would be viewed not as a redress of commemorative exclusion but as a special commemorative privilege offered to one particular race. The same objection was faced when a public subscription campaign appeared the same year for "a monument to commemorate the part which the African race took in our Civil War." An architectural periodical argued that it would be generally unfortunate for monuments to distinguish soldiers "by the accident of ancestry," implying once again that the standard soldier monuments were universal in their reference. But the editorial made an exception for the "the colored population" because its position "in relation to the great struggle was a peculiar one." Once again African Americans could be singled out because of their special identification with the national cause.[69]

The only proposal that appeared to make it to the drawing board was a project initiated in Illinois in 1889 and publicized by circular the following year.[70] A design preserved in the Library of Congress, copyrighted 1889 by the "National Monument Association of Springfield, Ill.," seems to correspond to this circular (fig. 6.8). The design has a large masonry tower inscribed at the base, "National Emancipation Monument," and surmounted by what looks to be the figure of a black Union soldier. Around the base are two tiers of figures, one of statesmen (including Lincoln holding the proclamation) and the other of soldiers. Here again the figure of the black soldier is connected or conflated with the cause of

NATIONAL EMANCIPATION MONUMENT.

6.8 Bullard and Bullard, architects, design for National
Emancipation Monument, 1889, lithograph.

emancipation. Yet the design is extraordinary for the figure's position at
the summit of the monument, above the white heroes arrayed at the base.
Not surprisingly, the project seems to have made little headway.

Clearly the debates over black-soldier monuments took place within
much larger ideological conflicts about race relations in America. Blacks
in Rochester argued against a monument for black soldiers probably because they felt that it smacked of black separatism and was therefore
incompatible with stated goals of racial integration and equality. Whites
resisted the idea probably because they needed to maintain the comfort-
ing illusion that their soldier monuments were race-free. To see their
monuments as racially exclusive would require a much deeper examination of the whole racial structure of power in society, which would involve, at the very least, a reexamination of the myth of a unified American
people with equal representation in political and cultural domains. At the
most basic level the monuments were white because the American polity
itself was structured as white. This left room for black representation

only in a "separate" monument, which, much like affirmative action programs today, whites could then reject as an unwarranted racial privilege. Even a separate monument to black soldiers segregated from the mainstream white monuments presented a serious problem because it threatened to expose and undermine the racial formation implicit in those monuments.

Only three monuments in the nineteenth century depicted blacks in military service, all appearing in the last decade of the century and none of them generic war memorials. Of the three, just one represented black soldiers in full military dress, and we shall take it up in more detail shortly. The other two were local monuments, but deliberately atypical: they were extremely ambitious projects located in large urban areas—Cleveland and Brooklyn. In both cases the size and complexity of the sculptural programs left some room for black representation; the branches of military service are represented by groups rather than single figures and so the black figures enter the picture as one member of a larger unit. Yet in both cases the black figures appear not as full-fledged recruits on a par with the white servicemen but as men in states of transition. Unlike their white comrades, they are seminude, without a complete or recognizable uniform; thus they fit within the conventional schema for representing the transition from slavery to freedom. Moreover, they are not standard line soldiers but men aboard ship, in naval groups; it is significant that they are placed there rather than in land-based groups (where most blacks actually served) because that helps reinforce the metaphor of liminality. Thus their status remains uncertain: like many actual black sailors during the war, they are easily assimilated into the category of "contrabands," fugitives from slavery pressed by circumstance into unofficial or ambiguous roles.

As it turns out, the one real opening for the full-fledged representation of black soldiers in a public monument came from an unexpected quarter—not from the local communities sponsoring soldier monuments, nor from black veterans seeking recognition, but from the cultural elite. Ironically it was the very marginality of the theme of black soldiers that made it attractive to this elite. To the cultural spokesmen who wrote for magazines like the *Atlantic*, the *Century*, and *Municipal Affairs*—men and women who were trying to nurture an American tradition of arts and letters—the standardization of the soldier monument was a cultural disaster. This was not because it created a new demographic of whiteness in public sculpture but because it industrialized, and cheapened, what was supposed to be the noblest of art forms. In their view the rise of the soldier monument was an assault on art itself and everything it was supposed to represent and achieve. Beginning in the 1880s critics began to assail the standard soldier monument and by the first decade of the next century, when the form was reaching its peak of popularity, the criticism was almost as standard as the monument.[71] While I have been arguing that the reproduction of a generic soldier figure over and over again is precisely what guaranteed its racial significance, the critics argued that reproduction made the figure meaningless,[72] that it drained the monuments of any of the sentiment that may have once inspired them. Art, in their way of thinking, was incompatible with standardization; meaning resided in difference, not in repetition. It was this antipopular way of thinking that legitimated the idea of a black-soldier monument. For in its very difference from the white norm lay its potential for artfulness. The same critic who disapproved of distinguishing soldier monuments by "ancestry" thus made an exception for the theme of the black soldier because it resisted the standardization of the ordinary monument:

> After the iron-foundries began keeping soldiers' monuments in stock, whatever sentiment had once attached to those structures evaporated, and it is a rare thing to be able to extract an idea from the compositions of granite obelisks and deformed lay-figures which occupy the most prominent positions in our larger towns, but the theme of the colored men's monument is full of suggestions. Fortunately, there is never likely to be more than one, so that the designer of it will not suffer the annoyance of seeing his ideas caricatured elsewhere, but with the strange, wild history of the Southern slaves in 1863–64 to inspire him, it would be strange if a man of decent abilities could not evolve a monument which should excite more attention, at least, than anything of the kind which now exists in Washington.[73]

The "strangeness" of racial difference was precisely what made the theme artistic and meaningful.

This theme finally bore artistic fruit in one extraordinary monument completed at the end of the century in the heart of what had once been the breeding ground of abolitionism. This was the so-called Shaw Memorial erected in 1897 in Boston Common across from the Massachusetts State House (fig. 6.9). There had never been an American monument more elite than this: designed by the nation's greatest sculptor, Augustus Saint-Gaudens, and a famous New York architect, Charles McKim; inscriptions composed by Harvard president Charles W. Eliott; dedication speeches delivered by philosopher William James and Tuskeegee President Booker T. Washington; and a list of sponsors that included prominent politicians, businessmen, and intellectual figures.[74] When the work was completed, it was touted in major magazines as the greatest monument the nation had ever erected,[75] and it remains one of the most widely reproduced and discussed monuments of the nineteenth century. Yet

6.9 Augustus Saint-Gaudens and Charles F. McKim, Shaw Memorial, 1897, Boston Common.

there is still much to be said about this unique work, because it has never been properly situated and read within the racial struggle of Civil War commemoration.

The commemorative subject of the monument was as exceptional as its artists and sponsors were. The memorial was a unique fusion of two apparently antithetical types—a monument to a famous officer and to the common soldiers he commanded. The officer was Colonel Robert Gould Shaw, a young Bostonian of wealth and high social position, whom John Greenleaf Whittier once described as "the very flower of grace and chivalry."[76] He was also an officer with a pedigree, a member of the Society of the Cincinnati, a hereditary organization of descendants of Revolutionary War officers (whose Latin motto appears prominently on the front panel of the monument). The regiment was the 54th Massachusetts, the first regiment of black troops mustered in the North. Though organized in Massachusetts, it drew its volunteers from across the North. The regiment earned its fame by leading one of the most desperate and ill-fated assaults of the Civil War, the attempt to capture Fort Wagner on the coast of South Carolina. Charging uphill without protection against the deadly long-range fire of rifle and artillery, a large portion of the regiment and Shaw himself perished.[77]

Soon after the loss at Fort Wagner, efforts were made to commemorate it in some way. From the beginning these efforts centered on the figure of Shaw, who in one stroke had become transformed from an obscure officer into an abolitionist martyr. On hearing of Shaw's fate, Massachusetts Senator Charles Sumner wrote, "that death will be sacred in history and in art."[78] Years later George Washington Williams echoed him, noting that "many brave soldiers fell in forlorn assault upon Fort Wagner, but when some great painter has patriotic inspiration to give this battle an immortal representation, Colonel Shaw will be the central figure."[79] The first actual campaign to commemorate Shaw apparently originated with freed slaves in Beaufort, South Carolina. Their contributions, collected by the Union military command in the area, were then supplemented by nearly $3,000 raised within the 54th itself and by additional contributions from Higginson's regiment. When Shaw's father was informed of their plans to erect a memorial near Fort Wagner, he wrote back that the monument should also include the names of those officers and soldiers who died with him. In effect, he wanted to transform the memorial from a hero monument into a battle monument, which was consistent with his stated wish that his son's body be left where it was, in a mass grave with the bodies of his fellow officers and troops. But for various reasons, including fears that the monument would not be "respected" by the local white population, this project failed to materialize and the funds were used instead for a free black school in Charleston. Shaw the hero retained precedence though: the school was named after him, as were other black schools in the South.[80]

It is true that Shaw showed unusual character in commiting himself to the 54th. He had begun his military career in the New York 7th, the same regiment commemorated by John Quincy Adams Ward's early standing-soldier monument, and was advancing in the ranks of the Massachusetts 2nd when he so dramatically shifted course. At the time there was still considerable resistance, both within the military and without, to the recruitment of black soldiers. It was unclear what opportunities the Union command would give to black soldiers to participate in combat, and whether they would be supported by white troops. And a few months before the battle of Fort Wagner, the Confederate government had officially announced its intention to treat the white officers of black regiments without the customary civilities due to enemy officers: if captured, they were subject to execution on the grounds of "inciting servile insurrection."[81] Yet the glorification of Shaw tends to obscure the even greater risks and challenges the black troops confronted. They faced still more fearful reprisals if captured: execution or enslavement, or perhaps worse. Unlike Shaw many of them left families behind dependent on them for support; they were promised the same pay given to white recruits but didn't get it, and they refused all pay on principle for over a year until stipends were finally equalized. And unlike Shaw, they volunteered knowing they would be denied advancement as commissioned officers, no matter how ably they served.[82]

Tactfully, it seems, Williams ascribed the elevation of Shaw not to the workings of white supremacy but to the more neutral operations of history and memory, which, he claimed, always exalt the lone hero over the collective mass. At Thermopylae, for example, 300 Spartans held their ground against a vast army "yet history has made Leonidas representative of them all." What Williams did not point out is that racial difference made this idea of representation problematic at best. Could Shaw, a highborn white man, represent a regiment of black troops? By association, perhaps: his name could summon up the historical presence of his black comrades in battle. Williams wrote that "in the humble huts of the unlettered blacks of the South his name is a household word," and Williams himself proposed to place his black-soldier monument in a park to be named after Shaw.

Likewise, a former slave living in Boston initiated the campaign that eventually produced Saint-Gaudens's celebrated monument. In the fall of 1865, Joshua B. Smith pledged $500 of his own money and raised additional funds by circular through the local African American community. From the beginning Smith envisaged the work as an equestrian monument to Shaw. As we have seen in the case of Lee, this was the most traditional hero monument possible, naturalizing command and rank in the relationship of rider to horse. When a public meeting was held on the idea, some objected to the pretensions of the equestrian format; one man even suggested that the best monument would be an "orphan house." But Smith beat those objections back. According to the newspapers, "he wanted to see [Shaw's] statue on horseback erected on Boston Common, as he last saw him at the head of his regiment on Beacon Street, and it must be done."[83] Smith enlisted the aid of white leaders, notably Charles Sumner, and together they established a committee to carry out the equestrian project.[84]

When the committee announced its intentions, however, it attempted to cast a wider commemorative net. The announcement declared that "the Monument is intended not only to mark the public gratitude to the fallen hero who at a critical moment assumed a perilous responsibility, but also to commemorate that great event, where he was a leader, by which the title of colored men as citizen-soldiers was fixed beyond recall."[85] The declaration of purpose shifts progressively from Shaw the hero to the attack he led to the black soldiers whose civic identity that attack supposedly secured. The ambiguity was no doubt intentional, for in the project there was already the sense that Shaw's personal reputation was intertwined with the wider civic recognition of African Americans. He was not a high-ranking officer, after all, and his claim to fame rested on the troops he commanded. Lincoln could stand alone, as he did in Saint-Gaudens's monument in Chicago; Shaw could not. Thus the Shaw campaign introduced the element of black recognition into the more conventional worship of white heroism.

Yet as the campaign progressed, the role of the African American community receded further into the background. Joshua Smith fell ill, and Sumner apparently took over the project, as he was wont to do. He told the papers that Smith had already collected several thousand dollars and that a "colored association of 800 members were all expected to contribute."[86] Sumner persuaded the committee to select an artist, his friend William Wetmore Story, the sculptor of the *Libyan Sibyl*.[87] But then the campaign disintegrated. When it was later revived in the 1870s, its origins in the efforts of Joshua Smith had been effectively erased. A movement that began in the African American community ended up in the hands of a few Boston Brahmins, and the original black contributors actually received less recognition here than they did in the case of the Freedmen's Memorial to Lincoln. Indeed, there is virtually no trace of them in the archive and the official history left by the Brahmin committee, and their early participation in the project can only be documented by looking elsewhere.[88]

The irony is that the traditional hero monument contemplated by Smith was transformed, in the hands of the Brahmins, into a monument commemorating black soldiery as well. A number of different events conspired to produce this surprising outcome, but they are all tied to the elite nature of the project. First of all, it is clear that the new committee—a group of four wealthy men—wanted to erect a work of art, and one with broad commemorative significance that went beyond the lone figure of Shaw himself. In early 1882, the committee members announced that they had found a design to their liking. It was to have have three large relief tablets illustrating the history of the black regiment—its departure, the battle at Fort Wagner, and the return of the survivors—surmounted by an equestrian statue of Shaw set into an arch. Shaw remained the leading figure in this design, of course, but the narrative history of the regiment extending even after Shaw's death foregrounded the issue of the black soldier's civic status. The newspaper account does not name the artist, but it was probably the celebrated Boston architect H. H. Richardson; a very similar design from his office survives (fig. 6.10). It was Richardson who brought Saint-Gaudens into the project, and both of them evidently worked on this plan.[89] Saint-Gaudens was particularly

6.10 Office of H. H. Richardson, design for Shaw Memorial,
circa 1882, pen and ink.

eager to do an equestrian, having never been commissioned to undertake
this most prestigious of sculptural assignments. But as he tells the story in
his memoirs, the Shaw family balked when they were presented with the
scheme. Consistent with their earlier objections to projects that sought to
separate Shaw from his troops, they argued that the honor of an equestrian was appropriate only for men of the highest rank.[90] Their son had
died a colonel, personally leading his troops into enemy fire, while high-
ranking commanders stayed out of action and led from command posts
in the rear; the calm equestrian image had, in fact, become symbolic of the
commander's withdrawal from the actual business of battle.

The committee had to rethink the design, and the burden clearly fell on
Saint-Gaudens's shoulders, especially after Richardson's death in 1886.
The sculptor embarked on a long search for a new form that would combine the noble equestrian figure he wanted to produce with the image of
the common soldiers Shaw commanded. In the process Saint-Gaudens
eventually hit upon the unique solution of representing an infantry march
with Shaw on horseback and his soldiers on foot, the whole scene in one
large relief panel. In effect, he proposed to integrate the two ideas that had
been separated in the earlier design announced in 1882. Shaw would still
remain the leading figure, but he was now part of a narrative image that
encompassed the departure and destiny of the regiment itself. Within this

6.11 Augustus Saint-Gaudens, plaster cast of sketch model
for Shaw Memorial, date unknown.

general solution the sculptor experimented with various possibilities, all
situating the equestrian figure of Shaw in the front center of the panel and
his troops in the background. One possibility he considered was a three-
quarter perspective in which Shaw would appear at the head of the march
leading his troops.[91] Eventually Saint-Gaudens settled on a profile scheme
in which Shaw's central position now meant that he was riding *beside* his
troops. The figure of Shaw thus retained the formal preeminence the artist
wanted without having to lead the march or guide the narrative. Saint-
Gaudens proposed a low-relief panel, since that was all the committee
could afford, and this compressed the troops into a very shallow background depth (fig. 6.11). The surviving sketch model for this low-relief
panel effectively merges the troops into a nearly indistinguishable mass in
order to bring the horse and rider into relief.[92] However, as years went by
and Saint-Gaudens continued to tinker, he began to increase the depth of
the relief so that more individual representation of the soldiers became
possible. As he explained later in his memoir, "through my extreme interest in it [the project] and its opportunity, [I] increased the conception until
the rider grew almost to a statue in the round and the negroes assumed far
more importance than I had originally intended."[93] The troops emerged
from the background screen Saint-Gaudens had devised and began to

6.12 Saint-Gaudens, relief panel of Shaw Memorial, 1897, bronze.

take on a shape and life of their own. By this long process of revision and experimentation, the first monument representing bona fide black soldiers in proper uniform came into being (fig. 6.12).

While the committee members were frustrated and at times angry with Saint-Gaudens's never-ending process of revision, they clearly approved of the changes because Saint-Gaudens was accomplishing what they had been struggling to do themselves, which was to bring the wider commemorative significance of the monument to the forefront. For the committee, the shift from the lone equestrian image to the narrative relief was not a compromise or a comedown, but an opportunity to enrich the monument's meaning. Committee member John M. Forbes wrote in 1892:

> The original intention was to have a statue. By tacit consent we have changed to a bas-relief, which includes soldiers differing to that extent from the original plan. Col. Lee asks what I think it is intended to record? I think the change from a statue to a bas-relief permits us to make it a memento for those who fell at Fort Wagner, and also to make it serve as a record of the Era which the outgoing of the regiment from Boston, and its only memorable battle some sixty days later, marks; but always with Col. Shaw the leading figure in the Memorial.[94]

Both the committee and the sculptor were trying to create a unique war memorial, one that radiated well beyond the military hero to the cause for which he and his men fought. The representation of the troops became the crux of the problem. As an artist, Saint-Gaudens was not content with simply multiplying a generic black soldier in order to create an undifferentiated mass of troops. Everything in his artistic makeup pushed him against the sort of repetition found in conventional war memorials. Deciding instead to represent the soldiers as distinct individuals, he became fascinated with the material reality of their own diversity. He wanted to defy military uniformity, on the one hand, and racial caricature, on the other; both in their own ways were strategies of standardization. For the sculptor, blackness did not become a leveling trait but a field in which to create a rich interplay of internal differences. He made dozens of life studies of black men, most of them encountered on the streets of New York. He worked to create a cross section based on age, facial structure, expression, and so on. The task of assembling these models into a matrix of soldiers, six rows up to four deep, was a daunting one. Saint-Gaudens ended up discarding many of the life studies because when placed into the panel they threw the whole subtly out of kilter.[95] He wanted to achieve difference and harmony in both dimensions, reading across the surface of the panel and reading into its depth. Thus if we examine the final work from right to left, we see the drummer boy juxtaposed with the sergeant behind him, the youngest member of the group with the oldest, smooth skin with beard, short stature with height; but if we read into depth, other more subtle contrasts emerge too, of facial hair, cheekbone, nose and eye shape. The procedure the sculptor used for faces is essentially the same he applied to every detail of the body and its uniform and equipment. Hat brims are flipped and twisted to create variations of pitch and curvature, guns are tilted at slightly different angles so that they cross or spread, blankets are rolled in various shapes and set on the pack in different ways. In this way the overall impression of uniformity—of identically clad soldiers marching perfectly in step, rhyming each other's body movements—is changed and enriched by a kind of contrapuntal rhythm of diversity.

It is fascinating that this exploration of black diversity came from the hands of a white man who shared the common racial prejudices of the white elite. In his memoirs, Saint-Gaudens writes quite disparagingly about his black models, who are brought into the story merely as comic relief. They come off as foolish, deceptive, and superstitious, though Saint-Gaudens is careful to say that he likes them for their "imaginative, though simple, minds."[96] In the text he creates caricatures; in the relief he gives them room to live as individuals. The disparity is striking enough to help explode some common misconceptions about the process of art-making. Saint-Gaudens's sympathetic portrait studies of black men do not imply a special sympathy for black men in the mind of the artist, nor does the lack of sympathy he showed in his memoirs invalidate the visual evidence of the sculpture. It was the self-imposed demands of art, not racial ideology, that compelled the sculptor to portray these men as he did.[97] The artistic imperative of difference over repetition was so powerful that it drove Saint-Gaudens to humanize his models in ways he had never originally intended.

But there is another issue of difference at work here, literally in the foreground, and that is the distinction between the soldiers and their commander. This is not only a distinction of facial type, of course, but a distinction of the body—its position, carriage, motion. There are really two rhythms in this march, masterfully interwoven: the steady tread of the foot soldiers carrying their gear, and the light but powerful step of the horse bearing Shaw. The soldiers lean their whole bodies slightly into the march, counterbalanced by the packstraps which pull against their shoulders. We are made to feel the weight they carry, and how they manage their burden in a series of controlled, disciplined movements; as they step forward, their trousers ride and fall in rumpled folds on heavily creased shoes. They are by no means "listless," as Albert Boime has recently argued.[98] The reason the soldiers do not dash or spring forward is that they are marching, conserving their strength as they carry themselves and their equipment in a measured tread. The horse, by contrast, fairly glides, its tail and raised leg moving in a perfectly timed pattern of opposing arcs. The animal naturally towers over the troops and moves with ease. The only strain betrayed by its sleek surface of vein and muscle is the pressure on its neck created by Shaw's taut reins, which check the horse's strength and keep it from outpacing the men beneath. Shaw thereby rides absolutely motionless, propelled not by his own body but by the superior energy of the steed. While everyone else angles forward, he remains fixed upright, ramrod straight, in the saddle. This creates perhaps the most startling effect of the whole panel: Shaw becomes a still center in the midst of an otherwise moving tableau. He is swept along, we know, by its collective movement, and yet abstracted from it.

It is this peculiar relationship of the commander to the surrounding movement that creates the tension and mystery of the panel. Boime, among others, tries to simplify that relationship by reading into it a clear racist hierarchy: Shaw towers above both the animal and the black men, who merge into one mass of inferior status. Boime points particularly to the visual rhyme between the horse's hind leg and the soldiers' retreating legs in back.[99] He overlooks the obvious ways in which the horse and the troops remain visually distinct, in their movements, in their surface quality. And, even more important, he does not see that this visual rhyme is one of a whole pattern of such rhymes meant to knit together all the various planes of the relief, including Shaw's. Look at the sword, for example, so prominent at the front of the relief. Its diagonal rhymes the horse's leg below and the rifle barrels above, thereby helping unite foreground and background—commander, horse, and troops—in one harmony. At the same time, however, that the sword helps to link Shaw with the rest of the march, it also marks his superior status. The sword is a deliberately antiquated weapon chosen to embellish the officer's regalia precisely because it signals the officer's removal from the actual business of killing, which the troops instead are trained to undertake. The detail of the sword reinforces what the interwoven rhythms of the whole have already established: Shaw at once belongs to the march and transcends it. He rides with his troops but elevated above them, his head reaching up into the realm of the angel who floats over the men and guides their march. For Saint-Gaudens the figure of the angel was crucial and he stood by it despite the opposition of committee members and even friends.[100] It enabled Shaw to become a mediating figure between the register of the real below—the concrete realm of the male body under physical strain—and the register of the ideal above, signified by the weightless female body divinely propelled. Shaw thus passes between the realms of mortality and immortality, between oblivion and eternity. While he moves ahead with his troops toward an inevitable death, he alone is singled out for everlasting fame.

In this monument Saint-Gaudens was able to elevate the white hero without demoting the black troops. He accomplished what other sculptors before him like Thomas Ball had failed to do, which was to make the black body more than a mere foil to whiteness. In the panel, officer and troops are absorbed in a common mission, and that mission is represented most profoundly by the men on the ground in all their compelling material presence. With Saint-Gaudens's revisions, the soldiers in effect moved forward out of the relief and into our space, acquiring a concreteness and individuality that African Americans had never before had in public sculpture—indeed, that common soldiers themselves had never had in the generic monuments erected to honor them. But while the soldiers moved forward into our world, Shaw moved upward into a different sphere. Like all of Saint-Gaudens's great hero figures—the Lincoln in Chicago being the preeminent example—Shaw represents a merger of the real and ideal. Ultimately, though he is directly connected to his troops and takes part in their movement and their fate, the figure of Shaw acquires a grace that the troops cannot and do not share.

This was its perfection for the white critics who yearned for an artistic and meaningful war memorial. It broke the mold of the standard soldier monument and spoke directly to the great issue of the war, which almost

all other memorials erased or belittled, the issue of slavery. It treated racial difference openly and with dignity, assserting a "brotherhood" of
man. And yet it registered, compellingly and beautifully, the transcen-
dence of the white hero in that brotherhood. Listen to the editorial of
Century Magazine, which declared the monument "the greatest work of
plastic art yet produced in America" and promoted it in a series of still
important articles published at the monument's dedication in 1897:

> In this sculptured picture we see the awakening of a race, the dark, deter-
> mined mass moved by a common impulse of daring endeavor; lifted above
> these, the high-bred form, the delicate, intense, intellectual visage, the fair
> Anglo-Saxon head of their heroic leader; and high above all, the everlasting
> ideal, the symbol of the spiritual purpose, which beckons, inspires, and glo-
> riously rewards.[101]

This description suppresses the concrete material presence of the soldiers—here they are no longer discrete individuals in all their diversity but
a "race," a "dark, determined mass"—in order to elevate Shaw the lone
individual, the Anglo-Saxon upper-class ideal of manhood. A three-tiered
hierarchy is devised: mass, hero, and ideal; black, white, divine. The old
racial hierarchy of chimp, negro, and Apollo is echoed but reconstructed
in a more "positive" light, so that the black man below can become part
of the human community even as he loses himself in the uniformity of a
"dark" mass.

The irony of this critical embrace is that it is purchased at the cost of
restandardizing the common soldier because of his race. While some critics did see the vitality and diversity of Saint-Gaudens's soldiers, many
important critics erased these qualities in order to sharpen the difference
between the black soldiers and Shaw, the white ideal. It is as if they refused to see the black soldiers except as a collective symbol, a "mass" or
a "vast, endless, countless host, moving like a huge human tide, hardly of
its own volition."[102] Their slaughter becomes the result of sheer collective
propulsion, the loss of individual will to the will of the mass or the will of
God. They transmute into a natural or even supernatural force, while the
hero's death remains a triumph of individual human will, a deliberate
stare into fate. In effect these critics refused to do what Saint-Gaudens
forced himself to do, and that is to make room for the black figures as
concrete individual agents in the larger historical narrative they helped
shape.

I am reserving the last word on the monument for its principal orator,
William James, because his text is probably the most unusual monument
oration ever delivered in the nineteenth century and because it speaks
directly to the relationship between the Shaw Memorial and the mainstream practice of soldier commemoration we have been discussing
here.[103] Like Howells, James had a palpable distaste for war, and it shows

through virtually every page of his text. While composing it James referred to his task as "a fearful job . . . an address on the unveiling of a military statue."[104] And indeed the speech can be read as a systematic critique of the whole business of erecting military statues. For James, the value of the Shaw lay in its difference from the run-of-the-mill military monument, from the monuments to generals and "the abstract soldier's-monuments . . . reared on every village green" (by abstract I take him to mean generic or anonymous). The subjects of the Shaw Memorial were neither distinguished military figures nor everyman common soldiers: they were "a particular set of comparatively undistinguished men." It was their particularity and their difference that allowed them to become types for something other than military prowess. "The very lack of external complication in the history of these soldiers"—an odd way of framing their distinctiveness, which was nothing if not complicated—"is what makes them represent with such typical purity the profounder meaning of the Union cause." That meaning, of course, was the final eradication of the great historical crime of slavery. It was a meaning that came through vividly in the sculpture itself—in "the dark outcasts, so true to nature that one can almost hear them breathing as they march," and in "the blue-eyed child of fortune" who led them.

James might easily have been content to rest with this single important point, that here finally was one monument that seemed to deliver what Howells had pleaded for some thirty years earlier. But it was still after all a "military statue," a form Howells had hoped to consign to oblivion. The weapons of war in this monument are carried with a purpose and a discipline far more palpable than anything in the standard soldier monuments, with their relaxed poses and their guns resting on the ground. And so James felt compelled in the end to explain how this most powerful of military monuments could be made to carry a different sort of moral lesson. "It is hard to end a discourse like this," he wrote, "without one word of moralizing." With this preamble, James launched into a critique of militarism and brought to a boiling point what had been quietly simmering throughout the rest of the oration:

> War has been much praised and celebrated among us of late as a school of manly virtue; but it is easy to exaggerate on this point. Ages ago, war was the gory cradle of mankind, the grim-featured nurse that alone could train our savage progenitors into some semblance of social virtue, teach them to be faithful one to another, and force them to sink their selfishness in wider tribal ends. War still excells in this prerogative; and whether it be paid in years of service, in treasure, or in life-blood, the war tax is still the only tax that men ungrudgingly will pay. How could it be otherwise, when the survivors of one successful massacre after another are the beings from whose loins we and all our contemporary races spring?

James thus distinguishes between two kinds of courage, both at play in the subject of the monument. The first and far more common is the military sort, bred into us as a fighting instinct, the kind of courage Shaw showed when he first enlisted in the New York 7th. The other "more lonely courage" is a kind of civic valor not bred into the species, which Shaw demonstrated when he decided to leave his white regiment and head the "dubious fortunes" of the "negroes of the 54th." Military valor needs no reinforcement, no monuments, because it is so inbred within us, while civic valor is "the kind of valor to which the monuments of nations should most of all be reared." And so the oration ends as a jeremiad, a warning that only the new Shaws of the nation can save it from all the "lesser powers of darkness" that threaten its domestic peace from within.

No wonder, then, that James had little use for the "abstract soldier's-monuments" scattered across the country, for they were erected to honor precisely the more common sort of valor—the simple willingness to kill and die for the tribe, for the nation writ small. While the whole idea of the citizen-soldier monument was to equate military and civic valor, James sought to separate them. One was merely instinctive, as promiscuous as the monuments erected to celebrate it, and the most it could hope to achieve was fidelity to a group. The other was principled, thus rare, and it involved fidelity to independent moral ideals that transcended the dictates of groups and the dynamics of tribalism. Shaw, the beautiful exemplar of what James finally lauds as the "English-speaking race" (at once a nod to and a retreat from the more overtly racialist concept of the Anglo-Saxon), stood for this precious commodity deliberately ignored in the standardized monuments erected to ordinary men.

What is finally striking about James's "moralizing" is the nearly complete disappearance of the black troops from its reckoning. They appear only momentarily as the sign or proof of Shaw's civic valor, their "dubious fortunes" serving to magnify Shaw's "lonely" courage. It is as if we have returned to Saint-Gaudens's original idea of the troops as a flat screen throwing the white hero into better relief. Indeed, James's image of loneliness seems as much a description of Shaw's position as a white commander marooned among black men, and the image also seems to register something of the peculiar relationship Saint-Gaudens fashioned when he made his hero a still center amid a moving file of men. Without coming right out and saying so, James reduces their assault on Fort Wagner to the typical sort of military adventure he despises. "Of five hundred of us who could storm a battery side by side with others, perhaps not one would be found ready to risk his worldly fortunes all alone in resisting an enthroned abuse." In this account the black soldiers become common soldiers after all, sharing the same simple fighting instinct. What James's sermon does not let them become is heroes in his sense: they have neither the loneliness nor the fortune on which civic valor seems to depend. They remain outcasts, even in uniform, from the republic of valor he is trying to construct.

As so many other white observers of the monument did, James restandardized the black soldiers even as he tried to turn their monument into a higher moral lesson. Yet, if Saint-Gaudens's monument can teach us anything, it does so by throwing attention on these men as *un*common soldiers. And in one crucial respect, they were not really common soldiers. Unlike most of their white comrades who wanted to fight a "white man's war," they fought for a national principle that transcended tribal loyalties, that was actually incompatible with the customary logic of those loyalties—this was the principle of equality, limited though it was then to an equality among men. Of all the men who fought in the war, the black soldiers were most clearly representative of a national purpose. The irony is that this made them unrepresentative of the common soldier and unrepresentable in public sculpture, even in a new class of monuments utterly motivated by nationalism.

"How extraordinary," W.E.B. Du Bois wrote in 1936, "and what a tribute to ignorance and religious hypocrisy, is the fact that in the minds of most people, even those of liberals, only murder makes men. The slave pleaded; he was humble; he protected the women of the South, and the world ignored him. The slave killed white men; and behold, he was a man."[105] In this stunning denunciation of militarism, Dubois, former student of William James, reflected on the absurd predicament of African American men during the Civil War. In order to persuade white culture of their humanity, they had to participate in the most inhumane of male rites. Yet, as we have seen, the transformation from slave to soldier to man turned out ultimately to be illusory. When the war ended African American veterans returned to a world in which manhood was still under construction, both for blacks and whites. It was a world in which, for the first time, no men were slaves and yet droves of men were soldiers or former soldiers. Out of this world emerged the citizen-soldier monument. It situated the ordinary white man for the first time in the symbolic economy of civic sculpture. There he stood, not as a murderer of other men, not as a slave of the military regime, not even as a hero in the conventional sculptural sense, but as an able, dutiful, moderate, self-disciplined individual. This singular achievement of white America could not be realized without suppressing the memory of slavery and of the black soldiers who fought specifically to eradicate it. The majority's concept of manhood was too inelastic, too uncertain of itself, to accommodate the very men who knew best what they were fighting for and what was at stake.

For all its novelty, the common-soldier monument was fundamentally reactionary. It evolved in reaction to a newly empowered nationality that had revealed itself first in the terrifying technological apparatus of warfare and then in an ideological program to reconstruct the racial order of society. While declaring undying allegiance to this national power, the monuments fought a rearguard battle against it, reasserting the primacy of the individual actor (the white male citizen) and the local community he represented. In the process the monuments came to terms with the new nationalism by reshaping its very face. They gave it a familiar face, a white face, a likeness this nation has yet to challenge with any real determination.

CHAPTER SEVEN

EPILOGUE

THIS BOOK has told the story of how a nation redefined itself in the most permanent form of self-reflection it had, the public monument. No single monument could accomplish this, although some did try. Their effect was cumulative. In the decades following the Civil War an unprecedented wave of monuments—to the great and the ordinary alike—spread across the country. As they did, they gradually mapped abstract notions of individual responsibility and collective purpose onto the material reality of the national landscape.

Some monuments never got built, for lack of support or money. Other monuments were built and imitated over and over again. This was a process of sifting, in which certain ideas proved themselves to be viable in the public sphere and others proved to be failures. When Ward's *Freedman* and Hosmer's proposal for the Freedmen's Memorial were dropped for good, the vast possibilities they represented were lost. The monuments that followed them shut old doors and opened new ones. The Freedmen's Memorial as it was finally built is a case in point. Ball's group, appearing at the end of Reconstruction, effectively closed the era of emancipation with the old image of a black man still mired in the ethos of slavery. At the same time, the very success of the monument helped a new imagery of white heroism to emerge. Ball's work was an important step in the process that ultimately freed Lincoln, and the white soldiers who fought for and against him, to stand alone in public space. With each succeeding monument to white valor, with each repetition of the common forms, the nation cemented its image and its power relations a bit more tightly.

Race was at the center of this process. Race was not always discussed but it was always there, at the most basic level of visual representation, the human body. Well before the Civil War, the racial formation of the human body had been mapped out. Even so, the black body had possibilities for representation in public space. In South Carolina, as we saw, the body of the slave became vital to the state's self-definition and self-defense. Later, as slavery turned to emancipation, African Americans found themselves suddenly in the national limelight. Lincoln's "new birth of freedom," if it meant anything at all, meant that the emancipated were the centerpiece of a new nationality. Black body and white nation were now intertwined dynamically, reshaping one another. The monuments commemorating the war were right in the middle of this dynamic relationship. They looked forward as much as backward. In the simple figures of slaves and soldiers, they were reinventing the very body of the nation.

Yet this was not a straightforward process. At the same time that public monuments went about building the new nation, they resisted it. Localities of various sorts, geographical and political, were coming to terms with the nation and redefining it in their own interests. Ultimately that process of push and pull succeeded in prying apart the black body from the white nation. The ideal of a new interracial order vanished from public space. The nation was recast more powerfully than ever before in the mold of the ordinary white man, leaving the black body once again on the margins—at its best, standing as the proud model of doomed manhood in Saint-Gaudens's unique war memorial, and its worst, kneeling in perpetual subordination in Ball's misnamed Emancipation Monument.

ONE of the most urgent questions of our time is why racial animosity and inequality persist in a nation dedicated to the ideals of freedom and opportunity. Despite the Civil War, Reconstruction, the Civil Rights movement, and affirmative action, the division between white and black seems as intractable as ever. To understand why, we must go beyond a history of politics and policy. We need a history of consciousness as well. We need to examine the inner life of culture as well as the external events that shape it.

The story of the public monument in America is uniquely revealing because it bridges these inner and outer realms. This is not to claim that the public monuments discussed in this book emanated from cultural consciousness in any direct way. They were built by specific people who claimed the right to speak for the collective, and to claim this right took power. But public monuments ultimately tested the limits and possibilities of collective consciousness. To be erected, monuments usually had to mesh with the beliefs and aspirations of the majority, even when those were so deep-seated that they were unspoken. And once monuments were erected, they reshaped those beliefs and aspirations simply by giving them a concrete form in public space. The image of a common soldier on a pedestal in the town green spoke eloquently, every day of every year, for the heroism of the ordinary white man defending the nation. The critics who called them meaningless were dead wrong. Though nobody spent much time looking at them, nobody needed to: they were simple forms, immediately understood, that worked precisely because they condensed life and death issues (what it meant to live and die for a community and a nation) into the most banal and uncontroversial form possible.

Though monuments were conservative, they were not so conservative that they resisted all innovation. Indeed, the glorification of the common soldier was itself an innovation. But the pace of monumental change was rather different from the pace of political events. If the history of current events before and after the Civil War looks like a rushing river full of twists and turns, the history of public monuments is more like a slow underground stream. From that slow stream it is easier to chart where the nation was heading. Traditions of racist thought entrenched in slavery acted as a drag on change, ultimately preventing public monuments from embracing and crystallizing a new interracial order. At the same time the catastrophe of mass warfare propelled public monuments into a new era of militarism. The demise of the one and the rise of the other went hand in hand, redefining both the meaning of patriotism and the identity of the patriots.

Monuments remain powerful because they are built to last long after the particular voices of their makers have ceased, long after the events of their creation have been forgotten. It is only then that truly they come to represent a common voice, for better or for worse. What power do these monuments to the Civil War era still have in today's world? Times have changed, yet the monuments, for the most part, remain. Some monuments continue to work in much the same way. Throughout the country common-soldier monuments have been supplemented by newer monuments to more recent wars or simply by new inscriptions that commemorate a seemingly never-ending record of sacrifice and death. Other monuments have become anachronistic and controversial. Ball's emancipation group in Boston has been the target of provocative counterinstallations. The Shaw Memorial went through a period of vandalism and neglect until it was rededicated in 1983 with the names of soldiers from the 54th added to the inscriptions. Confederate soldier monuments in the South have sometimes met with protests. Richmond's Monument Avenue, that public bastion of white supremacy, was finally "integrated" in the summer of 1996 with a monument to African American tennis player Arthur Ashe, designed by sculptor Paul D. Pasquale. The statue was added despite significant opposition and only after wrenching debate over the meaning of Confederate commemoration in today's South.[1]

The Ashe Monument offers a lesson in the continuing power of public monuments. On my many visits to Monument Avenue before the Ashe statue was contemplated, I never saw a soul—white or black—actually look at the Confederate heroes enshrined there. One might easily have thought that over time the monuments had lost all significance. But that appearance was deceiving. Even after the collapse of segregation and the demise of white rule in Richmond, the Confederate monuments remained powerful because they functioned within the civic landscape as a last

bastion of white privilege. Their importance was demonstrated most palpably when African American leaders, in the early 1990s, began to try
to alter Monument Avenue's image by proposing monuments to black
heroes—originally heroes of the Civil Rights movement. Many local
whites dug in to "protect" the Confederate landscape from such a direct
assault on its guiding principle. The ideas of a Civil Rights figure was then
dropped in favor of a popular icon whose appeal crossed racial lines. Yet
despite the compromise choice of Ashe, his monument has quietly undermined the avenue's aura of white supremacy. Driving down the avenue
today, one sees the familiar procession of Confederate heroes culminate,
unexpectedly, in a monument to exactly what the Confederacy feared and
fought against: an educated, articulate, powerful African American citizenry. Ashe's statue has succeeded in bringing all kinds of people to the
avenue who never visited in the past. In the months following its dedication it was common to find groups of people, white and black, standing
in front of it, marveling at its presence there, reading the beautiful inscription from Hebrews 12 with its exhortation to "lay aside every weight,
and the sin which so easily ensnares us, and let us run with endurance the
race that is set before us."[2]

In the slow stream of monumental history, the Ashe Monument is not
an insignificant step. One can only hope that it inspires us to imagine
other interventions that could further propel that history in a better direction. Consider Monument Avenue's counterpart, the Mall in Washington, D.C., and its gigantic monument to the Union, the Lincoln Memorial. Though it was not completed until 1922, it was still very much in the
ideological mold of Saint-Gaudens's *Standing Lincoln*. Daniel Chester
French's Lincoln, seated and colossal, appears alone; the central inscription behind his figure does not mention slavery or emancipation. But by
virtue of its grandeur and its location in the symbolic center of the nation's capital, the monument entered political history in a powerful and
unexpected way. It became the dramatic stage for several epochal events,
most notably Martin Luther King Jr.'s famous "I have a dream" speech
of 1963, which crystallized the moral cause of the Civil Rights movement.
Why not erect a monument to Reverend King within this great white
temple? Not just a plaque, which has already been proposed, but a life-
sized statue of King at the top of the memorial steps, where he gave
his speech—a companion figure to Lincoln's, as King indeed was in that
great hour of our nation's life.[3] Suggesting this is not meant to detract
from the memory of Lincoln but to expand it, to reimagine the landscape
of commemoration so that it can speak much more persuasively than it
has to the aspirations for peace and understanding that both King and
Lincoln once expressed so compellingly.

"Now is the time to make real the promises of democracy," King said on the steps of Lincoln's temple. One hundred years after the Emancipation Proclamation, King's speech commemorated it by reminding us that it was still not too late to reclaim the promise of emancipation, to reopen the doors that were closed after Reconstruction, and to march through toward a better destiny. In the future, our commemoration of history and our history of commemoration will help determine that destiny.

CHAPTER ONE
INTRODUCTION

1. Slavery was not a phenomenon unique to the Southern states. The national Constitution itself sanctioned slavery, and at the time of its ratification most states still permitted slave ownership. Although Northern states gradually abolished slavery in the late eighteenth and early nineteenth centuries, the Supreme Court as late as the 1850s confirmed and indeed strengthened the federal protection of slavery. This was, of course, one of the fundamental reasons why a Civil War became inevitable. See Leon F. Litwack, *North of Slavery: The Negro in the Free States, 1790–1860* (Chicago: University of Chicago Press, 1961).

2. See for example, "Sculpture, As a Means of Municipal Embellishment," *Cosmopolitan Art Journal* 1 (June 1857): 119. As late as 1888 an architectural journal could write: "We Americans to whom it is still a matter of much pride to have within the boundaries of the neighboring city even a single public statue, that we can go and gaze upon, cannot imagine the surroundings of a Greek or Roman citizen of even the lower class who was as free as the highest patrician to derive pleasure from the hundreds of statues in the public places of his native town." See *American Architect and Building News* 24 (July 28, 1888): 36.

3. There is still relatively little scholarship on monumentality in the nineteenth century. My remarks here build on earlier reflections in Kirk Savage, "Race, Memory, and Identity: The National Monuments of the Union and the Confederacy" (Ph.D. diss., University of California, Berkeley, 1990), and "The Politics of Memory: Black Emancipation and the Civil War Monument," in John R. Gillis, ed., *Commemorations: The Politics of National Identity* (Princeton: Princeton University Press, 1994), 127–49. For a study of monument proliferation in nineteenth-century France, see Maurice Agulhon, "La 'statuomanie' et l'histoire," *Ethnologie française* 8 (1978): 145–72.

4. Unlike Pierre Nora, I do not believe in any absolute distinction between memory and history. Still, the terms are not exactly interchangeable. I take the production of history to be one practice among many that constitute collective memory. When I refer to history, I mean generally to imply a narrative, a story about the past rooted in some claim to truth. For Nora's influential statement, see "Between Memory and History: *Les lieux de mémoire*," *Representations*, no. 26 (Spring 1989): 7–25.

5. "National Lincoln Monument," circular dated May 24, 1865, in National Lincoln Monument Association (NLMA Letters and Papers, Illinois State Historical Library, Springfield, Illinois.

6. The literature on collective memory is growing fast in a variety of disciplines. See, among others, James Fentress and Chris Wickham, *Social Memory* (Oxford: Basil Blackwell, 1992); David Middleton and Derek Edwards, eds.,

Collective Remembering (New York: Sage, 1990); Nora, "Between Memory and History"; Paul Connerton, *How Societies Remember* (Cambridge: Cambridge University Press, 1989); David Lowenthal, *The Past Is a Foreign Country* (Cambridge: Cambridge University Press, 1985). There have also been several ambitious historical surveys of American practices of remembrance which I have found useful: Merrill D. Peterson, *Lincoln in American Memory* (New York: Oxford University Press, 1994); John Bodnar, *Remaking America: Public Memory, Commemoration, and Patriotism in the Twentieth Century* (Princeton: Princeton University Press, 1992); Michael Kammen, *Mystic Chords of Memory: The Transformation of Tradition in American Culture* (New York: Knopf, 1991).

Much of the literature on collective memory is driven by structural oppositions: memory/history, internal/external (Nora); incorporated/inscribed (Connerton); living/dead (Lowenthal); vernacular/official (Bodnar). The first term of each pair is usually equated with "real" or "genuine" memory, whereas its opposite is therefore false or imposed memory. Although these oppositions can sometimes be useful in a heuristic way, they tend to break down when confronted with the actual operations of collective memory in the public sphere. The monuments I discuss in this book consistently problematize any such oppositions, whether they be African American monuments to Lincoln or white monuments to the ordinary soldier. This is because the ordinary people who entered the public sphere to participate in rituals of collective memory often did so because they wanted external recognition and civic legitimacy; they wanted to declare their allegiances. Conversely, sometimes the most elite participants in the process were the ones most concerned to express internal feelings rather than external loyalties. Kurt Piehler makes a similar point in his book *Remembering War the American Way* (Washington, D.C.: Smithsonian Institution Press, 1995), 193–94.

My reliance on the notion of the public sphere is of course indebted to Jürgen Habermas's pioneering book *The Structural Transformation of the Public Sphere: An Inquiry into a Category of Bourgeois Society*, trans. Thomas Burger (Cambridge, Mass.: MIT Press, 1989); but even more to some of the responses to his argument found in Craig Calhoun, ed., *Habermas and the Public Sphere* (Cambridge, Mass.: MIT Press, 1992), especially the essays by Mary P. Ryan and Geoff Eley. The newer literature on public art also invokes the concept of the public sphere, but its analyses tend to be ahistorical or to generalize from contemporary experience. Rosalyn Deutsche's work is an exception; her recent book, *Evictions: Art and Spatial Politics* (Cambridge, Mass.: MIT Press, 1996), came out too late for inclusion in this study.

7. Many of the works discussed in this study have provoked similar debates about the status of the public monument. Recently the struggle to erect a statue of black tennis star Arthur Ashe on Monument Avenue in Richmond, Virginia, home to several famous Confederate monuments, including the equestrian statue of Lee discussed in chapter 5, stimulated a very sharply delineated dispute. Many local white residents were outraged because for them the avenue's Confederate image was supposed to be eternal.

8. See, for example, Ivan Hannaford, *Race: The History of an Idea in the West* (Baltimore: Johns Hopkins University Press, 1996); Michael Banton, *Racial Theories* (Cambridge: Cambridge University Press, 1987); Stephen Jay Gould, *Mis-*

measure of Man (New York: Norton, 1981); Nancy Stepan, *The Idea of Race in Science: Great Britain, 1800–1960* (Hamden, Conn.: Archon Books, 1982); William Ragan Stanton, *Leopard's Spots: Scientific Attitudes toward Race in America, 1815–1859* (Chicago: University of Chicago Press, 1960); John S. Haller Jr., *Outcasts from Evolution: Scientific Attitudes of Racial Inferiority, 1859–1900* (Urbana: University of Illinois Press, 1971).

The term "race" was (and still is) used loosely, with a variety of meanings. Ambiguity and contradiction were inevitable since the concept embraced both biological and nonbiological characteristics, the bodily and the spiritual. Sometimes the term could even be used to describe a people or a nationality with no common physical characteristics (e.g., Americans), but I would argue that even in this case the appeal to the concept of race implied a certain bodily conformation (whiteness, to be sure). For more on the term, see for example George W. Stocking Jr., "The Turn-of-the-Century Concept of Race," *Modernism/Modernity* 1 (January 1994): 4–16. Kwame Anthony Appiah explores the philosophical contradictions of the modern biological concept of race in *In My Father's House: Africa in the Philosophy of Culture* (New York: Oxford University Press, 1992), esp. 10–13 and 34–46. Recently Michael Omi and Howard Winant have criticized Appiah's blunt conclusion that "there are no races" but their position is really consistent with his; they assert that race is a historical construct rather than biological truth, and as historical construct it has real effects on real populations, but Appiah does not deny this. See Omi and Wynant, *Racial Formation in the United States: From the 1960s to the 1990s*, 2d ed. (New York: Routledge, 1994), 54–56.

9. The sculptural mold, like a photograph, was a mechanical impression of form (in semiotic jargon, "indexical"). Unlike the photograph, however, the mold was three-dimensional and therefore transmitted special information. This gave the sculptural likeness a unique purchase on authenticity—for individual heroes as well as ethnographic types. As late as 1879, for example, the sculptor Clark Mills—about whom we will hear much more in chapter 4—was commissioned by the Smithsonian to take casts of the heads of native American students and prisoners for the purposes of scientific typology; see *U.S. National Museum Proceedings* 1 (1878): 201–14, and 2 (1879): 211.

10. The importance of antique sculpture in racial theorizing has not been sufficiently addressed in the secondary literature, but for some preliminary findings see Haller, *Outcasts from Evolution*, 9–11; Stepan, *The Idea of Race in Science*, 13–15; and Hugh Honour, *The Image of the Black in Western Art IV: From the American Revolution to World War I. Part 2: Black Models and White Myths* (Cambridge, Mass.: Harvard University Press, 1989), 12–21. See also Anders Retzius, "A Glance at the Present State of Ethnology, with Reference to the Form of the Skull," in Earl Wendel Count, ed., *This Is Race* (New York: Shuman, 1950), 75–89; and the remarks of Prof. Hermann Burmeister quoted in J. C. Nott and George R. Gliddon, *Types of Mankind* (Philadelphia: Lippincott, 1854), 415–17.

Not all racial theorists drew the same conclusions from the "evidence" of antique sculpture. Blumenbach, in particular, did not conclude that Negroes constituted an inferior race; he pointed out that just as many Europeans departed from the antique ideal as did Negroes. It was not until the nineteenth century that racial classifications hardened into definitive racial hierarchies thought to be immutable. See Hannaford, *Race*, 210–13, 255ff.

11. Nott and Gliddon, *Types of Mankind*, 457–58. Stephen Jay Gould has critiqued the cranial data (taken from Samuel Morton's collection of skulls) in *Mismeasure of Man*.

12. I am indebted to Henry Pisciotta for helping me see this now obvious point.

13. The basic source on the antique canon is Francis Haskell and Nicholas Penny, *Taste and the Antique: The Lure of Classical Sculpture, 1500–1900* (New Haven: Yale University Press, 1981).

14. It is of course crucial that the comparison is vertical rather than horizontal, since the diagram thereby capitalizes on the significance of the up/down opposition, which is a powerful sign not only in European cultures but many others as well; see Connerton, *How Societies Remember*, 73–74.

The use of this Greek head as a likeness of the white races does involve Nott and Gliddon in some internal inconsistencies, for in their racial hierarchy it is the northern or "Teutonic" races which are at the top of the totem pole; the modern descendants of the Greeks, being swarthier, would seem to be less "Greek" than the Anglo-Saxons, even though the authors are at pains to argue that racial characteristics remain constant over time.

15. Reproduced in Honour, *Image of the Black IV, Part 2*, 15; note also the illustration in Robert Knox's 1850 treatise *The Races of Men*, reproduced in Haller, *Outcasts from Evolution*, 10.

16. Gould in *Mismeasure of Man* makes the point but is unaware of the particular importance of sculpture.

17. The Southern sculptor Edward Valentine, for example, drew antique casts in the Medical College of Virginia; Elizabeth Gray Valentine, *Dawn to Twilight: The Work of Edward Valentine* (Richmond, Va.: William Byrd Press, 1929), 28.

18. Mikhail Bakhtin, *Rabelais and His World*, trans. Hélène Iswolsky (Bloomington: Indiana University Press, 1984), 24–29. In Bakhtin's formulation, the medieval forms of the grotesque had a liberating or regenerative function, which was then lost by the end of the Renaissance.

For more on the emergence of black bodies in popular media, see, among others, Robert C. Toll, *Blacking Up: The Minstrel Show in Nineteenth-Century America* (New York: Oxford University Press, 1974); Phillip Lapsansky, "Graphic Discord: Abolitionist and Antiabolitionist Images," in Jean Fagan Yellin and John C. Van Horne, eds., *The Abolitionist Sisterhood: Women's Political Culture in Antebellum America* (Ithaca, N.Y.: Cornell University Press, 1994), 201–30; Francis John Martin, "The Image of Black People in American Illustration from 1825 to 1925" (Ph.D. diss., University of California, Los Angeles, 1986); Guy C. McElroy, *Facing History: The Black Image in American Art, 1710–1940* (San Francisco: Bedford Arts, 1990); Honour, *Image of the Black IV, Part 2*.

19. David Wiles, *The Masks of Menander: Sign and Meaning in Greek and Roman Performance* (Cambridge: Cambridge University Press, 1991), 192–93. Wiles describes the code for slave movement, registered in antique frescoes, as follows: "the legs are apart, the knees are turned outwards, the buttocks are pro-

jected backwards and the stomach forwards." This could read equally well as a description of minstrel body language, from the figure of Jim Crow onward, though no one to my knowledge has made this connection. The sheet music example illustrated here was published in Toll, *Blacking Up*, 39.

20. According to a table in Nott and Gliddon (*Types of Mankind*, 450), the mean brain size in cubic inches for the "Barbarous tribes," tribes in U.S. territory, was 84; for native Africans the measurement was 83 and for "American-born Negroes" the measurement was 82. Indian skulls from Latin America were yet smaller. Nevertheless, the "Negro" receives the burden of the text's attention, as a paradigm of physical and mental inferiority; see pp. 259–63, 415–17, 456–60.

21. An engraving of the statuette was reproduced in Wayne Craven, "Henry Kirke Brown: His Search for an American Art in the 1840s," *American Art Journal* 4 (November 1972): 51. Another, more public, example is Thomas Crawford's seated figure of an Indian chief on the Senate pediment of the U.S. Capitol, modeled in the 1850s and based in part on the antique Torso Belvedere.

22. Note Alexis de Tocqueville's observation in *Democracy in America* (1835) that "the Negro transmits the eternal mark of his ignominy [slavery] to all his descendants; and although the law may abolish slavery, God alone can obliterate the traces of its existence"; quoted in Alexander O. Boulton, "The American Paradox: Jeffersonian Equality and Racial Science," *American Quarterly* 47 (September 1995): 467–92 (quotation from p. on 488).

23. Orlando Patterson in *Slavery and Social Death: A Comparative Study* (Cambridge, Mass.: Harvard University Press, 1982) discusses the universality of the slave stereotype across cultures (p. 96). The powerlessness and degradation of slaves are blamed on the slaves themselves, not on the masters responsible for enslaving them; to mask this naked act of domination the slaves must be represented as naturally dependent and incompetent even when they are in fact engaged in productive labor (pp. 335–39).

It is still worthwhile to read the remarks of Winthrop Jordan on how the English colonists represented and treated Indians and Africans differently; see Winthrop D. Jordan, *White over Black: American Attitudes toward the Negro, 1550–1812* (Chapel Hill: University of North Carolina Press, 1968), 89–91.

24. It is important to point out, however, that some proslavery spokesmen objected to *Types of Mankind* not only because it seemed inconsistent with scripture but also because it went too far in dehumanizing the "negro"; see George M. Fredrickson, *The Black Image in the White Mind: The Debate on Afro-American Character and Destiny, 1817–1914* (New York: Harper and Row, 1972), 29, 69–73, 84.

25. Patterson is careful to point out that slaves resisted their social death by creating family and community ties (*Slavery and Social Death*, 337–38), and that the slaveholders' ideology could not define how the slaves themselves thought or even behaved (p. 96). Nevertheless he puts great weight on the tactics used by slaveholders to construct the slaves' liminal existence; for example, the masters' practice of naming slaves (sometimes after Greek gods, a parodic inversion of the racial construct) served to strip them of social identity and ties of family. I would observe that such practices were doomed to fail at some level, for the simple reason that slaves still retained some power over meaning, the larger process of

signification. The master could never fully control the meaning of a name, or of the language he forced the slaves to learn; Henry Louis Gates's book, *The Signifying Monkey: A Theory of Afro-American Literary Criticism* (New York: Oxford University Press, 1982), among others, has taught us this. However difficult, however problematic, slaves could in important ways resist the master's language and redefine themselves as social beings.

26. For example, Vivien Green Fryd, *Art and Empire: The Politics of Ethnicity in the U.S. Capitol, 1815–1860* (New Haven: Yale University Press, 1992), details some of the specific reasons why references to slavery were suppressed in the decorative program of the U.S. Capitol.

27. Harriet Beecher Stowe, *Dred: A Tale of the Great Dismal Swamp* (Boston: Phillips, 1856), 1:240; quoted in Karen Sanchez-Eppler, "Bodily Bonds: The Intersecting Rhetorics of Feminism and Abolition," *Representations*, no. 24 (Fall 1988): 37. A similar trope operates in a much earlier attempt to ennoble the African, Aphra Behn's novel *Oroonoko* (1688); see Jordan, *White over Black*, 27–28.

28. Harriet Beecher Stowe, "Sojourner Truth, the Libyan Sibyl," *Atlantic Monthly* 11 (April 1863): 473.

29. Such a figure was more possible in European sculpture, though still rare. Victor van Hove's painted plasters of black male slaves, entitled *Esclave negre après la bastonnade* and *La vengeance* (1855), are sleekly heroic, if prostrate on the ground.

30. James C. Garman, "Viewing the Color Line through the Material Culture of Death," *Historical Archaeology* 28, no. 3 (1994): 74–93. Portrait images of anyone, white or black, were not common on New England gravestones, and these three examples were produced by an elite shop for presumably wealthy white masters.

31. There may have been some bas-reliefs (now lost) illustrating *Uncle Tom's Cabin* done perhaps in the 1850s by a black sculptor from New Orleans named Eugene Warburg, about whom little is known. See Samella Lewis, *Art: African American* (New York: Harcourt Brace Jovanovich, 1978), 30.

32. David H. Wallace, *John Rogers, the People's Sculptor* (Middletown, Conn.: Wesleyan University Press, 1967), 79–84.

33. William Dean Howells, "Question of Monuments," *Atlantic Monthly* 18 (May 1866): 647–48.

34. Cornel West, *Keeping Faith: Philosophy and Race in America* (New York: Routledge, 1993), 20. For a good recent survey of relevant literature, see Shelley Fisher Fishkin, "Interrogating 'Whiteness,' Complicating 'Blackness': Remapping American Culture," *American Quarterly* 47 (September 1995): 428–66.

35. Jordan, *White over Black*, 91–95; David R. Roediger, *Wages of Whiteness: Race and the Making of the American Working Class* (London: Verso, 1991), 133–63; Noel Ignatiev, *How the Irish Became White* (New York: Routledge, 1995).

36. The most notable essay in this direction is Albert Boime's *Art of Exclusion: Representing Blacks in the Nineteenth Century* (Washington, D.C.: Smithsonian Institution Press, 1990). I will have more to say about this work as my

argument comes more directly into contact with it. In general, the emerging literature on the "image of the black," while extraordinarily useful as historical exca-
vation, tends to segregate that imagery and reinforce its marginalization. In my
view, the image of the black cannot be separated from the image of the white.

CHAPTER TWO
EXPOSING SLAVERY

1. Hugh Honour, *The Image of the Black in Western Art IV: From the American Revolution to World War I. Part 1: From Slaves to Liberators* (Cambridge,
Mass.: Harvard University Press, 1989), 62–64.

2. The stooping image appears in M. M. Gravelot, *Iconologie par figures*
(Paris, 1791), 3:34. *Esclavage* is paired with *Servitude* and represents a more
extreme form of domination. A similar device appears in J. B. Boudard, *Iconologie* (Vienna, 1766; reprinted New York: Garland, 1976), 3:130. Ripa also distinguishes between *Servitu* and *Servitu Per Forza*, but illustrates only the former, as
a woman under a yoke; for the latter, he notes, chains are necessary. See Cesare
Ripa, *Iconologia*, ed. Piero Buscaroli (Milan: TEA, 1992), 404–5.

3. Quoted in Phillip Lapsansky, "Graphic Discord: Abolitionist and Antiabolitionist Images," in Jean Fagan Yellin and John C. Van Horne, eds., *The
Abolitionist Sisterhood: Women's Political Culture in Antebellum America* (Ithaca, N.Y.: Cornell University Press, 1994), 203.

4. Lydia M. Child, ed., *The Oasis* (Boston: Ticknor and Allen, 1834), 18. I am
indebted to MaryKate McMaster for drawing my attention to this passage.

5. Lapsansky, "Graphic Discord," 204–7. On its diffusion, largely by female
abolitionists, see Angelina Emily Grimké, "Appeal to the Christian Women of
the South," *Anti-Slavery Examiner* 1 (September 1836): 23; Jean Fagan Yellin,
Women and Sisters: The Antislavery Feminists in American Culture (New Haven:
Yale University Press, 1989), 3–23.

6. Lapsansky, "Graphic Discords," 202–13. See also Bernard Reilly Jr., "The
Art of the Antislavery Movement," in Donald M. Jacobs, ed., *Courage and Con-
science: Black and White Abolitionists in Boston* (Bloomington: Indiana University Press, 1993), 47–73.

7. Jean Fagan Yellin, "Caps and Chains: Hiram Powers' Statue of Liberty,"
American Quarterly 38 (Winter 1986): 798–826. See also Vivien Green Fryd,
"Hiram Powers's *America*: 'Triumphant As Liberty and in Unity,'" *American Art
Journal* 18, no. 2 (1986): 54–75.

8. Charles Avery, "Two Ornamental Bronzes from the Medicean Grand-
Ducal Workshop around 1600," *Burlington Magazine* 124 (July 1982): 428–30.
The tradition of the bound seated captive is familiar in ancient imagery, for exam-
ple in Roman statuettes of Ethiopian captives; see Jean Vercoutter, Jean Leclant,
Frank M. Snowden Jr., and Jehan Desanges, *The Image of the Black in Western
Art I: From the Pharoahs to the Fall of the Roman Empire* (Cambridge, Mass.:
Harvard University Press, 1976), 213. Other examples may be seen in Richard
Brilliant, *Gesture and Rank in Roman Art: The Use of Gesture to Denote Status
in Roman Sculpture and Coinage* (New Haven: Connecticut Academy of Arts and

Sciences, 1963). For the contemporary emblem of suffering ("Dolore"), see for example Cesare Ripa, *Iconologia* (Padua, 1611; reprinted New York: Garland, 1976), 125.

9. See for example the portrait of Maryland colonist Henry Darnall III by Justus Engelhardt Kuhn, circa 1710, reproduced in Guy C. McElroy, *Facing History: The Black Image in American Art, 1710–1940* (San Francisco: Bedford Arts, 1990), 3.

10. Lapsansky, "Graphic Discord," 216–30.

11. The "positive good" thesis as articulated by Calhoun appears in the *Congressional Globe*, 25th Congress, 2d Session, Appendix, January 10, 1838, 61–62. For more on proslavery thought in general, see Drew Gilpin Faust, ed., *The Ideology of Slavery: Proslavery Thought in the Antebellum South, 1830–1860* (Baton Rouge: Louisiana State University Press, 1981); Michael Banton, *Racial Theories* (Cambridge: Cambridge University Press, 1987); Paul Finkelman, ed., *Proslavery Thought, Ideology, and Politics* (New York: Garland, 1989).

12. "Slavery in the Southern States," *Southern Quarterly Review* 8 (October 1845): 317–60, quotation from p. 349.

13. On the universality of these slave stereotypes across cultures, see Orlando Patterson, *Slavery and Social Death: A Comparative Study* (Cambridge, Mass.: Harvard University Press, 1982), 96.

14. The statue was seen on exhibition by over 100,000 people in the late 1840s, and was exhibited to large crowds in the 1850s as well. See Richard P. Wunder, *Hiram Powers: Vermont Sculptor, 1805–1873*, 2 vols. (Newark: University of Delaware Press, 1991), 1:242–47.

15. As Yellin points out in *Women and Sisters*, Powers incorporated the motif of link chains even though he was aware that chains were not actually used in Turkish slave markets (p. 122). Chains were by now unavoidable since they had become the conventional sign of enslavement.

16. *Christian Inquirer* 1 (October 9, 1847): 207. For a discussion of the abolitionist response, see Vivien Green [Fryd], "Hiram Powers's *Greek Slave*: Emblem of Freedom," *American Art Journal* 14 (Autumn 1982): 31–39; Yellin, *Women and Sisters*, 99–124.

17. *The Complete Works of Elizabeth Barrett Browning*, ed. Charlotte Porter and Helen A. Clarke, 6 vols. (New York: Crowell, 1900), 3:178.

18. David Moltke-Hanson, ed., *Art in the Lives of South Carolinians: Nineteenth-Century Chapters* (Charleston: Carolina Art Association, 1979), RSa7, RSb5–7.

19. The *Greek Slave* was exhibited in Baltimore in 1848, in Louisville, Kentucky, and New Orleans in 1849, and in Augusta, Georgia, and Charleston and Columbia, South Carolina, in 1850–51; Wunder, *Hiram Powers*, 1:228–29, 235–37, 252.

20. Orville Dewey, "Powers' Statues," *Union Magazine of Literature and Art* 1 (October 1847): 160–61. For more discussion of this idealizing interpretation, see Joy S. Kasson, *Marble Queens and Captives: Women in Nineteenth-Century American Sculpture* (New Haven: Yale University Press, 1990), 50–63. Not everyone bought it, however: some were simply shocked; see Wunder, *Hiram Powers*, 1:232–33.

21. Quoted in Patterson, *Slavery and Social Death*, 13.

22. The allegory worked in two directions, more commonly to the then mainstream idea of woman as transcendent being, less commonly to the radical notion of woman as nothing but a slave to man; Yellin, *Women and Sisters*, 112.

23. Some contemporary observers actually criticized Powers for showing too little bone and muscle; Wunder, *Hiram Powers*, 1:239.

24. Patterson, *Slavery and Social Death*, 35–76.

25. For the active role of South Carolina in disseminating proslavery rhetoric, see for example *The Pro-slavery Argument* (1852; New York: Negro University Press, 1968), and Drew Gilpin Faust, *James Henry Hammond and the Old South: A Design for Mastery* (Baton Rouge: Louisiana State University Press, 1982).

26. The most important source on Brown is the biographical manuscript, consisting mostly of transcripts of letters to and from Brown, compiled by his nephew and adopted son Henry Kirke Bush-Brown, now in the Library of Congress, Washingon, D.C. (hereafter Brown Papers). Originals of some of the letters in the Brown Papers are in the Archives of American Art, Detroit, Michigan. Brown's views on slavery are most evident in correspondence with his abolitionist friend William Morris Davis, in the Brown Papers, 792–802, 831–32. The quotation is from p. 1357.

27. Brown to Daniel Huntington, December 24, 1852, quoted in Wayne Craven, "Henry Kirke Brown: His Search for an American Art in the 1840s," *American Art Journal* 4 (November 1972): 44–58, quotation from p. 48.

28. For example, as noted in chapter 1, Brown adapted the pose of the Apollo Belvedere for the bronze figurine of an Indian hunter. On a sketching trip in upstate New York, Brown referred to the Indian as "a poetic being, an ideal character"; Brown to Lydia Brown, September 16, 1848, in Brown Papers, 548–75.

29. For Brown's views on national sculpture, see his letter to M. C. Meigs of February 12, 1856, published in Charles E. Fairman, *Art and Artists of the Capitol of the United States of America* (Washington, D.C.: Government Printing Office, 1927), 191–92; and Brown's coauthored "Report of the United States Art Commission," February 22, 1860, Ex. Doc. No. 43, 36th Congress, 1st Session. See also Craven, "Henry Kirke Brown."

30. Brown Papers, 832–33f. Published in Vivien Green Fryd, *Art and Empire: The Politics of Ethnicity in the U.S. Capitol, 1815–1860* (New Haven: Yale University Press, 1992), 202.

31. This is how his friend William Morris Davis framed the enterprise, Brown Papers, 1356. For more on the historical context of the pediment commission, see Thomas P. Somma, The Apotheosis of Democracy, *1908–1916: The Pediment for the House Wing of the United States Capitol* (Newark: University of Delaware Press, 1995).

32. For Brown's description of the various figures, see the letter quoted in Fairman, *Art and Artsits of the Capitol*, 191–92.

33. Even the figure of Dolore in Ripa's *Iconologia* (Padua, 1611) is bound.

34. The conversation is reported in a fragment from Brown's notebook dated December 1855, transcribed in the Brown Papers, 826–826a.

35. The critique of Northern capitalism and its reliance on wage labor was a staple ingredient of the proslavery case; see Faust, *Ideology of Slavery*. A classic

interpretation of free-labor ideology is Eric Foner, *Free Soil, Free Labor, Free Men: The Ideology of the Republican Party before the Civil War* (New York: Oxford University Press, 1970).

36. On Brown's contact with South Carolina patrons in the 1840s, see Moltke-Hansen, *Art in the Lives of South Carolinians*, ARa6. In the late 1850s, Brown was actively seeking the commission for a statue of Calhoun in Charleston, South Carolina; see Brown Papers, 874, 896, 913, 939, and correspondence in 1858 in Henry Kirke Brown Papers, Archives of American Art.

37. *Art in the Lives of South Carolinians*, RSb4–8, RSa7.

38. Brown Papers, 1268–72, 1285b. *De Bow's Review* 4 (September 1860): 384. On art patronage in South Carolina, see Moltke-Hansen, *Art in the Lives of South Carolinians*. On the construction of the State House, see Mills Lane, *Architecture of the Old South: South Carolina* (Savannah, Ga.: Beehive Press, 1984), 247.

39. John R. Niernsee to Brown, April 2, 1859, Brown Papers, 1268.

40. William Morris Davis, "Heroism in Art," in Brown Papers, 1354–74, quotations from pp. 1357 and 1363. What little remains of the official archival record in Columbia is for the most part silent on Brown and the pediment. The official documents, if they existed at all, were probably destroyed in Sherman's sack of the capital in 1865.

41. Davis, "Heroism in Art," Brown Papers, 1364.

42. Brown Papers, 1268–1285d. The basic claim that Brown proposed the design and the slaveholder elite approved it is corroborated in correspondence from the architect of the State House, John R. Niernsee, who wrote Brown, March 10, 1860: "You have justified your reputation with General Jones [commissioner in charge of the building] and *all* who have seen what you have done and shewn them you intended to do . . . confirmed by the approval of such influential men *here*, as the Preston's, Hampton's, Manning's, Means' etc." [emphasis in original].

43. For identification of the allegories, see Brown Papers, 1282–83; letter from Johnson M. Mundy (Brown's studio assistant) to his sister, February 20, 1861, South Caroliniana Library.

44. Yellin, "Caps and Chains," 811. On Cruikshank's illustration, I am indebted to Janet McCall's unpublished paper "Conflicting Ideologies: Abolitionist Reform, the Erotic Body, and Social Order in the Carnegie's *Slave Market*."

45. Fryd, *Art and Empire*, 183–205.

46. Studying the ancient imagery of conquest or of daily life, it is hard to know when we are looking at slaves as opposed to indentured servants or free laborers or prisoners facing execution. Images of servants or laborers are sometimes labeled slaves in literature on ancient art, but T.E.J. Wiedemann points out that cues based on occupation or clothing or even racial difference are unreliable. See Wiedemann, *Slavery* (Oxford: Clarendon Press, 1987), 14–15. For a careful examination of the methodological problems involved in determining status, see Natalie Kampen, *Image and Status: Roman Working Women in Ostia* (Berlin: Mann, 1981). The problem is compounded by the fact that many intermediate categories between slavery and freedom existed in antiquity, categories that were actively suppressed in modern capitalist slave societies like America. For a fascinating account of the conventionalized image of the slave in Greek and Roman

theatrical masks and performance, see David Wiles, *The Masks of Menander: Sign and Meaning in Greek and Roman Performance* (Cambridge: Cambridge University Press, 1991).

47. "Agricultural Prospects of South-Carolina," *Southern Quarterly Review* 8 (July 1845): 118–47, esp. 127; T. A. Richards, "The Rice Lands of the South," *Harper's New Monthly Magazine* 19 (November 1859): 721–38; David O. Whitten, "American Rice Cultivation: A Tercentenary Critique," *Southern Studies* 21 (Spring 1982): 5–19; Charles Joyner, *Down by the Riverside: A South Carolina Slave Community* (Urbana: University of Illinois Press, 1984), 33–37.

48. Ulrich Phillips, *Life and Labor in the Old South* (1929; Boston: Little, Brown, 1963), 198–201; Kenneth Stampp, *The Peculiar Institution: Slavery in the Ante-Bellum South* (New York: Vintage Books, 1956), 327–31; Stanley M. Elkins, *Slavery: A Problem in American Institutional and Intellectual Life* (Chicago: University of Chicago Press, 1959), 82. On this as a cross-cultural phenomenon, see Patterson, *Slavery and Social Death*, 96.

49. *Harper's Weekly* 4 (December 1, 1860): 757.

50. Patterson, *Slavery and Social Death*, 483; Stampp, *Peculiar Institution*, 31–32; Ira Berlin, *Slaves without Masters* (New York: Pantheon Books, 1975), 137.

51. A good survey of the extant imagery of slave labor can be found in *Before Freedom Came: African-American Life in the Antebellum South* (Richmond, Va.: Museum of the Confederacy, 1991). For a more detailed discussion of one artist's imagery, see Sarah Burns, "Images of Slavery: George Fuller's Depictions of the Antebellum South," *American Art Journal* 15 (Summer 1983): 35–60.

52. Georg Wilhelm Friedrich Hegel, *The Phenomenology of Mind*, trans. J. B. Baillie (London: George Allen & Unwin, 1931), 239. For an excellent analysis, see Patterson, *Slavery and Social Death*, 97–100.

53. Ira Berlin and Phillip D. Morgan, eds., *Cultivation and Culture: Labor and the Shaping of Slave Life in the Americas* (Charlottesville: University Press of Virginia, 1993), 1–2. See also L. McDonnell, "Work, Culture, and Society in the Slave South, 1790–1861," in Ted Ownby, ed., *Black and White Cultural Interaction* 125–47.

54. W.L.G. Smith, *Life at the South, or Uncle Tom's Cabin As It Is in the Antebellum South* (Jackson: University Press of Mississippi, 1993) (Buffalo: George H. Derby, 1852), 30–40; the illustration appears opposite p. 38.

55. Richards, "Rice Lands of the South." A fascinating precursor of this article is T. B. Thorpe, "Cotton and Its Cultivation," *Harper's New Monthly Magazine* 8 (March 1854): 447–63. The article also includes images of slaves at work and also sets that imagery within a picturesque, horticultural context. One image shows the field "hands" in the picking season returning with baskets on their heads; the text reports that "they move along in the dim twilight of a winter day with the quietness of spirits rather than human beings" (p. 456). Like Richards's text, this one is mostly silent on slavery (the preferred term for laborer is "hand" or "Negro"), except toward the end when relations between masters and slaves are openly discussed, in a positive light. For more discussion, see Karin L. Zipf, "Imagining a Cotton South: Illustrations from New York's Popular Press, 1854–1888," *Georgia Historical Quarterly* 80 (Summer 1996): 358–74.

56. Wiedemann, *Slavery*, 3–4.

57. McDonnell, "Work, Culture, and Society in the Slave South, 1790–1861," 136–37; Joyner, *Down by the Riverside*, 43–45.

58. Brown Papers, 1273–1316, 1331–32, 1359–67.

59. Davis, "Heroism in Art," Brown Papers, 1370.

60. Ibid., 1370–71. One of the ironies here is that proslavery apologists who were in step with the pediment's program, like T. B. Thorpe, author of the *Harper's* 1854 article on cotton cultivation, could actually celebrate the black laborer's skill, while abolitionists felt compelled to deride it; see Thorpe, "Cotton and Its Cultivation," 453.

61. A passage in the *Freedmen's Record* (the organ of the New England Freedmen's Aid Society), 1 (March 1865): 1, is representative: "The freedman compared with the educated white man is a child needing instruction and guidance. . . . He must unlearn much: not only the vices of slavery, but its thriftlessness and improvidence. He must unlearn not only old ideas that freedom from work is a blessing; but also old ways of doing work with clumsy implements, and sluggish effort, not caring to do it better."

62. The "modernization" of slavery, as some envisaged it, involved precisely such a drastic clarification of the slave's status, a transformation of slavery itself into a kind of industrial apartheid; see Bertram Wyatt-Brown, "Modernizing Southern Slavery: The Proslavery Argument Reinterpreted," in Finkelman, *Proslavery Thought*, 485–507.

63. Clemson to Brown, December 19, 1860, Mrs. Clemson to Mrs. Brown, April 28, 1861, Robert W. Gibbes to Brown, May 13, 1861, Brown to Davis, July 14, 1861, August 7, 1861; Brown Papers, 1304, 1333, 1343–47. On the destruction of Columbia and Brown's studio, see William Gilmore Simms, *The Sack and Destruction of the City of Columbia, S.C.* (Atlanta: Oglethorpe University Press, 1937), 76–79.

64. Brown Papers, 2379–80.

Chapter Three
Imagining Emancipation

1. James M. McPherson, *Battle Cry of Freedom: The Civil War Era* (New York: Oxford University Press, 1988), 557–59. For an interesting selection of contemporary documents relating to the proclamation and its significance, see Ira Berlin, ed., *Free at Last* (New York: New Press, 1992), 95–129, and C. Peter Ripley, ed., *Witness for Freedom: African-American Voices on Race, Slavery, and Emancipation* (Chapel Hill: University of North Carolina Press, 1993), 221–31.

2. The standard source on Ward's work is Lewis I. Sharp, *John Quincy Adams Ward: Dean of American Sculpture* (Newark: University of Delaware Press, 1985).

3. *Independent*, June 11, 1863, p. 6.

4. Ibid. See also *New York Times*, May 3, 1863, p. 5, and June 24, 1863, p. 2. A more comprehensive selection of press clippings can be found in the John Quincy Adams Ward Scrapbook (hereafter Ward Scrapbook) in the Ward Papers, Albany Institute of History and Art, Albany, N.Y.; see especially New York *Evening Post*, November 3, 1865.

5. James Jackson Jarves, *The Art-Idea* (1864; Cambridge, Mass.: Belknap Press, Harvard University Press, 1960), 225–26. See also *Independent*, June 11, 1863.

6. The bronze probably appeared in 1864, judging from a clipping which announces its arrival in Goupil's gallery. "For more than a year we have patiently awaited its reproduction in some permanent material"; unidentified clipping in Ward Scrapbook. For the various bronze versions of the work, see Sharp, *John Quincy Adams Ward*, 154–56.

7. *New York Times*, June 24, 1863, p. 2. An unidentified newspaper clipping from the same period found in the Ward Scrapbook calls the figure "a very 'likely' contraband"; see also the fan letter to Ward from A. M. Powell, April 8, 1863, also in the Ward Papers. Most reviewers placed the figure in some kind of fugitive narrative.

For more on the "contrabands," see McPherson, *Battle Cry of Freedom*, 354–58, 494–510.

8. Ward to J. R. Lambdin, April 2, 1863, in Albert Rosenthal Papers, Archives of American Art, Roll D34, frame 1302, Detroit, Michigan.

9. For example, at the same National Academy of Design exhibition in the spring of 1863 the academic painter Henry Peters Gray showed his *America in 1862*, which one critic described as follows: "a kneeling manly figure of a slave looks up into the eyes of the genius of America, who breaks his chains with one hand and offers him a sword with the other." See *Harper's Weekly* 7 (May 2, 1863): 274.

The Library of Congress holds several prints showing Lincoln raising a kneeling slave, for example, the print entitled *Emancipation of the Slaves* by J. Waeshle published in Philadelphia and a Currier and Ives image entitled *Freedom to Slaves*, circa 1863 (fig. 3.2).

10. Sharp, *John Quincy Adams Ward*, 42.

11. Ward traveled to Georgia before the war to do a portrait of Alexander H. Stephens, later to be vice-president of the Confederacy; there Ward had the "opportunity to study Southern types" according to J. Walker McSpadden, *Famous Sculptors of America* (New York: Dodd, Mead, 1927), 10–11. McSpadden also claims that Ward's first experiment in sculpture was "to fashion [in clay] a negro's head, giving it the features of an old slave who lived in the vicinity [Ohio in the 1840s]."

12. For example, in the illustrations of popular news magazines: "A Typical Negro," *Harper's Weekly* 7 (July 4, 1863): 429. In the published notices of runaway slaves, identifying scars and brands figured routinely. These notices were in turn publicized by abolitionists to demonstrate the physical cruelty of slavery; see, for example, Lydia Maria Child, *The Patriarchal Institution As Described by Members of Its Own Family* (New York: American Anti-Slavery Society, 1860).

13. "An American Sculptor," *Harpers New Monthly Magazine* 57 (June 1878): 66.

14. *Evening Post*, November 3, 1865, clipping in Ward Scrapbook. On the before-and-after images, see "A Typical Negro," and William A. Gladstone, *United States Colored Troops, 1863–1867* (Gettysburg, Pa.: Thomas Publications, 1990), 44.

15. It is interesting to note here that both of Ward's types—seated black man and Indian with dog—were represented in the pediment design made by Henry Kirke Brown in the 1850s when Ward was Brown's principal studio assistant; see chapter 2.

16. William Dean Howells, "Question of Monuments," *Atlantic Monthly* 18 (May 1866): 646–49, esp. 647.

17. In using the terms "drama" and "indeterminacy," I am evoking concepts made familiar by Victor Turner; see, for example, "Social Drama and Stories about Them," *Critical Inquiry* 7 (Autumn 1980): 141–68.

18. Jan M. Seidler, "A Critical Reappraisal of the Career of William Wetmore Story (1819–1895), American Sculptor and Man of Letters" (Ph.D. diss., Boston University, 1985), 502–22. Story was an expatriate from Boston living in Rome, and his *Libyan Sibyl* was first exhibited in 1862 in London. The work became well known in the United States through critical remark and reproductions in print. On Whitney's piece, see Elizabeth Rogers Payne, "Anne Whitney: Art and Social Justice," *Massachusetts Review* 12 (Spring 1971): 245–60; Whitney was actually criticized by her friend Thomas Wentworth Higginson for avoiding racial signifiers.

19. Harriet Beecher Stowe, "Sojourner Truth and the Libyan Sibyl," *Atlantic Monthly* 11 (April 1863): 473–81. At least one critic actually compared the *Freedman* to the *Libyan Sibyl* and found Story's piece wanting because it "dodges" the reality of Truth herself, while Ward succeeded in "rendering all"; unidentified clipping in Ward Scrapbook.

20. Seidler, "A Critical Reappraisal of the Career of William Wetmore Story," 504.

21. *Evening Post*, November 3, 1865, clipping in Ward Scrapbook.

22. *Independent*, June 11, 1863, p. 6. See also *New York Times*, June 24, 1863, p. 2, and miscellaneous unidentified clippings in Ward Scrapbook.

23. In general, African Americans in New York City at this time were barred from the institutions and events of high culture; see George E. Walker, *The Afro-American in New York City, 1827–1860* (New York: Garland, 1993), 24–26.

24. Michael Hatt, " 'Making a Man of Him': Masculinity and the Black Body in Mid-Nineteenth-Century American Sculpture," *Oxford Art Journal* 15 (1992): 21–35, quotation from p. 31. The paradox is not exactly resolved, he argues, but rather defused or displaced by the erotic objectification of the black male body. Although his argument leans heavily on psychoanalytical theory, it does have a historical dimension, which has to do with his reading of the changing status of the black body in white society before and after emancipation. While slavery lasted, he claims, the black body was "anthropological curiousity, animal, or chattel" and thereby available for inspection to the mastering white gaze; but

"after emancipation, a new logic of the spectacle was needed, a new codification of the body and its audiences to allow scrutiny and visual discipline of the black, but one which would mitigate the dangerous, potentially erotic allure of gleaming black muscles. . . . It is the very medium of public sculpture that provided the answer. The sculpted body of bronze or marble was an essential means of exposing and classifying the male form without at the same time exposing the flesh, its weaknessess and its pleasures." There are several problems with Hatt's argument, interesting as it is. On an empirical level, given how rarely the black male body appeared in public sculpture (Hatt himself cites only two examples—the *Freedman*, which was never erected in public, and Ball's *Emancipation*), it could hardly be considered a historically effective or even commonly experienced "answer" to the problem of the black body. The black body never did become a spectacle in public sculpture, even after emancipation; indeed, its very failure to become spectacular must be explained. On a theoretical level, his argument assumes that public sculpture must inevitably serve the demands of oppression. He forecloses from the start even the possibility of a genuinely emancipating work, one that did not simply serve to reinforce "the visual discipline of the black."

25. Hatt is right, I think, to emphasize this issue, though my analysis differs significantly from his.

26. *Evening Post*, November 3, 1865, and unidentified clipping [1863], both in Ward Scrapbook.

27. *New York Times*, May 3, 1863, p. 5.

28. *Evening Post*, November 3, 1865, in Ward Scrapbook.

29. See, for example, Alexander H. Everett, "Greenough's Statue of Washington," in Henry T. Tuckeremna, ed., *A Memorial of Horatio Greenough* 1853; (New York: Benjamin Blom, 1968), 215–25.

30. The cast owned by the Metropolitan Museum of Art in New York, for example, has clearly been rubbed by human hands; this has changed the patina and the modeling in subtle but easily visible ways. One might draw a disturbing analogy here between the possessor of the sculpture, who probes the object with hands and eyes, and the slaveowners and traders who inspected the black body in similar ways if not for similar reasons. I would argue, however, that the owner's aesthetic engagement with the bronze remains qualitatively different from the slaveholder's engagement with chattel and more properly belongs to the old and venerated custom of handling small bronzes—be they gods, humans, or animals.

31. Lynda Roscoe Hartigan, *Sharing Traditions: Five Black Artists in Nineteenth-Century America* (Washington, D.C.: Smithsonian Institution Press, 1985), 85–98. See also James A. Porter, "Versatile Interests of the Early Negro Artist: A Neglected Chapter of American Art History," *Art in America* 24 (January 1936): 16–27.

32. Hartigan, *Sharing Traditions*, 93.

33. See letters reproduced in James A. Porter, *Modern Negro Art* (Washington, D.C.: Howard University Press, 1992), 162–63; and *Boston Daily Evening Transcript*, October 18, 1869, p. 2, and October 19, 1869, p. 4, both clippings kindly supplied by Merl M. Moore Jr. from his personal archive.

34. Jarves, *The Art-Idea*, 225–26; Henry Tuckerman, *Book of the Artists* (New York: G. P. Putnam & Son, 1867), 582. Tuckerman attributes this suggestion to Jarves's *Art-Idea* but it does not appear there.

35. *Atlantic Monthly* 18 (May 1866): 648.

36. Charles de Kay, "Ward and His Art," *New York Tribune*, March 11, 1994, clipping, in John Quincy Adams Ward Scrapbook, New York Historical Society, New York.

37. Joseph T. Wilson, *Black Phalanx* (1890; New York: Arno Press, 1968), 90.

38. Thomas F. Paige, ed., *Twenty-two Years of Freedom: An Account of the Emancipation Celebration by the Freedmen of Norfolk, Virginia, and Vicinity on January 1, 1885* (Norfolk: Barron's Presses, 1885), 8–15.

39. "National Lincoln Monument, Address to the Public," circular dated January 24, 1868, in Vinnie Ream Hoxie Papers, Library of Congress, Washington, D.C.; "National Lincoln Monument," circular dated May 24, 1865, in NLMA Letters and Papers, Illinois State Historical Library, Springfield, Illinois. For more on this point, see Kirk Savage, "Race, Memory, and Identity: The National Monuments of the Union and the Confederacy" (Ph.D. diss., University of California, Berkeley, 1990).

40. Charles Eliot Norton, "Something about Monuments," *Nation* 1 (August 3, 1865): 154–56; Howells, "Question of Monuments," 649.

41. Henry Kirke Brown to James R. Wallace [Jan. 1866?], in Brown Papers, 1768, Library of Congress, Washington, D.C.

42. Note especially Chantrey's standing statue of Washington in Boston and Canova's destroyed seated statue in Raleigh, North Carolina.

43. Marianna Griswold van Rensselaer, "Saint Gaudens's Lincoln," *Century* 35 (November 1887): 37–39, quotation from p. 37.

44. See Savage, "Race, Memory, and Identity," 49–51.

45. See, for example, *New York Times*, July 8, 1865, p. 4, and Howells, "Question of Monuments," 647.

46. "A Visit to Avery's Tomb," *Christian Recorder*, January 16, 1869, p. 1. The monument does not appear in Freeman Henry Morris Murray's otherwise exhaustive catalog *Emancipation and the Freed in American Sculpture: A Study in Interpretation* (Washington, D.C.: Murray Brothers, 1916), or in any later surveys of black landmarks. For the information that follows, I am indebted to Henry Pisciotta's unpublished paper, "The Avery Memorial: Sculpting a New Political Party on the Brink of the Civil War."

47. In a brief notice appearing in the *Scientific American* in December 1859, the hero and his monument were represented as procolonization. That interpretation was promptly repudiated by the monument's sponsors and a "correction" was published in the *Pittsburgh Daily Dispatch* on December 6. More on this story appears in Pisciotta, "The Avery Memorial."

48. John Rogers to Charles Stillé, December 18, 1866, in Charles Stillé Papers, Historical Society of Pennsylvania, Philadelphia (hereafter Stillé Papers). The letter is quoted in Wayne Craven, "Abraham Lincoln," in Fairmount Park Art Association, *Sculpture of a City: Philadelphia's Treasures in Bronze and Stone* (New York: Walker, 1974), 47–48.

49. The angle of the photograph hides Lincoln's left hand from view; it may in fact be holding something suggestive of the Emancipation Proclamation.

50. Orlando Patterson, *Slavery and Social Death: A Comparative Study* (Cambridge, Mass.: Harvard University Press), 241–46.

51. A. M. Duff, *Freedmen in the Early Roman Empire* (New York: Barnes and Noble, 1958), 23–24. A Roman relief that illustrates the ceremony does survive; see *Les antiquités égyptiennes, grecques, etrusques, romaines et gallo-romaines du Musée de Mariemont* (Brussels: Editions de la Librarie Encyclopedique, 1952), 138.

52. *Freedmen's Record* 1 (March 1865): 32.

53. The design Rogers proposed had a third figure, a demon representing the rebellion, according to the letter he sent Charles Stillé, March 25, 1867, Stillé Papers. Other plaster models relating to this commission once existed in the University of Michigan Museum of Art, but have long since been destroyed and no archival photographs remain to document them. See the catalog in Millard F. Rogers Jr., *Randolph Rogers: American Sculptor in Rome* (Amherst: University of Massachusetts Press, 1971) 209.

54. Letter from Ball to Charles Stillé, January 18, 1867, Stillé Papers. Photos and a sketch of the model also survive in the Stillé Papers.

55. In another version made in the same time period, Ball had Lincoln actually holding the Emancipation Proclamation; photographs of this alternative model survive in the Stillé Papers. Ball returned to this solution when he was eventually commissioned to enlarge the group as an outdoor monument (see chapter 4).

56. Thomas Ball, *My Three Score Years and Ten* (Boston: Roberts Brothers, 1891), 253.

57. For more on the *Arrotino*, see Francis Haskell and Nicholas Penny, *Taste and the Antique: The Lure of Classical Sculpture, 1500–1900* (New Haven: Yale University Press, 1981), 154–56; and Anne Weis, *The Hanging Marsyas and Its Copies: Roman Innovations in a Hellenistic Sculptural Tradition* (Rome: G. Bretschneider, 1992), 46–55.

Although the *Arrotino* is now identified as an executioner waiting to flay Marsyas, the figure still appears on the cover of a modern textbook on slavery, Kenneth Hughes, *Slavery* (London: George Allen & Unwin, 1975).

58. Wayne Craven is the only other scholar to have written about the pose in depth, and his description comes close to mine: "[Ball's] image was not to represent one of jubilant triumph. Rather, the 'feel' of it was to be one of hesitancy and uncertainty, for the condition of freedom was so unfamiliar to this Black man that only slowly was the full impact of the Emancipation Proclamation to dawn upon him." Wayne Craven, "Thomas Ball and the Emancipation Group," *Elvehjem Art Center Bulletin* (1976–77): 43–51, quotation from p. 45.

59. New York *Evening Post*, September 18, 1866, p. 2; Boston *Daily Evening Transcript*, March 28, 1867, p. 2. Both clippings are from Merl Moore's personal archive, Falls Church, Virginia.

60. William Greenleaf Eliot, *The Story of Archer Alexander: From Slavery to Freedom* (Boston: Cupples, Upham and Company, 1885), 14. As we shall see, Eliot asked Ball to remodel the facial features after photographs of Alexander, in order to introduce "the representative form of a negro." Thus the solution was to alter the face, not the body.

61. Ball, *My Three Score Years and Ten*, 253.

62. Henry Kirke Brown to his wife, April 30, 1867, Brown Papers, 1840.

63. Brown Papers, 1856a.

64. Quoted in Carmine A. Prioli, " 'Wonder Girl from the West': Vinnie Ream and the Congressional Statue of Abraham Lincoln," *Journal of American Culture* 12 (Winter 1989): 1–20, quotation from p. 12. This interpretation was idly reprinted in the Washington newspapers—*National Intelligencer*, February 22, 1869, and *Washington Evening Star*, January, 7, 1871, p. 1—and in many other

unidentified papers clipped and preserved in the Vinnie Ream Hoxie Scrapbooks, Library of Congress.

65. Pencil draft of letter sent to "several American artists in Europe," December 15, 1866, in Stillé Papers.

66. Hiram Powers to Charles Stillé, January 9, 1867, in Stillé Papers. In addition to the press notices already mentioned, there are clippings from the Boston *Daily Evening Transcript*, January 11, 1866, p. 2; September 20, 1866, p. 4; November 19, 1866, p. 2; New York *Evening Post*, April 4, 1867, p. 2; all in the Merl Moore archive.

67. Draft of letter from Charles Stillé to Randolph Rogers, May 6, 1867, in Stillé Papers.

68. Ibid.

69. Nathaniel B. Brown to Charles Stillé, April 11, 1868, in Stillé Papers.

70. Rogers, *Randolph Rogers*, 101–7. Also in 1866, Hammatt Billings included a bas-relief illustrating the theme in his proposed design for a monument to Boston soldiers, but ultimately the design was rejected. My thanks to Thomas J. Brown for sharing his paper "Civil War Monuments of New England," delivered at the 1996 meeting of the Organization of American Historians in Chicago.

71. Rogers's letter of November 5, 1866, describes the four reliefs as "representing War, Victory, Peace, and History"; the letter was published in the appendix of *Report of the Committee on a Monument to the Rhode Island Soldiers and Sailors Who Perished in Suppressing the Rebellion, Made to the General Assembly, at Its January Session, 1867*, Public Document no. 4 (Providence, 1867), located in the Soldiers and Sailors Monument Scrapbook, Rhode Island Historical Society, Providence (hereafter Providence Scrapbook). The new description as emancipation first appears in the *Providence Journal*, June 24, 1870, clipping in Providence Scrapbook. The photograph of the plaster model is also preserved in this scrapbook.

72. Robert Freeman and Vivienne Lasky, *Hidden Treasure: Public Sculpture in Providence* (Providence: Rhode Island Bicentennial Foundation, 1980), 41.

73. Rogers, *Randolph Rogers*, 108–12.

74. "Negro Shrines," *Ebony* 10 (July 1955): 42–45; "Monuments and Landmarks," *Ebony* (18 (September 1863): 109.

75. Hugh Honour, *The Image of the Black in Western Art IV: From the American Revolution to World War I. Part 1: From Slaves to Liberators* (Cambridge, Mass.: Harvard University Press, 1989), 256–58; *Frank Leslie's Historical Registrar of the United States Centennial Exposition 1876* (New York: Frank Leslie's, 1877), 133, 162.

CHAPTER FOUR
FREEDOM'S MEMORIAL

1. *Final Report of the Western Sanitary Commission* (St. Louis: R. P. Studley & Co., 1866), 131. The origin story is told in the *Final Report*, 130–38. The details about local response in Ohio are given in a newspaper report, "Proposed Monuments by Colored Citizens," in the *Cleveland Daily Leader*, October 10,

1865, this reference kindly supplied by William and Aimee Lee Cheek. The commission's version of the story says nothing about this early fund raising; its story is of a single five-dollar seed blossoming through white patronage. The account published by the abolitionist newspaper the *Independent* left out the mediating role played by the former master and had the "old freedwoman" giving her contribution directly to "one of our generals"; see "A National Monument," *Independent*, December 27, 1866, p. 1.

2. "Freedom's Memorial," undated circular, circa 1865, in St. Louis Sanitation Papers, Missouri Historical Society, St. Louis. It is worth noting that, in the actual letter from Scott's former master (*Final Report*, 132–33), he quotes her rather differently: "The colored people have lost their best friend on earth; Mr. Lincoln was our best friend, and I will give five dollars of my wages towards erecting a monument to his memory."

3. Letter from James Yeatman to Rev. Hawkins, in *National Freedman* 1 (October 15, 1865): 304; *Final Report*, 131, 134–38.

4. "Freedom's Memorial," *National Freedman* 1 (August 15, 1865): 231.

5. "Freedmen's Monument to Lincoln," circular in Harriet Hosmer Collection (unprocessed papers), Schlesinger Library, Radcliffe College, Cambridge, Mass. (hereafter Hosmer Collection). For more on Langston's fund-raising activities, see *Missouri Daily Democrat*, February 7, 1866; (Oberlin, Ohio) *Lorrain County News*, February 21, 1866; Nashville *Colored Tennessean*, March 31, 1866; Cincinatti *Gazette*, March 26, 1866; *Lorrain County News*, April 25, 1866. Many thanks to William and Aimee Lee Cheek for supplying me with these references.

6. Douglass's sentiments appear in a letter published in the *Anglo-African*, September 3, 1865, p. 1. The phrase of Langston's appears in his autobiography, John Mercer Langston, *From the Virginia Plantation to the National Capitol* (Hartford, Conn.: American Publishing Co., 1894), 336. During the fund-raising campaign he was quoted as saying, "Show the world we appreciate the fact that Lincoln was our emancipator," Cincinatti *Gazette*, March 26, 1866.

7. "Freedom's Memorial," St. Louis Sanitation Papers, Missouri Historical Society.

8. William E. Parrish, "The Western Sanitary Commission," *Civil War History* 36 (March 1990): 17–35.

9. His speech entitled "Higher-Law Doctrine," delivered in St. Louis January, 27, 1861, advocated gradual abolition; after war broke out he shifted his stance and argued for immediate abolition in Missouri, but he still maintained in a speech of 1862 that "a more gradual and peaceful method would have been far better for the enslaved race." See Charlotte Eliot scrapbook in William Greenleaf Eliot Papers, Washington University, St. Louis; and *A Discourse Delivered before the Members of the "Old Guard" of St. Louis* (St. Louis: E. P. Studley & Co., 1862), 20.

10. Dolly Sherwood, *Harriet Hosmer: American Sculptor, 1830–1908* (Columbia: University of Missouri Press, 1992), 25, 37, 244–53, 274.

11. *Celebration by the Colored People's Educational Monument Association in Memory of Abraham Lincoln on the Fourth of July, 1865 in the Presidential Grounds* (Washington, D.C.: McGill & Witherow, Printers, 1865). Their fund-raising broadside is preserved in the National Archives, Washington, D.C.,

Microfilm M371 (Records of the Commissioner of Public Buildings and Grounds), reel 27, frame 331. This association went by several names, one of which was the National Lincoln Monument Association.

12. *Anglo-African*, September 3, 1865, p. 1.

13. *Anglo-African*, October 21, 1865, p. 1. See also September 16, p. 2; October 7, p. 1; November 4, p. 1; November 18, p. 1. For background on the dispute between Douglass and Garnet, see Sterling Stuckey, "A Last Stern Struggle: Henry Highland Garnet and Liberation Theory," in *Going through the Storm: The Influence of African American Art in History* (New York: Oxford University Press, 1994), 103–19. For a broader overview of Douglass's efforts to shape the memory and meaning of the Civil War era, see David W. Blight, *Frederick Douglass's Civil War: Keeping Faith in Jubilee* (Baton Rouge: Louisiana State University Press, 1989).

14. Among the many fund-raising appeals issued by the Springfield association was one addressed to "the colored population of our country"; see National Lincoln Monument Association (NLMA) Minutes, 3, Illinois State Historical Library, Springfield, Illinois. The association had at least one agent fund-raising in African American communities; see letters from agent Morrill, July 26, 1865, and July 31, 1865, in NLMA Letters and Papers. See also the letter from Colonel Clark E. Carr to Governor Oglesby, August 11, 1865, on the wish "either to build a monument by themselves or some particular portion of the monument." On the soldiers' contributions, see John Carroll Power, *Abraham Lincoln, His Life, Public Services, Death and Great Funeral Cortege, with a History and Description of the National Lincoln Monument* (Chicago: H. W. Rokker, 1889), 263.

15. "Freedmen's Monument to Lincoln," Hosmer Collection.

16. "Freedmen's Monument to Abraham Lincoln," *Freedmen's Record* 3 (January 1867): 2–3. *Harper's New Monthly Magazine* 34 (February 1867): 389–90 and (March 1867): 804.

17. The photographs and stereo are preserved in a compilation made by Joseph Leo Curran Jr., ed., "Harriet Goodhue Hosmer: Collected Sources," 5a: 31–33, Watertown Free Library, Watertown, Massachusetts; London *Art-Journal* 7 (January 1, 1868): 8.

18. Hosmer's description of the model is included in "Freedmen's Monument to Lincoln," Hosmer Collection.

19. Quoted in Eric Foner, *Reconstruction: America's Unfinished Revolution, 1863–1877* (New York: Harper & Row, 1988), 8.

20. General Howell Cobb, quoted in Leon F. Litwack, *Been in the Storm So Long: The Aftermath of Slavery* (New York: Vintage Books, 1979), 43.

21. Sargent Prince Rivers, quoted in ibid. 64.

22. Ibid., 96–103, 268–70.

23. For examples see William A. Gladstone, *United States Colored Troops, 1863–1867* (Gettysburg, Pa.: Thomas Publications, 1990), 44, 47; and *Harper's Weekly*, July 4, 1863, p. 429, and July 2, 1864, pp. 422–28.

24. Thomas Wentworth Higginson, *Army Life in a Black Regiment* (1870; East Lansing: Michigan State University Press, 1960), 201.

25. "Freedmen's Monument to Lincoln," Hosmer Collection.

26. *Independent*, December 27, 1866, p. 1; "Freedmen's Monument to Abra-

ham Lincoln," *Freedmen's Record* 3 (January 1867): 2; *Harper's New Monthly Magazine* 34 (February 1867): 389–90.

27. Letter from Harriet Hosmer to James Yeatman, included in his letter to Governor Oglesby, August 18, 1868, NLMA Letters and Papers.

28. The negotiations between the two groups in the summer of 1868 are documented in letters from James Yeatman and Wayman Crow, NLMA Letters and Papers. Bellows's letter to Governor Oglesby, dated July 27, 1868, also appears here. Hosmer's role in the scheme is described in Sherwood, *Harriet Hosmer*, 274–92.

29. For an overview of the competition, see William J. Hosking, "Lincoln's Tomb: Designs Submitted and Final Selection," *Journal of the Illinois State Historical Society* 50 (Spring 1957): 51–61. The surviving documents appear in the NLMA Letters and Papers.

30. The other surviving designs are by Larkin Mead, the winner, and by Vinnie Ream. Hers is preserved in the Prints and Drawing Division, Library of Congress, Washington, D.C.

31. "Description of the Design for Lincoln Monument, As Proposed by C. G. Volk, Quincy, Illinois"; undated notes on the board's meeting with competing artists; both in NLMA Letters and Papers.

32. Letter from A. E. Harnische, August 25, 1868, in NLMA Letters and Papers.

33. Harnische's proposal did not include a vault for Lincoln's remains, which may also explain its failure to get votes.

34. The records of this association do not survive, but its activities are documented in several pamphlets published by the association and in contemporary newspaper accounts. Some notations of correspondence and subscriptions received do survive in Record Group 50 (Treasurer), Register of Letters Received by the Treasurer of the United States, National Archives.

35. *Congressional Globe*, March 26, 1867, pp. 345–46.

36. *National Lincoln Monument Association* (Washington, D.C.: Great Republic Office, 1867), 3.

37. It is hard to determine how much involvement Douglass actually had with the project. Nothing about the monument seems to survive in his voluminous personal papers. By 1870, however, some of the association's publicity materials were being printed from the offices of his newspaper, the *New National Era*. The newspaper itself does not seem to have given much attention to the monument campaign.

38. *Anglo-African*, November 4, 1865, p. 1.

39. *National Lincoln Monument Association: Organization and Design . . .* (Washington, D.C.: New National Era, 1870), 8–11. A letter from James Yeatman of the Western Sanitary Commission to Jesse Dubois of the Springfield association, February 3, 1871, NLMA Letters and Papers, confirms the details of the arrangement.

40. The stereo is in the Prints and Photographs Division, Library of Congress.

41. *New York Tribune*, December 10, 1863, p. 5. Quoted in part by Vivien Green Fryd, *Art and Empire: The Politics of Ethnicity in the U.S. Capitol, 1815–1860* (New Haven: Yale University Press, 1992), 200. The most complete source

on Mills is still Rosemary Hopkins, "Clark Mills: The First Native American Sculptor" (Master's thesis, University of Maryland, 1966). See also Michael Edward Shapiro, *Bronze Casting and American Sculpture, 1850–1900* (Newark: University of Delaware Press, 1985), 34–44. My thanks to Dr. Shapiro for lending me his informative files on Mills.

42. *Washington Star,* March 22, 1865, p. 1, and March 23, 1865, p. 2; *New York Times,* March 25, 1865, p. 2. The informer's accusation appears in a letter from John L. Lake to C. A. Dana, assistant secretary of war, March 28, 1865, National Archives, Microfilm M371, Reel 27, frame 264. The commissioner of public buildings, Benjamin B. French, wrote back to Dana on April 5, 1865, reporting that Mills would lose his studio; Microfilm M371, reel 7, frames 541–42.

43. Stephen Douglas's oration is in *Oration of the Hon. Stephen A. Douglas on the Inauguration of the Jackson Statue* (Washington, D.C.: Lemuel Towers, 1853), 5–6. Henry Bellows defended Mills in similar terms despite his acknowledgment that it was "the fashion" to deprecate the sculptor; Henry W. Bellows, "The National Lincoln Monument," *Old and New* 1 (January 1870): 9–12, esp. 12. Perhaps the most wicked deprecation came from Nathaniel Hawthorne, who wrote that in the history of sculpture there were "the two inclusive extremes of Phidias and Clark Mills"; see *Passages from the French and Italian Note-books* (Boston: Riverside, 1883), 306. For other criticism of Mills, see, for example, James Jackson Jarves, *Art-Hints: Architecture, Sculpture, and Painting* (New York: Harper and Brothers, 1855), 308–9; Henry James, *William Wetmore Story and His Friends* (New York: Kennedy Galleries, 1969), 2:48; and various magazine and newspaper clippings in the Mills file at the Office of the Architect of the Capitol, Washington, D.C. Sometimes even the same periodical voiced both the opposing viewpoints: see *Round Table,* May 14, 1864, and September 8, 1866.

44. Bellows, "The National Lincoln Monument," 12.

45. Letter to Governor Oglesby, dated July 27, 1868, NLMA Letters and Papers.

46. *National Lincoln Monument Association: Organization and Design,* 6.

47. Ibid. A recollection in the hand of Mills's younger son, Fisk Mills, is in the Clark Mills file at the Office of the Architect of the Capitol; this states that Mills's eldest son Theodore A. Mills returned from Munich in 1865 to work on the plaster model of the Lincoln monument. Moreover, Mills took a life mask of Lincoln on February 11, 1865, and this may have been in connection with the monument project; Lloyd Ostendorf, "A Relic from His Last Birthday: The Mills Life Mask of Lincoln" *Lincoln Herald* 75 (Fall 1973): 79–85.

48. For general remarks on Rauch's monument and its context, see H. W. Janson, *19th-Century Sculpture* (New York: Abrams, 1985), 92–93. The proposal for the Washington pedestal is published in James M. Goode, *The Outdoor Sculpture of Washington, D.C.: A Comprehensive Historical Guide* (Washington, D.C.: Smithsonian Institution Press, 1974), 385. Only an illustration of the Lee statue survives; the pedestal can be visualized from the descriptions Mills provided the monument committee in 1877, which are preserved in the Virginia State Library, Archives Division, Records of the Lee Monument Association, Correspondence 1871–93, Richmond, Virginia.

49. *Every Saturday*, February 2, 1871, quoting from the *New York Tribune*, clipping in the Clark Mills file at the Office of the Architect of the Capitol. "Genuine artists, who have seen the plan on paper, pronounce it a monstrous humbug," reported the *Springfield Republican*, undated clipping in Vinnie Ream Hoxie Papers, Library of Congress. An unidentified clipping in the Matthew Simpson Papers, Library of Congress, called the plan "a national misfortune" and "a clever Yankee notion, by which soldiers, philanthropists, statesmen and divines are to be conglomerated in one monumental pile at wholesale price."

50. *National Lincoln Monument Association: Organization and Design*, 4, 7–13.

51. Ibid., 9.

52. Ibid., 5, 9.

53. *Proceedings of the National Convention of the Colored Men of America* (Washington, D.C., 1869), 27.

54. *National Lincoln Monument Association: Organization and Design*, 5. However, the general agent in charge of fund raising, in early 1869, was still describing the figure as time; *New York Times*, March 12, 1869, p. 2. So did Henry Bellows in his January 1870 essay in *Old and New*. Their descriptions depart in several other respects from the details given in the association's 1870 pamphlet.

55. *National Lincoln Monument Association: Organization and Design*, 10.

56. Ladies' Union Aid Society, *Minute Book, 1865–1868*, 91–92, Missouri Historical Society, St. Louis. This is discussed in Paula Coalier, "Beyond Sympathy: The St. Louis Ladies' Union Aid Society and the Civil War," *Gateway Heritage* 11 (Summer 1990): 38–51.

57. Letter from Eliot to James Yeatman, November 8, 1869, in Correspondence, William Greenleaf Eliot Papers, Washington University, St. Louis.

58. *New York Times*, November 6, 1883, p. 2; *National Lincoln Monument Association: Organization and Design*, appendix, iii.

59. The two statues were of Salmon Chase and Matthew Simpson. On the fate of the Simpson statue, see James E. Kirby, "The Bishop Who Almost Stood with Lincoln," *Methodist History* 7 (October 1968): 31–37. On the fate of the Chase, see Boston *Evening Transcript*, October 29, 1880, p. 6, and *Monumental News* 10 (February 1898): 127. In later years, several attempts were made to track down the original subscribers and the whereabouts of the remaining funds, but without success; these are documented in clippings from April 1910 preserved in the vertical files of the Columbia Historical Society, Washington, D.C., and in a clipping of July 28, 1929, in the Lincoln Memorial vertical file at the Martin Luther King Jr. Public Library in Washington, D.C.

60. Clark Mills's son Fisk Mills tried in the late 1860s to get a massive congressional appropriation for an emancipation group he designed for the House pediment, the very same commission that Henry Kirke Brown had tried to secure in the 1850s. A schematic description survives, but no model does, and the project never seems to have garnered much support beyond a congressman or two. See Thomas P. Somma, The Apotheosis of Democracy, *1908–1916: The Pediment for the House Wing of the United States Capitol* (Newark: University of Delaware Press, 1995), 40–41.

61. Letter from Eliot to Yeatman, November 8, 1869, in Correspondence, William Greenleaf Eliot Papers.

62. This is documented in a series of letters sent back and forth from January to June 1871 in NLMA Letters and Papers. See especially the letter of Jesse Dubois to Yeatman January 30, 1871, and of D. L. Phillips to Dubois, May 22, 1871.

63. *Inaugural Ceremonies of the Freedmen's Memorial Monument to Abraham Lincoln* (St. Louis: Levison & Blythe, 1876).

64. William G. Eliot, *Story of Archer Alexander: From Slavery to Freedom* (1885; Westport, Conn.: Negro Universities Press, 1970), 14.

65. *Inaugural Ceremonies*, 8.

66. Ibid., 9.

67. Eliot, *Story of Archer Alexander: From Slavery to Freedom.*

68. Ibid., 59.

69. Ibid., 54–73. Ira Berlin, Barbara J. Fields, Thavolia Glymph, Joseph P. Reidy, and Leslie S. Rowland, eds., *The Destruction of Slavery*, series 1, vol. 1 of *Freedom: A Documentary History of Emancipation, 1861–1867* (Cambridge: Cambridge University Press, 1985), 403–8, 441–44, 457–58. General Curtis and Provost Marshal Dick—the latter man personally signed the protection papers for Archer Alexander, pursuant to Curtis's policy—were replaced in May 1863 by General Schofield and Colonel Broadhead.

70. Eliot, *Story of Archer Alexander: From Slavery to Freedom*, 88.

71. Ibid.

72. Cromwell reported this in Freeman H. M. Murray, *Emancipation and the Freed in American Sculpture* (Washington, D.C.: Murray Brothers, 1916), 198–99.

73. *Inaugural Ceremonies*, 21.

74. Letter from Douglass to W. J. Wilson published in the *Anglo-African*, November 4, 1865, p. 1.

75. That first narrative becomes even harder to read in the monument as erected because once the group is elevated on a pedestal the key motif of the chains lying on the ground becomes invisible.

76. *Inaugural Ceremonies*, 10; *Southern Workman* 5 (May 1876): 39; New York *Evening Post*, April 14, 1876, p. 3. Descriptions of the slave figure as kneeling or crouching include Boston *Evening Transcript*, January 11, 1886, p. 3, September 20, 1866, p. 4, April 14, 1873, p. 7, June 7, 1879, p. 4; New York *Tribune*, July 7, 1873, p. 5; New York *Evening Post*, September 18, 1866, p. 2. The *Post* in a notice of April 4, 1867, p. 2, however, wrote that the slave "is apparently in the act of rising to his feet." The *Transcript* on May 23, 1871, suppl., p. 1, described Lincoln as "beckoning a slave to rise." All these clippings were kindly supplied to me by Colonel Merl Moore from his personal archive. One interesting twist comes in Benjamin Quarles's assertion that the figure looks "like a sprinter getting set"; Quarles imagines the motion forward as well as upward. See Benjamin Quarles, *Lincoln and the Negro* (New York: Oxford University Press, 1962), p. 9.

77. *Inaugural Ceremonies*, 19, 25–26.

78. *Boston Evening Transcript*, June 7, 1879, p. 4, July 9, 1879, p. 4; both

clippings in Merl Moore archive. The full inscription reads, "A Race set free / and the country at peace / Lincoln / rests from his labors."

79. Joseph T. Wilson, *Emancipation: Its Course and Progress* (Norfolk, Va.: Normal School Steam Press, 1882), 157.

80. Murray, *Emancipation and the Freed*, 26–28.

81. *A Description of United States Postage Stamps, 1847–1942* (Washington, D.C.: Post Office Dept., 1942), 129; Quarles, *Lincoln and the Negro*; "Monuments and Landmarks," *Ebony* 18 (September 1963): 107; Scott A. Sandage, "A Marble House Divided: The Lincoln Memorial, the Civil Rights Movement, and the Politics of Memory, 1939–1963," *Journal of American History* 80 (June 1993): 135–67, quotation from p. 140. Marianna Griswold van Rensselaer wrote about the Boston version that the black man was "apparently . . . blacking Lincoln's boots"; Boston *Evening Transcript*, July 2, 1892, p. 6.

82. For example, when Rose Strunsky published her leftist biography of Lincoln in 1915 she wrote that "the picture of Lincoln looking out upon space with sad and loving eyes, his right hand outstretched presenting the Emancipation Proclamation, his left resting tenderly upon the head of a newly-freed and grateful slave kneeling at his feet, can no longer be satisfactory." This description, with a few details embellished for proper effect, is clearly based on Ball's group. See Herbert Aptheker, ed., *Book Reviews by W.E.B. DuBois* (Millwood, N.Y.: kto press, 1977), 50.

83. Merrill D. Peterson, in his magisterial volume *Lincoln in American Memory* (New York: Oxford University Press, 1994), writes that "the image of Emancipator belonged particularly to American Negroes" (p. 29); I would argue that the Freedmen's Memorial was instrumental in shaping that association, and in reshaping white memory in other directions.

84. Perhaps the best statement of the problem comes from Marianna Griswold van Rensselaer, "Saint Gaudens's Lincoln," *Century* 35 (November 1887): 37–39.

85. For some of the initial sketches, see John H. Dryfhout, *The Work of Augustus Saint-Gaudens* (Hanover, N.H.: University Press of New England, 1992), 159.

86. The archives of the monument fund trustees are in the Chicago Historical Society; there is no correspondence about the bronze globes, except for a short note from Thomas Withrow to Saint-Gaudens, dated December 9, 1887, reporting that "the balls are in place and are very handsome." Similarly, the Saint-Gaudens Papers at Dartmouth College, Hanover, N.H., shed no light on the issue.

87. Eli Bates left $40,000 for the purpose of erecting a monument to Lincoln in Chicago; the implementation of the bequest is documented in the archives of the Chicago Historical Society. The negotiations with Ball are discussed in a letter from George Payson to Thomas Withrow, March 3, 1882. The trustees' decision to hire Saint-Gaudens received some unfavorable publicity, but they seem to have left the sculptor free to work out the design anyway.

88. F. Lauriston Bullard, *Lincoln in Marble and Bronze* (New Brunswick, N.J.: Rutgers University Press, 1952), 82–83. "Saint-Gaudens's standing 'Lincoln' . . . probably has stirred the enthusiasm of more people in the country than

any other"; James William Pattison, "The Art of Sculptors: Saint-Gaudens and Others," *World To-Day* 17 (October 1909): 1056–62, quotation from p. 1060. My thanks to Henry Pisciotta for drawing my attention to this latter source.

89. *Catalogue of a Collection of Engraved and Other Portraits of Abraham Lincoln* (New York: Grolier Club, 1899), 7, in Abraham Lincoln vertical file at the National Museum of American Art Library, Washington, D.C.; John Coleman Adams, "Lincoln's Place in History," *Century* 47 (February 1894): 595–96.

90. Lorado Taft, "American Sculpture and Sculptors," *Chautauquan* 22 (January 1896): 387–95, quotation from p. 390.

91. Thus Saint-Gaudens's Lincoln seems the perfect sculptural image of the "statist" Lincoln, which, according to Peter Karsten, emerged as the ideal in poetry and oratory toward the end of the nineteenth century; see his *Patriot-Heroes in England and America: Political Symbolism and Changing Values over Three Centuries* (Madison: University of Wisconsin Press, 1978), 98–100.

92. van Rensselaer, "Saint Gaudens's Lincoln."

93. Letter from Hosmer to Norman Williams, November 22 [1889?], in Crerar Library Records, University of Chicago Library.

94. The tortuous correspondence documenting Hosmer's efforts over a period of seven years is preserved in the Crerar Library Records.

95. *Saint Louis Daily Globe-Democrat*, December 13, 1888, clipping in Hosmer Collection.

96. Ibid.

97. Ibid.

98. See Dryfhout, *The Work of Augustus Saint-Gaudens*, 278–79.

<h2 style="text-align:center">CHAPTER FIVE</h2>

<h3 style="text-align:center">SLAVERY'S MEMORIAL</h3>

1. Drew Gilpin Faust, *The Creation of Confederate Nationalism: Ideology and Identity in the Civil War South* (Baton Rouge: Louisiana State University Press, 1988), 59–60.

2. One of the most sophisticated accounts of the image of Lee is in Gaines Foster, *Ghosts of the Confederacy: Defeat, the Lost Cause, and the Emergence of the New South* (New York: Oxford University Press, 1987), 51, 101–3, 120–21. Also helpful are Mark E. Neely Jr., Harold Holzer, and Gabor S. Boritt, *The Confederate Image: Prints of the Lost Cause* (Chapel Hill: University of North Carolina Press, 1987), 139–54; Thomas L. Connelly, *The Marble Man: Robert E. Lee and His Image in American Society* (New York: Knopf, 1977); Charles Bracelen Flood, *Lee: The Last Years* (Boston: Houghton Mifflin, 1981). Important and widely read contemporary speeches on Lee's character include Jubal Early's oration at Lexington, January 19, 1872; John Daniel's at Lexington, June 28, 1883; Archer Anderson's in Richmond, May 30, 1890. The vertical files on Lee at the Valentine Museum in Richmond and the files of the Lee Monument Association in the Archives Division, Virginia State Library, Richmond, are largely unplumbed treasure troves of material on the Lee image.

On the Jefferson Davis story, see Nina Silber, "Intemperate Men, Spiteful Women, and Jefferson Davis: Northern Views of the Defeated South," *American*

Quarterly 41 (December 1989): 614–35. On Davis's problematic status as "national" leader, see Paul D. Escott, *Many Excellent People: Power and Privilege in North Carolina, 1850–1900* (Chapel Hill: University of North Carolina Press, 1985), 36–37. For a comparison of Lee's and Davis's reputations, see Paul H. Buck, *Road to Reunion, 1865–1900* (Boston: Little, Brown, 1937), 250–55.

3. Quoted in Alan T. Nolan, *Lee Considered: General Robert E. Lee and Civil War History* (Chapel Hill: University of North Carolina Press, 1991), 9.

4. For a recent reexamination of Lee's views on slavery, see Nolan, *Lee Considered*, 9–29; see also Douglas Southall Freeman, *R. E. Lee: A Biography*, 4 vols. (New York: Scribner's Sons, 1935), 1:371–73. For a direct example of the postwar efforts to use Lee to prove that slavery was not the cause of the war, see the 1904 report of the History Committee of the United Daughters of the Confederacy, in *Minutes of the Eleventh Annual Meeting of the United Daughters of the Confederacy*, October 4–8, 1904, 199.

5. Norfolk *Landmark*, July 23, 1886; *Richmond Dispatch*, June 6, 1886; Richmond *State*, August 7, 1886; all clippings in Edward Valentine Papers, Valentine Museum.

6. Marianna Griswold van Rensselaer, "Saint Gaudens's Lincoln," *Century* 35 (November 1887): 37–39, quotation from p. 37.

7. For example, *Richmond Dispatch*, August 13, 1886, clipping in Valentine Papers.

8. Quoted in Flood, *Lee: The Last Years*, 161.

9. My thanks to Elizabeth Thomas for giving me this idea and suggesting the line of inquiry that follows.

10. "General R. E. Lee's War-Horse," *Richmond Dispatch*, August 10, 1886, clipping in Valentine Papers. Reprinted in *Southern Historical Society Papers* 35 (1907): 99–101.

11. "General R. E. Lee's War-Horse"; *Richmond Dispatch*, August 13, 1886, clipping in Valentine Papers.

12. Curry to Samuel Bassett French, November 14, 1877, Lee Monument Association Correspondence, 1871–93, Archives Division, Virginia State Library, Richmond (hereafter LMA Correspondence). The same idea was repeated in the Virginia press, for example in Richmond *State*, August 3, 1886, clipping in Valentine Papers.

13. See Jack P. Maddex Jr., *The Virginia Conservatives, 1867–1879* (Chapel Hill: University of North Carolina Press, 1970), and for the wider Southern context the classic account is C. Vann Woodward, *Origins of the New South, 1877–1913* (Baton Rouge: Lousiana State University Press, 1951).

14. For a full account of the complex history of the Lee Monument campaign, see Kirk Savage, "Race, Memory, and Identity: The National Monuments of the Union and the Confederacy" (Ph.D. diss., University of California, Berkeley, 1990). Partial accounts of the campaign include Foster, *Ghosts of the Confederacy*, 52–61, 98–101; Connelly, *Marble Man*, 28–47; Jay Killian Bowman Williams, *Changed Views and Unforeseen Prosperity: Richmond of 1890 Gets a Monument to Lee* (Richmond: printed by author, 1969); and Joseph T. Knox, "Le général Lee: A Design for the Future," *Virginia Cavalcade* 38 (Autumn 1988): 76–85.

15. "To the Survivors of the Army of Northern Virginia," broadside in LMA Correspondence.

16. Letter from Jubal Early to Governor Holliday, March 11, 1878, LMA Correspondence. Early scorned agents who "wanted to make a living in the memory of the dead Lee," and he put a stop to paid agents after he discovered that some were pocketing over half the contributions they collected. See also Early to Governor Fitzhugh Lee, March 27, 1886, in Executive Papers—Fitzhugh Lee, Archives Division, Virginia State Library.

Agents from rival associations competed with one another, rushing all over the South to canvass towns before any of the others arrived. Samuel Bassett French, secretary of the governor's association, wrote to an agent in February 1876 that "General Lilly of the Lee Memorial Association [a rival group in Lexington] . . . is now in the South and has crossed me at Charleston—I should like to get ahead of him in cities further south"; Letterpress books of Samuel Bassett French, Lee Monument Association, 1:128–29, Eleanor S. Brockenbrough Library, Museum of the Confederacy, Richmond (hereafter French Letterpress).

17. French Letterpress, 1: 151, 255.

18. John D. Couper to S. B. French, October 20, 1876; I. Critcher to French, November 1, 1876; Mary Roberts to French, December 20, 1877; Mr. Bacon to French, December 21, 1877; Louise King to French, December 28, 1877; Laura Hockaday to French, February 6, 1879; B. H. Rutledge to French, February 11, 1879; William P. Chilton to French, January 3, 1879, May 5, 1879, June 6, 1879, September 3, 1879, October 23, 1879, November 3, 1879; all in LMA Correspondence. See also French Letterpress, 2:211–15.

19. Ledgers are filed in LMA Correspondence. The transfer of the charter from Early to Governor Kemper is documented in Early to Holliday, March 10, 1878, LMA Correspondence, and French Letterpress, 1:12–21.

On Kemper see Robert R. Jones, "Conservative Virginian: The Post-war Career of Governor James Lawson Kemper" (Ph.D. diss., University of Virginia, 1964); and Jones, "James L. Kemper and the Virginia Redeemers Face the Race Question: A Reconsideration," *Journal of Southern History* 38 (1972): 393–414.

20. French Letterpress, 1:198.

21. Ibid., 1:199.

22. *Richmond Dispatch*, January 18, 1871, and January 20, 1871.

23. Maddex, *Virginia Conservatives*, 188–202. See also Jones, "Conservative Virginian," 199–202, 224.

24. Jones, "Conservative Virginian," 119–29, 201–2, 224; Maddex, *Virginia Conservatives*, 121–37, 184–95.

25. On Mahone, see Nelson Morehouse Blake, *William Mahone of Virginia: Soldier and Political Insurgent* (Richmond, Va.: Garrett & Massie, 1935). On the French-Mahone relationship, see ibid., 135–45; Jones, "Conservative Virginian," 162, 334; Maddex, *Virginia Conservatives*, 112.

26. French Letterpress, 1:90, 221.

27. Ladies' Lee Monument Committee to Lee Monument Association, March 3, 1877, in Minute Books of the Lee Monument Association (hereafter LMA Minutes), 1:27, Archives Division, Virginia State Library.

28. French Letterpress, 1:377–79, 391–93. LMA Minutes, 1:35–36.

29. Randolph to Fitzhugh Lee, April 16, 1886, Executive Papers—Fitzhugh Lee. The ladies' committee at this time consisted of E. H. Brown, Imogen Lyons, Elizabeth Byrd Nicholas, and Randolph, all well connected in elite society and the latter two from prominent old families.

30. The committee's letter of March 3, 1877, LMA Minutes, explained that the process of recruiting the best artistic talent in the world would mean delay, but the delay was worth it. "When such a work is designed to go down to posterity as an exponent of the nation's devotion and admiration for our immortal Lee the task of selecting the author must be considered a solemn as well a sacred one," the letter argued. This was the antipragmatic, antitemporal mission of high culture. For a good discussion of the concepts of culture and genitlity during this period, see Alan Trachtenberg, *The Incorporation of America: Culture and Society in the Gilded Age* (New York: Hill and Wang, 1982), 140–52.

31. French Letterpress, 1:340.

32. LMA Minutes, 1:35. Several of the competitors did not realize how important the likeness would be considered at this stage; Moses Ezekiel complained that he thought "the *spirit* and not the letter would have its weigh"; see Ezekiel to French, December 18, 1877, LMA Correspondence.

33. Letters from the judges are preserved in LMA Correspondence; the letter from General John B. Gordon, a popular ex-Confederate, to French, November 12, 1877 is typical: "If I had not been told that [Vinnie Ream's model] was designed for General Lee I should have instantly recognized it. This at last is the highest test of merit."

34. J. Proctor Knott to French, November 9, 1877. Other letters examining the relationship of form to visual memory came from General C. M. Wilcox, November 13, 1877; G. A. Peple, November 9, 1877; Carroll Spence, November 12, 1877; Colonel G. T. Fry, November 10, 1877; Alex Q. Holladay, November 14, 1877; Colonel T. A. Washington, November 13, 1877; all in LMA Correspondence. Also significant is a letter from Carleton McCarthy to Edward Valentine, October 31, 1877, reporting on Jubal Early's observations, Valentine Papers.

35. Colonel G. T. Fry to French, November 10, 1877; George Jacob to French, November 6, 1877; both in LMA Correspondence.

36. Colonel R. E. Withers to French, November 5, 1877; George Jacob to French, November 6, 1877; in LMA Correspondence.

37. Fry to French, November 10, 1877. Examples of letters arguing for the horse at rest are Spence to French, November 12, 1877, and Dr. J.L.M. Curry to French, November 14, 1877; all in LMA Correspondence.

38. Augustus Saint-Gaudens to Sarah Randolph, January 12, 1887, Executive Papers—Fitzhugh Lee.

39. *Richmond Whig*, March 26, 1886, clipping in Valentine Papers.

40. Early to Fitzhugh Lee, March 27, 1886, Executive Papers—Fitzhugh Lee.

41. Lynchburg *Weekly Virginian*, July 29 [1886]; *Norfolk Landmark*, July 23, 1886; *Richmond Dispatch*, June 6, 1886; Richmond *State*, March 20, 1887; clippings in Valentine Papers. This criticism is already articulated in the 1870s, for example, in the *Southern Planter and Farmer*, December 1877, p. 783.

42. *Norfolk Landmark*, July 23, 1886, clipping in Valentine Papers.

43. By insisting on an accurate likeness even at the preliminary stage and setting a relatively brief turnaround time for entries, the 1877 competition procedures heavily favored local entries.

The most important lightning rods in this long dispute over American public sculpture are probably Clark Mills's Andrew Jackson Monument in Washington, D.C. (1853), and Vinnie Ream's Abraham Lincoln statue in the U.S. Capitol (1871); for a discussion of the latter and the rhetorical debate it inspired, see Carmine A. Prioli, " 'Wonder Girl from the West': Vinnie Ream and the Congressional Statue of Abraham Lincoln," *Journal of American Culture* 12 (Winter 1989): 1–20.

44. The scholarly literature on Ream is still minimal and confined mostly to her Lincoln statue; see Prioli, " 'Wonder Girl from the West,' " and Joan A. Lemp, "Vinnie Ream and *Abraham Lincoln*," *Woman's Art Journal* 6 (Fall 1985–Winter 1986): 24–29.

Ream's brother fought for the Confederacy in the southwestern theater, and the letters Ream wrote as a teenage girl during the war reveal her to be a Confederate sympathizer; Correspondence 1862–64, Vinnie Ream Hoxie Papers, Library of Congress, Washington, D.C. Nevertheless, her family moved to Washington, and she soon immersed herself in its official life and established connections with men like Thaddeus Stevens from the radical Republican elite. Meanwhile, according to an undated newspaper clipping in her Scrapbooks, Library of Congress, her mother traveled behind enemy lines in Missouri, rescued her brother from the Confederate service, and had him paroled by the secretary of war in Washington.

45. See Savage, "Race, Memory, and Identity," 79–81.

46. *Richmond Dispatch*, November 21, 1877, clipping in Valentine Papers. On Ream's reputation, see Lemp, "Vinnie Ream and *Abraham Lincoln*."

47. *Richmond Dispatch*, February 16, 1886, p. 1, and February 18, 1886, p. 4.

48. "Alleged Art in the Lee Monument," unidentified clipping in Valentine Papers; "Mercié Talks about Lee," undated clipping [May 1890?] from *Richmond Dispatch*, Vertical File, Monuments—Lee, Valentine Museum. Other descriptions of Mercié's first model include *Richmond State*, March 20, 1887, clipping in Valentine Papers; and "Equestrian Monuments—XLIV," *American Architect and Building News* 34 (November 14, 1891): 104.

49. Sarah Randolph to Fitzhugh Lee, April 16, 1886, Executive Papers—Fitzhugh Lee.

50. There is no recent monograph on Mercié and virtually no scholarship on his Lee commission; a popular account is Joseph T. Knox, "Le général Lee: A Design for the Future." On Saint-Gaudens's relationship with Mercié, see Homer Saint-Gaudens, ed., *Reminiscences of Augustus Saint-Gaudens*, 2 vols. (New York: Century Co., 1913), 1:74–78, 110. For Saint-Gaudens's thoughts on the profession and the academic French model, see ibid., 2:262–64; further information can be found in John H. Dryfhout, *The Work of Augustus Saint-Gaudens* (Hanover, N.H.: University Press of New England), and Michele Bogart's review of the book in *Winterthur Portfolio* 18 (Spring–Autumn 1983): 219–22. In 1887, Saint-Gaudens listed Mercié among seven sculptors he consid-

ered major influences on him; see Burke Wilkinson, *Uncommon Clay: The Life and Works of Augustus Saint Gaudens* (San Diego: Harcourt Brace Jovanovich, 1985), 377.

51. Savage, "Race, Memory, and Identity," 89, 92–93. The minutes of the joint boards' meetings indicate that the ladies' committee and the governor's people were at odds over the site; the ladies agreed to the governor's site on June 18, 1886, only after failing to get approval from him for their preferred sites; LMA Minutes. This did not stop Sarah Randolph from complaining about the site for some time afterward; letter to Archer Anderson, November 11, 1887, Archer Anderson Papers, Virginia Historical Society, Richmond.

52. *Richmond Dispatch*, May 6, 1890, p. 1.

53. Ibid., August 21, 1888, p. 1, and May 25, 1890, p. 1; *Richmond Whig*, August 19, 1888, clipping in Vertical File, Monuments—Lee, Valentine Museum.

54. Henry James, *The American Scene* (1907; Bloomington: Indiana University Press, 1968), 393.

55. Sarah Randolph to Fitzhugh Lee, April 16, 1886, Executive Papers—Fitzhugh Lee.

56. *Richmond Dispatch*, October 12, 1886, p. 1. See Savage, "Race, Memory, and Identity," 92–94, 189–91.

57. Photos from the Valentine Museum circa 1907 show earthworks, cut to accommodate the street and sidewalk, in the vicinity of the Davis Monument; one of these is published in Kathy Edwards, Esme Howard, and Toni Prawl, *Monument Avenue: History and Architecture* (Washington, D.C.: National Park Service, 1992), 73. As the avenue was developed, these were replaced by cannon in the median strip to mark the line of defense. On the development of the avenue and its social composition, see ibid.

58. *New York Herald*, quoted in *Richmond Dispatch*, May 30, 1890, p. 4. See also *Dispatch*, June 1, 1890, p. 7, and Williams, *Changed Views and Unforeseen Prosperity*, 47.

59. *Richmond Dispatch*, October 29, 1887, p. 2.

60. *Southern Historical Society Papers* 17 (1889–90): 312.

61. *Richmond Dispatch*, September 6, 1887, p. 1. For the political context in the 1880s, see Michael B. Chesson, *Richmond after the War, 1868–1890* (Richmond: Virginia State Library, 1981).

62. *Southern Historical Society Papers* 17 (1889–90): 317. See Foster, *Ghosts of the Confederacy*, 101–3; *Southern Historical Society Papers* 17 (1889–90): 262–311; *Richmond Dispatch*, May 28, 1890, p. 2, and May 30, 1890, pp. 1–2.

63. *New York Times*, May 30, 1890, p. 2. See Savage, "Race, Memory, and Identity," 149–52.

64. *Richmond Planet*, May 24, 1890, p. 2.

65. Ibid., May 10, 1890, p. 2.

66. Ibid., June 7, 1890, p. 2.

67. Ibid.

68. *New York Times*, May 30, 1890, p. 4. See also *Harper's Weekly*, June 3, 1890, p. 470, and for a useful sampling of Northern press reactions, see *Richmond Dispatch*, June 1, 1890, p. 5. There were, of course, some Northern papers that expressed outrage, like the *New York Sun* and the *Boston Transcript*.

69. *Southern Historical Society Papers* 17 (1889–90): 312. The transformation of Lee from Confederate hero into American hero is discussed in Buck, *Road to Reunion*, 251.

70. *New York Times*, March 4, 1890, p. 2; *Richmond Dispatch*, March 4, 1890, p. 1.

71. *Richmond Planet*, June 7, 1890, p. 2.

72. James, *American Scene*, 367–71.

73. Ibid., 394.

74. Ibid., 375, 378.

75. Critics have recently taken up the issue of James's response to the black body. See Eric Haralson, "The Person Sitting in Darkness: James in the American South," and Walter Been Michaels, "Jim Crow Henry James?" in *Henry James Review* 16 (Fall 1995): 249–56, 286–91, both of which are responses to Kenneth Warren, *Black and White Strangers: Race and American Literary Realism* (Chicago: University of Chicago Press, 1994).

76. *Charlotte Observer*, May 22, 1896, p. 1; *Rock Hill Herald*, May 23, 1896, p. 3.

77. Leon F. Litwack describes some of the family lore in *Been in the Storm So Long: The Aftermath of Slavery* (New York: Vintage Books, 1980), 17–18. The tradition of erecting gravestones to faithful slaves stretched back long before the war but evidently continued after it. The author has seen examples documented in Gable, South Carolina, Hopewell, South Carolina, Tippah County, Mississippi, and elsewhere. For the Tippah County headstone, inscribed simply "Jennie the Faithful Slave," I am in debt to William W. Thomas Jr. for sharing a family manuscript by Will Ticer dated July 4, 1960.

78. Reynolds J. Scott-Childress, "Richard Watson Gilder and the Editing of the New Nation: The Antebellum South As Racial Model for Postbellum America," forthcoming in *Race and the Invention of Modern American Nationalism* (New York: Garland). See also Buck, *Road to Reunion*, chap. 9.

79. A twenty-foot obelisk was erected in 1894 in a park in Canton, Mississippi, to commemorate a faithful body servant of a Confederate soldier; see George Cantor, *Historic Landmarks of Black America* (Detroit: Gale Research, 1991), 169–70. A plaque was erected on the courthouse grounds in Lexington, Virginia, to the "colored servants of Rockbridge County," and was removed in 1979; telephone conversation with Keith Gibson of Rockbridge Historical Society, March 10, 1992. There was even a faithful-slave monument erected in the North, in Barrington, Rhode Island, in the form of a boulder with a bronze plaque; see Freeman Henry Morris Murray, *Emancipation and the Freed in American Sculpture: A Study in Interpretation* (Washington, D.C.: Murray Brothers, 1916, 219.

The question of a larger monument campaign was discussed in the *Confederate Veteran* 12 (1904): 443, 525; 13 (1905): 123–24. For efforts in the 1910s, see Murray, *Emancipation and the Freed*, 218. On the proposed "Mammy" monument, see *New York Age*, January 6, 1923, p. 4.

80. See *Natchitoches: Oldest Settlement in the Louisiana Purchase* (Natchitoches: Association of Natchitoches Women for the Preservation of Historic Natchitoches, 1958), 17–18. The statue is illustrated in an official tourist guide to

Lousiana from the 1930s, *Do You Know Louisiana?* ed. Rex Laney (Baton Rouge: n.p., n.d.), 238. The statue was removed from public view in the 1960s, and is now in the collection of the Rural Life Museum, Baton Rouge, Louisiana; telephone conversation with John Dutton, curator, March 24, 1992.

81. *Charlotte Observer*, May 22, 1896, p. 1.

82. *Rock Hill Herald*, May 23, 1896, p. 3.

83. Unidentified clipping, dated March 9, 1911, from Elliott White Springs Scrapbook, kindly furnished to me by Louise Pettus.

84. March 9, 1911, clipping; Louise Pettus, "Fort Mill's Confederate Monument," unpublished paper; William R. Bradford Jr., *Out of the Past: A History of Fort Mill, South Carolina* (Fort Mill: by author, 1980), 38–40.

85. Doug Seroff, "Polk Miller and the Old South Quartette," *JEMF Quarterly* 18 (Fall–Winter 1982): 147–50.

86. Polk Miller, "Krismus 'Fo De Wah," *Richmond Dispatch*, December 22, 1895, clipping in Polk Miller Scrapbooks, 2:34, Country Music Foundation Library, Nashville, Tenn. See also 1:3–4, 31, 45, 61, 117.

87. See Eric J. Sundquist, *To Wake the Nations* (Cambridge: Cambridge University Press, 1994), 294–323, 472–80; W.E.B. DuBois, *The Souls of Black Folk* (New York: Penguin Books, 1989), 204–6.

88. "The Aspiring Negro," Richmond *Dispatch*, August 21, 1895, clipping in Polk Miller Scrapbooks, 2:15; see also 1:46.

89. DuBois, *Souls of Black Folk*, 206; Seroff, "Polk Miller and the Old South Quartette," 148.

90. *Charlotte Observer*, May 22, 1896, p. 1; *Rock Hill Herald*, May 23, 1896, p. 3.

91. Murray, *Emancipation and the Freed in American Sculpture*, 119. The black newspapers and magazines I have consulted did not cover the event. The closest black newspaper, the *Star of Zion* published by the Charlotte A.M.E. Church, has no issues surviving in 1896 before June 11.

92. Seroff, "Polk Miller and the Old South Quartette," 147–49. Opposition to the idea of a faithful-slave monument was sometimes articulated on these grounds, that it presented a positive type when in every state there was "some beautiful woman whose life has been strangled out by some black fiend"; *Confederate Veteran* 12 (1904): 525.

CHAPTER SIX
COMMON SOLDIERS

1. Studies of soldier monument patronage are typically local and fragmentary at best. However, even a cursory examination of the Inventory of American Sculpture—a national database of both public and private sculpture, located in the National Museum of American Art in Washington, D.C.—demonstrates that in the North the Grand Army of the Republic (the major veterans' organization) and its ladies' auxilliaries were responsible for erecting many if not most soldier monuments. For the rise of the veteran in American life, see Wallace Evan Davies, *Patriotism on Parade: The Story of Veterans' and Heridilary Organizations in America, 1783–1900* (Cambridge, Mass.: Harvard University Press, 1955); and

Stuart McConnell, *Glorious Contentment: The Grand Army of the Republic, 1865–1900* (Chapel Hill: University of North Carolina Press, 1992). In the South veterans organized later and they preferred to have soldier monuments erected by women's organizations. An early work setting forth the goals and accomplishments of this female movement is Confederated Southern Memorial Association, *History of the Confederated Memorial Associations of the South* (New Orleans: Graham Press, 1904).

Studies that document the shift in type of monument from funereal shaft to realistic effigy are also for the most part fragmentary. The only statistical surveys compiled to date are for Confederate monuments to 1912, in Gaines Foster, *Ghosts of the Confederacy: Defeat, the Lost Cause, and the Emergence of the New South* (New York: Oxford University Press, 1987), 273; and Lewis Waldron Williams II's partial inventory of Union and Confederate monuments to 1915 in "Commercially Produced Forms of American Civil War Monuments" (M.A. thesis, University of Illinois, 1948), 160–75. The earliest example of the funereal type of Civil War memorial appears to be in a cemetery in Somerville, Massachusetts, from 1863; see Alfred S. Roe, *Monuments, Tablets, and Other Memorials Erected in Massachusetts to Commemorate the Services of Her Sons in the War of the Rebellion* (Boston: Wright and Potter, 1910), 105.

2. Unidentified newspaper clipping, circa 1869, John Quincy Adams Ward Scrapbook, Albany Institute of History and Art, Albany, New York.

3. Ward's earlier design for the 7th Regiment Memorial actually included a subsidiary figure of a wounded soldier, but this was never executed; see Lewis I. Sharp, *John Quincy Adams Ward: Dean of American Sculpture* (Newark: University of Delaware Press, 1985), 174–77. By contrast, figures of wounded or dying soldiers were standard in France, for example; see David G. Troyansky, "Monumental Politics: National History and Local Memory in French *Monuments aux Morts* in the Department of the Aisne since 1870," *French Historical Studies* 15 (Spring 1987): 121–41, and Daniel J. Sherman, "Art, Commerce, and the Production of Memory in France after World War I," in John R. Gillis, ed., *Commemorations: The Politics of National Identity* (Princeton: Princeton University Press, 1994), 186–211. Soldier figures in active combat poses were common on battlefield monuments but not in towns; see Michael Wilson Panhorst, "Lest We Forget: Monuments and Memorial Sculpture in National Military Parks on Civil War Battlefields, 1861–1917" (Ph.D. diss., University of Delaware, 1989), 222–24.

4. For example, some have assumed that the bowed head was a distinctive Confederate type, but it is relatively rare and the same type appears on some Union monuments as well. The easiest way to compare monuments is to consult the two most recent pictorial catalogs of local Confederate and Union monuments: Ralph W. Widener Jr., *Confederate Monuments: Enduring Symbols of the South and the War between the States* (Washington, D.C.: Andromeda, 1982); and Mildred C. Baruch and Ellen J. Beckman, *Civil War Union Monuments: A List of Union Monuments, Markers, and Memorials of the American Civil War, 1861–1865* (Washington, D.C.: Daughters of Union Veterans of the Civil War, 1978). The Union catalog is woefully incomplete, but it will soon be rendered

obsolete by the on-line inventory of outdoor sculpture being amassed and entered into the Smithsonian's Inventory of American Sculpture.

5. Still the best source on the monument industry is Lewis Waldron Williams II, "Commercially Produced Forms of American Civil War Monuments." Panhorst's "Lest We Forget" updates this earlier study to some extent.

6. William Dean Howells, "Question of Monuments," *Atlantic Monthly* 18 (May 1866): 646–49.

7. John Keegan, *Mask of Command* (New York: Elisabeth Sifton Books, 1987), 187; Russell F. Weigley, *History of the United States Army* (New York: Macmillan, 1967), 37–43, 104–5; Marcus Cunliffe, *Soldiers and Civilians: The Martial Spirit in America, 1775–1865* (Boston: Little, Brown, 1968), 37–56.

8. Benson J. Lossing, *Pictorial Field-Book of the Revolution*, 2 vols. (New York: Harper and Bros., 1852).

9. Ibid., 1:552–59.

10. Janet A. Headley, "The Monument without a Public: The Case of the *Tripoli Monument*," *Winterthur Portfolio* 29 (Winter 1994): 247–64.

11. Randolph Rogers was commissioned in 1863 to produce a standing-soldier monument for Spring Grove Cemetery, Cincinnati. The colossal bronze figure was cast in Munich in 1865, and the model was on view in Rogers's studio in Rome; see Millard F. Rogers Jr., *Randolph Rogers: American Sculptor in Rome* (Amherst: University of Massachusetts Press, 1971), 92, 208. When it was actually installed in Cinncinati is harder to determine for the cemetery publication quoted by Williams mistakenly gives the date as 1864 (p. 31); Panhorst, "Lest We Forget," 217, gives the date as 1867 but without documentation. A report in a magazine of June 1866 suggests that the monument was already complete by then; see "American Studios in Rome and Florence," *Harper's New Monthly Magazine* 33 (June 1866): 102.

Boston was not far behind. Probably the first standing-soldier monument erected in urban space was Martin Milmore's design, dedicated in front of the city hall in February 1867 but soon removed to a cemetery in Roxbury; my thanks to Thomas J. Brown for showing me his paper, "Civil War Monuments of New England," delivered at the 1996 meeting of the Organization of American Historians in Chicago. Howells may well have seen designs for this or similar monuments at the time of his writing.

12. See Widener, *Confederate Monuments*, and Baruch and Beckman, *Civil War Union Monuments*, and the statistical surveys in Foster, *Ghosts of the Confederacy*, 273, and Williams, "Commerically Produced Forms of American Civil War Monuments," 160–75.

13. Cunliffe, *Soldiers and Civilians*, 53–54, 68–70.

14. Weigley, *History of the United States Army*, 75, 104–5, 153–57.

15. Cunliffe, *Soldiers and Civilians*, 70, 215–44.

16. Weigley, *History of the United States Army*, 42, 62–64, 74.

17. Keegan, *Mask of Command*, 177; Cunliffe, *Soldiers and Civilians*, 101, 111–26, 172–76. For an interesting collection of documents on attitudes of and toward soldiers, see Peter Karsten, *The Military in America: From the Colonial Era to the Present* (New York: Free Press, 1980).

18. Kenneth M. Stampp, *The Peculiar Institution: Slavery in the Ante-Bellum South* (New York: Vintage Books, 1956), 144–45. See also the proslavery novel by J. P. Kennedy, *Swallow Barn* (Philadelphia: J. B. Lippincott, 1860), 453.

19. Joseph T. Glatthaar, *Forged in Battle: The Civil War Alliance of Black Soldiers and White Officers* (New York: Free Press, 1990), 20.

20. Reid Mitchell, *The Vacant Chair: The Northern Soldier Leaves Home* (New York: Oxford University Press, 1993), 51.

21. Reid Mitchell, "The Creation of Confederate Loyalties," in Robert H. Abzug and Stephen E. Maizlish, eds., *New Perspectives on Race and Slavery in America: Essays in Honor of Kenneth Stampp* (Lexington: University of Kentucky Press, 1986), 98–99.

22. Stampp, *Peculiar Institution*, 144; Weigley, *History of the United States Army*, 63, 231.

23. John Keegan argues that "inside every army is a crowd struggling to get out," in *Face of Battle: A Study of Agincourt, Waterloo and the Somme* (Middlesex: Penguin Books, 1976), 175.

24. Cunliffe, *Soldiers and Civilians*, 112.

25. Mitchell, *Vacant Chair*, 51.

26. Ibid., 7, and Cunliffe, *Soldiers and Civilians*, 112.

27. Statistics for the Confederate army are less precise and make these figures only rough estimates.

28. The most sensitive study of the disillusionment of the volunteer is Gerald F. Linderman, *Embattled Courage: The Experience of Combat in the American Civil War* (New York: Free Press, 1987). Keegan's quotation is from *Face of Battle*, 181.

29. Henry T. Johns, *Life with the Forty-Ninth Massachusetts Volunteers* (1864; Washington, D.C.: Ramsey and Bisbee, 1890), 167.

30. Thomas Wentworth Higginson, *Army Life in a Black Regiment* (1870; East Lansing: Michigan State University, 1960), 8, 23. In "Colored Troops under Fire," *Century Magazine* 54 (June 1897): 200, Higginson later wrote, "Their antecedents as slaves were not in themselves, as many supposed, a good preparation for the life of a soldier; for military discipline is of a higher grade than plantation discipline, and appeals throughout to a man's self-respect." It is easy to see why a dedicated abolitionist like Higginson would make such a distinction, but the fact remains that even his own account of his troops lends support to the very argument he is trying to combat.

31. For the threat to white manhood, see Leon F. Litwack, *Been in the Storm So Long: The Aftermath of Slavery* (New York: Vintage Books, 1980), 66. This helps explain why so many white troops were openly hostile and even violent toward their black comrades in arms; see Bell Irvin Wiley, *The Life of Billy Yank: The Common Soldier of the Union* (New York: Bobbs-Merrill, 1952), 119–21.

32. Wiley, *The Life of Johnny Reb: The Common Soldier of the Confederacy* (New York: Bobbs-Merrill, 1943), 314, 329–30.

33. For two recent analyses of the picture, see Marc Simpson, *Winslow Homer Paintings of the Civil War* (San Francisco: Fine Arts Museums of San Francisco, 1988), 180–87; Peter H. Wood and Karen C. C. Dalton, *Winslow Homer's Images of Blacks: The Civil War and Reconstruction Years* (Austin: University of

Texas Press, 1988), 48–51. For a description of the Petersburg and the new realities of trench warfare, see Linderman, *Embattled Courage*, 146–55.

34. This traditional image of battle persisted in much of the painting and prints of the Civil War; see Harold Holzer and Mark E. Neely Jr., *Mine Eyes Have Seen the Glory: The Civil War in Art* (New York: Orion Books, 1993).

35. Wood and Dalton argue that the picture calls to mind the battle of the Crater, begun by a huge explosion planted beneath the Confederate lines, and that for Northern viewers the black figure specifically would evoke "immediate thoughts of the black soldiers who fought and died there" (*Winslow Homer's Images of Blacks*, 50). I find this interpretation strained because it downplays what actually goes on in the picture and because the caricaturing of the black figure seems calculated to *avoid* any allusion to black soldiering.

36. Keegan, *Face of Battle*, 322–23.

37. Wiley, *Yank*, 39–40; *Reb*, 309.

38. Higginson, "Colored Troops under Fire," 200.

39. Some even compared military service, especially under despotic white officers, with reenslavement; see Glatthaar, *Forged in Battle*, 113.

40. James McPherson, *The Negro's Civil War: How American Negroes Felt and Acted during the War for the Union* (New York: Pantheon Books, 1965), 171; Glatthaar, *Forged in Battle*, 79.

41. *New York Times*, June 23, 1874, clipping in John Quincy Adams Ward Scrapbook.

42. Linderman, *Embattled Courage*, 266–77.

43. Some Northern veterans did argue that the erection of Confederate monuments "makes treason and loyalty equally commendable," but their voice was overwhelmed by the larger movement to promote sectional reconciliation. See Davies, *Patriotism on Parade*, 256–80 (quotation from 263); McConnell, *Glorious Contentment*, 189–92; G. Kurt Piehler, *Remembering War the American Way* (Washington, D.C.: Smithsonian Institution Press, 1995), 64–72; Oscar Handlin, "The Civil War As Symbol and Actuality," *Massachusetts Review* 3 (Autumn 1961): 133–43, esp. 135; Paul H. Buck, *The Road to Reunion, 1865–1900* (Boston: Little, Brown, 1937), 236–46.

44. An emerging documentary source of monument inscriptions is the Inventory of American Sculpture, which is gradually incorporating numerous outdoor sculpture surveys conducted throughout the nation. Inscriptions are recorded in their entirety and are searchable by key words. So far, many cities and a couple of states have completed inventories. Examples of soldier monuments referring to liberty or freedom include those in Buffalo, N.Y. (1884), Brattleboro, Vt. (1887), Watertown, N.Y. (1890), Kewaunee, Wis. (c. 1989), and Philadelphia (1921). Examples referring specifically to the abolition of slavery are fewer, for example, Boston (1877), Yonkers, N.Y. (1891), Mt. Carroll, Ill. (1891), and Sycamore, Ill. (1897). Examples of Confederate inscriptions referring to Constitutional government or sovereignty principles include Darlington, S.C. (1880), Fort Mill, S.C. (1891), Lewisburg, Tenn. (1904), Raymond, Miss. (1908), Charlottesville, Va. (1909), and St. Louis (1914). Sometimes, of course, the same terms could appear on both Union and Confederate monuments; for example, "Constitutional government" actually appears on one Union monument in New Haven, Conn.

(1905). The only example I have found of a Confederate monument that refers to slavery is in Columbia, N.C. (1912), which includes the inscription "In appreciation of our faithful slaves."

For a case study that confirms these general observations, see Will Lee, "Post-Civil War Soldiers' Monuments in New Haven County, Connecticut," *Journal of the New Haven Colony Historical Society* 36 (Fall 1989): 25–51.

45. See the memorial volume by Thomas Astley Atkins and John Wise Oliver, *Yonkers in the Rebellion of 1861–1865* (Yonkers, N.Y.: Yonkers Soldiers' and Sailors' Monument Association, 1892).

46. Atkins and Oliver, *Yonkers,* 221–22.

47. The first two were designed by Randolph Rogers; see chapter 3. The Buffalo and Brattleboro monuments are recorded in the Inventory of American Sculpture. For the Cleveland and Indianapolis monuments, see Freeman Henry Morris Murray, *Emancipation and the Freed: A Study in Interpretation* (Washington, D.C.: Murray Brothers, 1916), 37–39.

48. Joseph Anderson, *History of the Soldiers' Monument in Waterbury, Conn.* (Monument Committee, 1886), 49–50.

49. "American Monumental Art," *Century* 28 (August 1884): 630–31; Karl Bitter, "Municipal Sculpture," *Municipal Affairs* 2 (March 1898): 75; *Monumental News* 10 (August 1898): 450; William Jean Beauley, "The Acute Problem of the Soldier's Monuments," *New York Herald,* magazine, May 29, 1904, p. 3. For a discussion of the industry's marketing and distribution tactics, see Williams, "Commerically Produced Forms of American Civil War Monuments," 84–86.

50. Williams, "Commercially Produced Forms of American Civil War Monuments," 52, 74–90.

51. "Grant's Memorial: What Shall It Be?" *North American Review* 141 (September 1885): 282.

52. See Williams, "Commercially Produced Forms of American Civil War Monuments," 55–59 for an overview. Detailed examples include *Proceedings at the Unveiling of the Soldiers' Monument on the Site of Fort Stephenson, Fremont, Ohio* (Fremont, Ohio.: Democratic Messenger, 1885), 6; *Watertown Enterprise,* November 1, 1889, clipping in Parks and Monuments Vertical File, Watertown Free Library, Watertown, Massachusetts.

53. Roe, *Monuments, Tablets, and Other Memorials Erected in Massachusetts,* 72. The allegorical monument in Lynn was supplemented by a standing-soldier monument several decades later; in Savanna, Georgia, the allegorical figure was actually replaced by a soldier figure. See Bettie A. C. Emerson, *Historic Southern Monuments, Representing Memorials of the Heroic Dead of the Southern Confederacy* (New York: Neale Publishing, 1911), 119–20.

In New Haven, Connecticut, a "realistic" soldier monument was erected in 1905 to supplement the allegorical monument erected in 1887; see Lee, "Post-Civil War Soldiers' Monuments."

54. This dispute was chronicled in some detail in *Monumental News* 10 (January 1898): 15–16; (March 1898): 161; (June 1898): 337; (July 1898): 394. See also *New York Times,* January 25, 1898, p. 11; May 27, 1898, p. 12.

55. The dedication of the standing-soldier monument in Watertown, Massachusetts, in 1889 illustrates this in exemplary fashion. The newspaper account is

careful to stress what the monument shares in common with other war memorials and also where it distinguishes itself. The account does not shy from remarking that the soldier figure "is a copy of one in New Bedford," but maintains that "the pedestal and base are of an entirely new design." It goes on to verify the authenticity of the pose—a slight variation from parade rest—and to explain its precise tactical significance. Yet the description does not end without commending the "artistic grouping" of emblems on the pedestal. *Watertown Enterprise*, November 1, 1889. See also Lee, "Post-Civil War Soldiers' Monuments," 36–38.

56. See Gerald F. Linderman, *The Mirror of War: American Society and the Spanish-American War* (Ann Arbor: University of Michigan Press, 1974), esp. 60–90. My thanks to Peter Karsten for drawing my attention to this important study.

57. *Proceedings at the Unveiling of the Soldiers' Monument on the Site of Fort Stephenson, Fremont, Ohio*, 32.

58. John W. Thompson, *An Authentic History of the Douglass Monument* (1903; Freeport, N.Y.: Books for Libraries Press, 1971), 39–40. The campaign did fail to erect a soldier monument, but unlike other campaigns it did succeed in erecting a statue of a black man—a monument to Frederick Douglass (1899)—the first freestanding portrait statue of an African American in the United States.

59. This racial system was and is unique to the United States. In Central and South American societies, white and black carry different meanings; gradations are recognized and accepted. A person who is considered "black" in the U.S. is not necessarily black in Cuba or Brazil or elsewhere.

60. *Proceedings at the Dedication of the Soldiers Monument at Pittsfield, Mass., September 24, 1872*, quoted in Williams, "Commercially Produced Forms of American Civil War Monuments," 147.

61. Rev. Joseph N. Green, "History of the Monument Erected by the Norfolk Memorial Association," undated brochure in author's possession. See also George Cantor, *Historic Landmarks of Black America* (Detroit: Gale Research, 1991), 257.

62. George Washington Williams, *A History of the Negro Troops in the War of the Rebellion, 1861–1865* (1888; New York: Bergman, 1968), 328.

63. John Hope Franklin, *George Washington Williams: A Biography* (Chicago: University of Chicago Press, 1985), 172. On the GAR's policies of segregation, see McConnell, *Glorious Contentment*, 213–18.

64. In the South, most Confederate soldier monuments were organized by ladies' memorial associations and later by the United Daughters of the Confederacy. Their organizational role is documented relatively early by catalogs of Confederate monuments; see especially Confederate Southern Memorial Association, *History of the Confederated Memorial Associations of the South*. For a local case study, see W. Stuart Towns, "Honoring the Confederacy in Northwest Florida: The Confederate Monument Ritual," *Florida Historical Quarterly* 57 (1978): 205–12. In the North, evidence of women's participation is much more piecemeal, but is nevertheless overwhelming. A search of the Inventory of American Sculpture turns up numerous examples of Union monuments sponsored or aided by women's organizations such as the Women's Relief Corps or the Ladies' Auxilliary of the GAR; many others not yet in the inventory also exist.

These same organizatons were also often accorded a visible presence in the dedication ceremonies.

65. Franklin, *George Washington Williams*, 171–73.

66. Williams, *History of the Negro Troops*, 328–29.

67. Ibid., 331–32.

68. Franklin, *George Washington Williams*, 172.

69. *American Architect and Building News* 23 (January 7, 1888): 2.

70. *Washington Bee*, June 28, 1890, p. 2.

71. "American Monumental Art," *Century* 28 (August 1884): 630–31; *American Architect and Building News* 22 (July 30, 1887): 46, and 23 (January 7, 1888): 2; Bitter, "Municipal Sculpture," *Municipal Affairs* 2 (March 1898): 75; *Monumental News* 10 (August 1898): 450; Charles Mulford Robinson, *The Improvement of Towns and Cities* (New York: G. P. Putnam's Sons, 1901), 236; Beauley, "The Acute Problem of the Soldier's Monuments," *New York Herald* magazine, May 29, 1904, p. 3; James Barnes, "Soldier's Monuments," *Art and Progress* 7 (May 1910): 185–89.

72. Bitter, "Municipal Sculpture," 76.

73. *American Architect and Building News* 23 (January 7, 1888): 2.

74. The most important secondary literature on the monument includes Stephen T. Riley, "A Monument to Colonel Robert Gould Shaw," *Proceedings of the Massachusetts Historical Society* 75 (January–December 1963): 27–38; Lincoln Kirstein, *Lay This Laurel* (New York: Eakins Press, 1973); Lois Goldreich Marcus, "The *Shaw Memorial* by Augustus Saint-Gaudens," *Winterthur Portfolio* 14 (Spring 1979): 1–23; Stephen J. Whitfield, "'Sacred in History and in Art': *The Shaw Memorial*," *New England Quarterly* 60 (March 1987): 3–27; Albert Boime, *The Art of Exclusion: Representing Blacks in the Nineteenth Century* (Washington, D.C.: Smithsonian Institution Press, 1990), 199–219.

75. James Barnes, "The Shaw Memorial," *Harper's Weekly* May 29, 1897, p. 546; "The Hero," *Century* 54 (May 1897): 312.

76. Quoted in Whitfield, "Sacred in History and in Art," 5.

77. Luis F. Emilio, *A Brave Black Regiment: History of the Fifty-Fourth Regiment of Massachusetts Volunteer Infantry, 1863–1865* (1894; New York: Arno Press, 1969); McPherson, *Negro's Civil War*, 173–91.

78. Quoted in Whitfield, "Sacred in History and in Art," 8.

79. Williams, *History of the Negro Troops*, 202.

80. Emilio, *A Brave Black Regiment*, 228–30. Kirstein, *Lay This Laurel*, sec. 4. Another example was Shaw University in Holly Springs, Mississippi; see William C. Harris, *The Day of the Carpetbagger: Republican Reconstruction in Mississippi* (Baton Rouge: Louisiana State University Press), 343.

81. Robert Duncan, ed., *Blue-Eyed Child of Fortune: The Civil War Letters of Colonel Robert Gould Shaw* (Athen: University of Georgia Press, 1992); Emilio, *A Brave Black Regiment*, 6–7.

82. McPherson, *Negro's Civil War*, 174–76, 193–203.

83. Boston *Daily Advertiser*, October 9, 1865. See also Boston *Evening Transcript*, October 7, 1865. Both clippings were kindly supplied to me by Thomas Brown. Smith's ex-slave status is reported by Alfred Roe in his *Monuments, Tablets and Other Memorials*, 32.

84. Boston *Evening Transcript*, October 7, 1865.

85. This statement of purpose was printed on the subscription books themselves and reprinted in the local newspapers; Boston *Daily Advertiser*, November 6, 1865, and Boston *Evening Transcript*, November 4, 1865. See also Edward Atkinson, "The History of the Monument," *Century Magazine* 54 (June 1897): 176.

86. Boston *Evening Transcript*, October 17, 1865.

87. Boston *Evening Transcript*, November 4, 1865.

88. According to the treasurer, Edward Atkinson, merely thirty-five people subscribed to the campaign in all, for a total amount of $7,521. His history of the monument makes no mention of Smith's early fund-raising and organizational efforts; he merely lists Smith as one of the original committee members; Atkinson, "The History of the Monument," 176. The archival material from the later committee is located primarily in Atkinson's papers and the papers of Henry Lee, both in the Massachusetts Historical Society, Boston.

89. Boston *Evening Transcript*, April 25, 1882; Marcus, "The *Shaw Memorial*," 8. The Richardson design is published in John H. Dryfhout, *The Work of Augustus Saint-Gaudens* (Hanover, N.H.: University Press of New England, 1982), pl. 166–7, along with a similar sketch by Saint-Gaudens (pl. 166–8). Edward Atkinson, treasurer for the committee, was already corresponding with Saint-Gaudens about his design in 1882; letter from Atkinson to Saint-Gaudens, December 9, 1882, in Atkinson Family Papers, Massachusetts Historical Society.

90. Homer Saint-Gaudens, ed., *The Reminiscences of Augustus Saint-Gaudens*, 2 vols. (New York: Century Co., 1913), 1:332. It is impossible to know precisely when or even whether this event took place. The committee did consult the wishes of the Shaw family, as a letter from Atkinson to Saint-Gaudens of November 5, 1886, makes clear (Atkinson Family Papers). By April 1883 Saint-Gaudens had prepared a model, which was approved (Atkinson to Saint-Gaudens, April 12, 1883, Atkinson Family Papers). Saint-Gaudens then signed a contract with the committee in early 1884, and the contract specifies only "a life size memorial in bronze and stone in alto and bas relief of Colonel Robert G. Shaw according to the sketch submitted" (Papers of Augustus Saint-Gaudens, Dartmouth College, Hanover, N.H., Reel 36, frame 62). This model may or may not have included figures of black soldiers.

91. Marcus, "The *Shaw Memorial*," 16.

92. See Dryfhout, *The Work of Augustus Saint-Gaudens*, pl. 166–9, p. 225.

93. Saint-Gaudens, *Reminiscences*, 1:333.

94. Letter from John M. Forbes to Henry Lee and M. P. Kennard, September 30, 1892, Lee Family Papers, Massachusetts Historical Society. Forbes's comments were part of the committee's long debate over the monument's inscriptions. The committee members fought hard with each other and in the process reflected openly on the meaning of the monument. But for all their differences over details, they agreed on the essentials—that the monument commemorated far more than Shaw himself, and that the black troops were critical to its significance.

95. William A. Coffin, "The Sculptor St. Gaudens," *Century* 54 (May 1897): 181.

96. *Reminiscences*, 1:333–35.

97. Albert Boime argues, mistakenly I believe, that the attitudes Saint-Gaudens revealed toward his models inform the sculpture as well, as if the art were an unmediated transcription of prejudice; this argument cannot be sustained without a serious misreading of the sculpture itself. See *Art of Exclusion*, 206–9.

98. Ibid., 209. I could not disagree more with Boime's observation that the black soldiers' "expressions, hand gestures, and postures are less certain and less energetic than Shaw's." It is the horse that is energetic; Shaw is still. There is no uncertainty in the postures or gestures of the troops: they are all calculated to show discipline.

99. Ibid., 209–11.

100. John M. Forbes, in particular, disliked the angel figure and the way in which Shaw's hat intersected with it: "I should like to make it a condition that that dev[lish] angel should be got out of the way of Robert Shaw's hat" (Forbes to Henry Lee, June 15, 1892, Lee Family Papers). Saint-Gaudens's artist-friend Paul Bion told him to remove the figure and wrote that "your priestess merely bores me"; *Reminiscences*, 1:344.

101. "The Hero," *Century* 54 (May 1897): 312.

102. William Howe Downes, quoted in Lorado Taft, *The History of American Sculpture* (1903; New York: MacMillan, 1925), 303. See also Charles Caffin, *American Masters of Sculpture* (Garden City, N.Y.: Doubleday, 1913), 11. Taft himself recognizes "the varied African types" of the soldiers, but sees them as marks of "workmanship," which by themselves "could not thrill us thus" (p. 304); he prefers to be swept up by the thrilling rhetoric of Downes. For a subtle, alternative reading, stressing the physical diversity of the soldiers, see Barnes, "The Shaw Memorial," *Harper's Weekly*, May 29, 1897, p. 546.

103. The text of the oration is reprinted in full in *Exercises at the Dedication of the Monument to Colonel Robert Gould Shaw* (Boston: Municipal Printing Office, 1897), 39–53. Booker T. Washington gave a shorter address at the ceremony, arguing that, despite the memorial's physical beauty, the "real monument" was being built in the South by the emancipated race itself, in the efforts to "justify all that has been done and suffered for it"; ibid., 60–61.

104. Quoted in Whitfield, "Sacred in History and in Art," 17.

105. W.E.B. DuBois, *Black Reconstruction* (New York: Harcourt, Brace, 1935), 110.

CHAPTER SEVEN
EPILOGUE

1. Blake Stimson, "Slow Provocation: An Interview with Dennis Adams," *Views: The Journal of Photography in New England* 12–13 (Winter 1992): 3–7; my thanks to Daniel Younger for sending me this essay. Stephen J. Whitfield, "'Sacred in History and in Art': *The Shaw Memorial*," *New England Quarterly* 60 (March 1987): 3–27.

The recent history of Monument Avenue needs to be written. The Ashe controversy was much discussed in the *Richmond Times-Dispatch* and the *Washington Post* in 1995–96. But the idea of erecting monuments to black heroes on the avenue goes back several years earlier; see John F. Harris, "Monumental Issue Divides Old Dominion," *Washington Post*, September 29, 1991, p. B3.

2. The full inscription reads, "Since we are surrounded by / so great a cloud of witnesses / let us lay aside every weight, and / the sin which so easily ensnares us, / and let us run with endurance / the race that is set before us."

3. On the proposed plaque, see Scott A. Sandage, "A Marble House Divided: The Lincoln Memorial, the Civil Rights Movement, and the Politics of Memory, 1939–1963," *Journal of American History* 80 (June 1993): 135–67, esp. 166–67.

INDEX

PAGE NUMBERS in bold italic refer to illustrations.

abolitionism, 21; in Boston, 64, 75; in Britain, 21; gradual, 93; as paternalistic, 87. *See also* abolitionist ideology; abolitionist imagery; abolitionists; emancipation; *Greek Slave*; U.S. Congress

abolitionist ideology, 35, 49, 72, 75; and convergence with proslavery ideology, 51; and ideal of racial uplift, 72, 75, 78. *See also* abolitionism; abolitionist imagery; abolitionists; emancipation; slave stereotypes

abolitionist imagery: in popular prints, *22, 23, 24*, 40, 43, *45*; in sculpture, 15–17, 21, *22*, 23, 28. *See also* abolitionism; abolitionist ideology; abolitionists; emancipation; slavery

abolitionists, 21, 23, 64, 75, 93; racial prejudices of, 81. *See also* abolitionism; abolitionist ideology; abolitionist imagery; Brown, Henry Kirke; emancipation; women

affirmative action, 192, 210

Africa: missionaries to, 72; personifications of, *59, 126,* 128; as primitive, 126, 155. *See also* African colonization

African American body, 31, 49; classicized, 53–54, 57, 81; and eroticism, 61–62, 77; indeterminacy of, 58–59, 69, 125; marked by slavery, 14; and masculinity, 61–62, 77–78, 117–19; and nudity, 53, 57–58, 61, 73; public invisibility of, 70, 88, 99; in public sculpture, 18, 66, 70, 81–83, 117; as sculptural subject, 14–16, 47, 69, 73, 77, 81, 87, 90, 96, 106, 114, 118, 126; and white nation, 209–10; whitened ideal of, *59*. *See also* African American soldiers; African Americans; slavery; white body

African American history: representation of, in sculpture, 89, 95–96, 104–5. *See also* African Americans; Hosmer, Harriet; Mills, Clark

African American soldiers, 128, 132; absence from common-soldier monuments, 167, 174–75, 184, 186, 188; absence from public memory, 189–90; as artistic theme, 193; civic status of, 97, 174–75, 196–97; as donors to Lincoln monuments, 92, 94; as emblems of emancipation, 97, 181, 190–91; as emblems of nation-state, 180, 184, 190, 207; experience in Civil War, 174; in folk memory, 189; and masculinity, 96–98, 174–75, 181, 207; Norfolk monument to, 187; and personal agency, 174; proposed national monuments to, 189–90, 191; represented in common-soldier monuments, 187, 192, 200; risks faced by, 195–96; and social identity, 98, 174, 181. *See also* African American body; African Americans; Shaw, Robert Gould; U.S. Congress

African Americans: in antebellum sculpture, 16–17, 70–72; caricature of, 9, 12, 26–27, 59, 97, 160, 172, 201; countermemory of, 138, 152; cranial measurements of, 13–14; as donors to monument campaigns, 90–92, 94, 137–38, 196–97; folklore of, 160; in local politics, 184–85, 191; in monument ritual, 138, 151, 153, 161, 188; as monument sponsors, 93–94, 114, 119–20, 186, 187, 189–191, 195, 196–97, 211–212; as national citizens, 3–4, 17, 94, 98, 111, 113, 118, 152, 174–75, 209, 212; in national monuments, 114; as part of public for monuments, 84, 90, 92, 93, 94, 137–38; in popular imagery, 12, 13, 26–27, 45–46, 160; in public sculpture, 86–87, 114, 117–19; in scientific illustration, 9–10, 12; stereotypes of, 12, 27, 158–60, 172, 201. *See also* African American body; African American soldiers; Lincoln tomb; Native Americans;

African Americans (*cont.*)
　　public space; Saint-Gaudens, Augustus;
　　slavery; slaves
African colonization, 72. *See also* Africa
Ahearn, John, 5
Alexander, Archer, 115, 116–17, 119
allegory: as monumental sign system, 108;
　　in public sculpture, 32, 40, 47, 62, 86–
　　87, 96, 99, 105, 165, 183, 126; and ra-
　　cial difference, 86–87, 101. *See also*
　　racial equality; realism; sculpture;
　　veterans
Anderson, Archer, 150–51, 152
Apollo Belvedere, 9, *11*, 12, 14, 15, 53,
　　81, 204. *See also* sculpture
architects, role in public monuments, 66,
　　142, 147, 190, 193, 197
Army of Northern Virginia, 130, 135, 136.
　　See also Confederate veterans; Lee,
　　Robert E.
Arrotino, 79, *80*
art, nineteenth-century idea of, 107–8; vs.
　　authenticity, 108–9, 183; vs. industry,
　　192–93; vs. nature, 145; vs. the popular,
　　108, 145; vs. standardization, 193; vs.
　　truth, 145, 147. *See also* African Ameri-
　　can soldiers; allegory; public monu-
　　ments; sculpture
Ashe, Arthur, monument to, 5, 211, 212
Atlanta Cotton States Exposition, 158
Avery, Charles, monument to, 70, *71*, 72,
　　82

Bakhtin, Mikhail, 12
Ball, Thomas, 73, 95, 124, 203; design for
　　monument to Lincoln, 77, *78*, 79–81,
　　83, 84, 114; *Emancipation Group* (Bos-
　　ton), 120, *121*; racial attitudes of, 81.
　　See also Eliot, Reverend William Green-
　　leaf; Freedmen's Memorial to Abraham
　　Lincoln; Lincoln monuments
Bandinelli, *Hercules and Cacus*, 79
Barton, Clara, 112
battle. *See* warfare
Beaufort, South Carolina, 195
Beecher, Henry Ward, 65, 110
Bellows, Henry, 110, 113; on Hosmer's de-
　　sign for the Freedmen's Memorial, 100–
　　101; on Mills's design for the National
　　Lincoln Monument, 107–108. *See also*
　　Freedmen's Memorial to Abraham Lin-
　　coln; Hosmer, Harriet; Mills, Clark; Na-

tional Lincoln Monument Association
　　(Washington, D.C.)
Bickerdyke, Mary, 112
Bingham, William, 137, 138, 139
Birth of a Nation (Griffith), 161
Bissell, George, 180
Blumenbach, Johann Friedrich, 9, 79,
　　217n.10
Boime, Albert, 202, 203, 256nn. 97, 98
Boston, 64, 75, 92, 196, 197. *See also* abo-
　　litionism; Boston Brahmins; Boston Com-
　　mon; *Emancipation Group*; Lincoln
　　monuments; Shaw Memorial
Boston Brahmins, 164, 192, 197
Boston Common, 193, 196
Brattleboro, Vermont, 180
Brooklyn, New York, 67, 69, 192. *See also*
　　Lincoln monuments
Brown, Henry Kirke, 17, 52, 57; as aboli-
　　tionist, 31, 36, 41, 48, 50; as advocate
　　of national sculpture, 32; *Choosing
　　of the Arrow*, *14*; as critic of Lincoln,
　　50; determination to make "Negro"
　　visible in public sculpture, 31, 36, 51,
　　54; final design for Lincoln monument
　　in New York, 81–82; Lincoln monu-
　　ment in Brooklyn, 67, *68*, 69; model for
　　pediment of South Carolina State
　　House, 36, *37*, *38*, *39*, 40–43, 47–51,
　　157; proposal for House pediment of
　　U.S. Capitol, 31–32, *33*, 34–35, 40, 48,
　　106; proposal for Lincoln monument in
　　New York, 73, *74*, 75–77; racial atti-
　　tudes of, 81. *See also* Lincoln monu-
　　ments; South Carolina State House;
　　U.S. Capitol
Brown, John, 48
Browning, Elizabeth Barrett, 28–29, 127
Brunt, Henry Van, 182, 184
Buffalo, New York, 180
Buffon, George, 10
Bullard and Bullard, architects, 190
Bush-Brown, Henry Kirke, 50–51, 81–82

Calhoun, John C., 27, 41, 129
Camper, Petrus, 9
Catawba Indians (South Carolina), 159
Centennial Exhibition, Philadelphia, 87
Charleston, South Carolina, 195
Chase, Salmon, 110
Chesnutt, Charles, 160
Chicago, Illinois, 124, 126, 128, 197, 203.

See also Hosmer, Harriet; Lincoln monuments; Saint-Gaudens, Augustus

Child, Lydia Maria, 93

citizen-soldier, 19, 163, 188; African American, 98, 196; and American nationalism, 167–68; generic body of, 176–77; mythology of, 167–68, 177; redefinition of, 176–77, 207; sculptural proliferation of, 182. *See also* common soldier; nationalism; volunteer soldiers

Civil War, 3, 210; casualties in, 162, 166; moral cause of, 67, 165; and nationalism, 184; and sectional reconciliation, 132, 150; transformation of warfare, 173; becomes war on slavery, 52, 173. *See also* African American soldiers; commemoration; common soldier; nationalism; proslavery ideology; war memorials; warfare

Clark, Edward, 142

Clay, Edward W., 27

Cleveland, Grover, 152

Cleveland, Ohio, 180, 192

Coffin, F. M., 45

collective memory: distinct from history, 215 n.4; in nineteenth-century U.S., 6–7; and ritual, 136; theory of, 6–7, 216 n.6. *See also* commemoration; emancipation; public monuments; slavery

Colored People's Educational Monument Association, 93–94, 104. *See also* Douglass, Frederick; Garnet, Henry Highland

Columbia, North Carolina, 158

Columbia, South Carolina. *See* Brown, Henry Kirke; South Carolina State House

commemoration: as closure, 4, 64, 65, 70, 75, 87, 121; and history, 66, 98, 101–102, 213; landscape of, 20, 212; Northern vs. Southern, 130, 178–79; process of, 4, 7; role of sculpture in, 66; surge of interest in, after the Civil War, 69–70. *See also* collective memory; Confederate commemoration; emancipation; history; Lincoln, Abraham; Massachusetts 54th regiment; Union commemoration; white supremacy

common soldier: appearance in public sculpture, 162, 166, 176; changing role in warfare, 173; duality of image, 168; experience in Civil War, 169–70, 173;

and loss of personal agency, 170, 173–74, 177; and masculinity, 167, 170, 172, 174; in national monument to Lincoln, 111–12. *See also* soldiering

common-soldier monuments: and authenticity, 183–84; criticism of, 182, 192–93, 210; demographics of, 185; and emancipation, 84–87, 180; equate military and civic valor, 178, 206; inscriptions on, 178–180; in local communities, 178, 183, 185, 210; and masculinity, 167, 177, 188, 207; modern invention of, 19, 162, 166; moral neutrality of, 178, 206; and nationalism, 183, 184, 207–208; parade rest pose of, 164, 176–77; and patriotism, 178, 211; and physiognomy, 163, 187; popularity of, 166, 182, 184, 193; proliferation of, 162, 164, 166, 178, 181–82; as racial construct, 181, 186–88, 190; as reactionary, 208; redefinition of heroism, 177; as representation of warfare, 183–84; ritual of, 188; siting of, 162; standardization of, 163–64, 177, 182–83, 193; in twentieth century, 211; as vernacular idiom, 184; and whiteness, 162–63, 167, 181–82, 186–88, 190, 209. *See also* African American soldiers; ethnicity; nationalism; New England; veterans; women

Confederacy, 52, 62, 129, 130, 131, 212, 135. *See also* Confederate commemoration; Confederate veterans; Lee, Robert E.; proslavery ideology

Confederate commemoration, 18, 152; disavowal of slavery, 129–31, 149, 157–58; and progress, 148–50; in recent times, 211–212. *See also* Confederacy; Confederate veterans; Union commemoration

Confederate veterans, 135–36, 137, 145, 147, 155. *See also* Lee Monument; veterans

contrabands. *See* fugitives from slavery

Copperheads, 84

countermemory. *See* African Americans

Craven, Wayne, 231 n.58

Crawford, Thomas, 32

Cromwell, John, 117

Crow, Wayman, 93

Cruikshank, George, 40

Cumberworth, Charles, 15

Currier and Ives, 72
Curry, Jabez, 134–35
Cuvier, Georges, 9

Davis, Jefferson, 131, 148
Davis, William Morris, 36, 48–49
Declaration of Independence, 120
Defiance: Inviting a Shot before Petersburg
    (Homer), 170–73, *171*
de Kay, Charles, 64
Democratic Party, 180
design competitions. *See* Lee Monument;
    Lincoln tomb
Detroit, Michigan. *See* Michigan Soldiers'
    and Sailors' Monument
Dix, Dorothea, 112
Douglas, Stephen, 107
Douglass, Frederick, 30, 92, 122; on inte-
    gration versus separatism, 93–94, 104;
    on masculinity, 117–18; monument to,
    253 n.58; as sculptural emblem of eman-
    cipation, 110–11; speech at Freed-
    men's Memorial, 114, 117–20. *See also*
    Colored People's Educational Monu-
    ment Association; Freedmen's Memorial
    to Abraham Lincoln; Lincoln, Abraham
DuBois, W. E. B., 161, 207; *Souls of Black
    Folk*, 160

Early, Jubal, 135, 136, 137, 138, 144
École des Beaux-Arts, 146, 147, 148
Eliot, Reverend William Greenleaf, 93,
    112; and Archer Alexander, 115, 116–
    17; and Thomas Ball, 114
Eliott, Charles W., 193
emancipation, 63; African American cele-
    brations of, 65; as challenge to nation,
    3, 17, 89–90; in collective memory, 5,
    65, 122, 128; as commemorative sub-
    ject, 18, 19, 65, 84–87, 100–101, 113,
    120–21, 125, 128, 213; and femininity,
    59, 77; as incomplete historical process,
    18, 56–57, 65, 98, 102–103; as manu-
    mission, 74–75, 77, 80, 83, 87; marginal-
    ization of, 19, 121–22, 124–25; and mas-
    culinity, 59, 77–78, 118–19; as narrative
    orchestrated by Lincoln, 65–66, 72, 77,
    79, 83, 87, 99–100, 117, 118; and na-
    tional memory, 5, 100–101; negative im-
    agery of, 27, 160; popular imagery of,
    56, 72, 120–21; as rebirth, 59, 80; as
    sculptural subject, 54, 63–64, 65–66,

72, 85–87, 90, 96–97, 101–3, 105–6,
117–19, 126; subordinated to idea of
Union, 84, 100, 122. *See also* African
American soldiers; common-soldier mon-
uments; Douglass, Frederick; *Freedman*;
Union commemoration; Ward, John
Quincy Adams
Emancipation Group (Ball), 18, 120, *121*,
211. *See also* Ball, Thomas; Freedmen's
Memorial to Abraham Lincoln; Lincoln
monuments
Emancipation Monument. *See* Freedmen's
Memorial to Abraham Lincoln
Emancipation Proclamation, 52–56, 67,
103, 213; in Missouri, 116 ; in monument proposals, 77, 83, 95, 102, 104,
122, 124; in public monuments, 81,
101. *See also* emancipation; Lincoln,
Abraham
equestrian monuments: to Andrew Jackson
(Mills), 107; to Frederick the Great
(Rauch), 66, 109; to Marcus Aurelius,
39; as metaphor of dominance, 133,
150, 196; and modern warfare, 198. *See
also* Lee, Robert E.; Lee Monument;
Shaw Memorial
ethnicity, in common-soldier monuments,
186. *See also* race
Ezekiel, Moses, proposal for Lee Monument, 141–42, *143*, 146

faithful slaves: Fort Mill monument to,
155, *156*, 157–61, 162; and mammy figure, 158–59; proposed monuments to,
158; white memory of, 157–59. *See also*
slavery, slaves
Faust, Drew Gilpin, 129
Ferdinand, Grand Duke, monument to, 23,
26
Fisk Jubilee Singers, 160
folk memory, 7, 189. *See also* African
American soldiers; collective memory
Forbes, John M., 200
Fort Mill, South Carolina, 159. *See also*
faithful slaves
Fort Wagner, South Carolina, 194–95,
197, 206. *See also* Massachusetts 54th
regiment; Robert Gould Shaw
Foster, Stephen, 172; *My Old Kentucky
Home*, 158
Fourteenth Amendment, 62, 103
Franklin, Benjamin, 21

free labor ideology, 35. *See also* abolitionist ideology; proslavery ideology

Freedman (Ward), 53, 209; as agent of his own emancipation, 56; and classical canon, 53–54, 57, 60, 62; as commemorative object, 54, 64, 87, 165; comparisons of other works with, 63–64, 73, 81, 87, 98; eroticism of, 61–62, 73; as liminal figure, 55, 59, 62, 64; masculinity of, 61–62; nudity of, 53, 57–62; as promise of new sculptural order, 54, 62, 125; realism of, 54, 57, 60; reception of, 52, 53–54, 55, 60–62, 64; title of, 56–57. *See also* Howells, William Dean; Ward, John Quincy Adams

Freedmen's Bureau bill, 92

Freedmen's Memorial to Abraham Lincoln (Ball), 18, 19, 91, 122, 125, 128, 197, 209; Ball's designs for, 78, 114, 115, 118; dedication of, 114, 117–20; as enactment of Reconstruction, 89–90, 92, 119; fundraising campaign for, 89–92, 94; Hosmer's designs for, 94–100, 95, 99; as image of domination, 90, 119, 129; and National Lincoln Monument Association (Springfield, Illinois), 100–1, 103, 111, 114; and National Lincoln Monument Association (Washington, D.C.), 103–4, 111, 114; as portrait of Archer Alexander, 115–17; public for, 92, 94, 120; repetition of, 120–21; white sponsorship of, 92–93. *See also* Ball, Thomas; Bellows, Henry; Douglass, Frederick; Hosmer, Harriet; Lincoln tomb; National Lincoln Monument Association (Washington, D.C.); Reconstruction; U.S. Congress; Western Sanitary Commission

Frémont, John Charles, 116

Fremont, Ohio, 185

French, Daniel Chester, Lincoln Memorial, 128, 212

French, Samuel Bassett, 137, 138, 139, 140

fugitives from slavery, 52, 55, 62, 63, 93, 115–16; as heroic, 15; imagery of, 57, 58, 73, 96, 192, 227n.12. *See also* slavery, slaves

Fuller, James, 187

Garfield, James, 169, 170

Garnet, Henry Highland, 93

Garrison, William Lloyd, 64

Gettysburg: battle of, 62, 166; national soldiers cemetery, 4

Gettysburg Address (Lincoln), 3, 4, 54, 124, 178

Gliddon, George R. *See Types of Mankind*

Grand Army of the Republic, 188, 247 n.1

Grant, Ulysses S., 106, 110

Greek Slave (Powers), 29, 59; abolitionist interpretations of, 28–29; comparisons of other works with, 34, 57; as ideal sculpture, 29–31, 50, 54; as phantasm of slavery, 30; slaveholders' acceptance of, 29, 36; whiteness of, 30

Greeley, Horace, 124, 160

Greenough, Horatio, *George Washington*, 54, 58, 62

Griffith, D. W., 161

Grotesque, 12, 59, 160

Habermas, Jürgen, 216 n.6

Hampton, Wade, 36

Harnische, A. E., 102–3

Harrison, Benjamin, 152

Hart, Charles Henry, 124–25

Hatt, Michael, 61, 228 n.24

Hayne, Robert, 36

Hegel, Georg Wilhelm Friedrich, 43

heroism: African American, 15, 57, 59, 62, 111, 132, 189, 206; redefinition of, 18–19, 176–77, 207; sculpture and, 23, 55, 58, 67, 69, 73, 108, 125, 133, 176–77, 207; in warfare, 168, 170, 171–72; white, 54, 58, 83, 88, 96, 125, 130, 132, 197, 203–4, 206. *See also* common-soldier monuments; fugitives from slavery; history; Lee, Robert E.; sculpture; slaves; valor; warfare

Higginson, Thomas Wentworth, 98, 170, 174, 195

history: and commemoration, 66; as heroic tale of great men, 66, 69

Hoen, A. and Co., 134

Homer, Winslow. *See Defiance: Inviting a Shot before Petersburg*

Hosmer, Harriet: *African Sibyl*, 127; in design competition for Lincoln tomb, 101–3; designs for Freedmen's Memorial, 94–100, 95, 99; design for Lincoln monument in Chicago, 125–28, 127; failure to realize designs, 103, 113, 128, 209; as

Hosmer, Harriet (*cont.*)
  high artist, 107–8, 109, 145; on slavery,
  93. *See also* Bellows, Henry; Freedmen's
  Memorial to Abraham Lincoln; Mills,
  Clark
Houdon, Jean Antoine, 130
Houston, Sam, 136
Hove, Victor van, 220n.29
Howard University, 189
Howells, William Dean: and critique of
  militarism, 164, 204; on *Freedman*, 58–
  59, 64, 165–66; on nature of public
  monuments, 66; on new national order,
  17, 18; on war memorials, 19, 84, 164–
  66, 167, 182, 205
Hunt, Richard Morris, *163*

Ignatiev, Noel, 19
Indianapolis, 180
Indians. *See* Native Americans
Irish-Americans, 81–82, 89, 186

Jackson, Andrew, 107, 167
James, Henry: on Lee Monument, 148,
  154; on the "Negro," 154–55; on
  Richmond, 154
James, William: on civic valor, 206–7; on
  militarism, 205; oration at Shaw Memo-
  rial, 193, 204–7
Jarves, James Jackson, 54, 61, 64
Jefferson, Thomas, 130, 167
Jim Crow, 128, 152
Johns, Henry T., 170
Johnson, Andrew, 92
Jordan, Winthrop, 19

Keegan, John, 170, 173
Kemper, James, 137, 138, 139, 145–46,
  151
Kimball, Moses, 120
King, Martin Luther, Jr., 212, 213

Ladies Union Aid Society of St. Louis,
  111–12
Langston, John Mercer, 92
Lee, Colonel Henry, 200
Lee, Fitzhugh, 146, 148, 150
Lee, Robert E., 162; African American attitudes toward, 132, 138; as "American"
  hero, 139, 152, 161; as embodiment
  of Confederacy, 130–31, 135, 140;
  equestrian image of, 133, *134*, 135,

141–44, 146, 150, 196; and horse
  Traveller, 133–35; Northern attitudes
  toward, 132; popular memory of, 137;
  as racial icon, 132 ; as sculptural subject, 132, 140–41, 143–44; and slavery,
  131; and white mastery, 133–35, 142,
  146. *See also* Lincoln, Abraham; white
  supremacy
Lee Monument (Mercié): African American participation in, 137–38, 151–53;
  African American reception of, 151–53;
  and class division, 151; and Confederate
  veterans, 135, 136, 137, 145, 147; design competitions for, 109, 139–46; design proposals for, 109, *142*, *143*, *144*;
  fundraising for, 136–39; and gender division, 135, 139–40, 145–46, 150; as
  image of "the people," 150–51; Mercié's
  final design for, *147*, 148; as national
  monument, 136, 152; Northern reception of, 152; and racial division, 151–
  52; ritual of, 136–38, 150–52; siting of,
  148–50; and slavery, 130, 150, 152,
  154, 157; and white supremacy, 135,
  138–39, 150–52, 155, 157; women's
  participation in, 135, 139–40, 145–146,
  148, 150. *See also* Ezekiel, Moses;
  James, Henry; Mercié, Antonin; Mills,
  Clark; Ream, Vinnie; Saint-Gaudens, Augustus, Ward, John Quincy Adams
Leonidas, 196
Lewis, Edmonia, *Forever Free*, *63*, 64
Lincoln, Abraham, 50, *56*, *68*, 72, *74*, *76*,
  78, *82*, *91*, *105*, *115*, *121*, *123*; as art
  critic, 108–09; assassination, 70, 90; as
  commemorative subject, 65–66, 67, 70,
  81, 87–88, 90, 101, 119–20, 121–22,
  124–25, 212; compared to Lee, 131–32;
  compromises with proslavery Unionists,
  116–17; early monument campaigns for,
  69–70; as embodiment of Union, 125,
  130; Frederick Douglass on, 119; as
  ideal figure, 80, 122, 124–25; as master,
  74–75, 91, 133; noncanonical body of,
  67, 69, 114, 131–33; physiognomy of,
  69; as prophet, 126; as savior of Union,
  122, 124–25, 180; as sculptural subject,
  69, 73–74, 83, 96, 99–100, 114, 122,
  131; as white man's President, 119, 122.
  See also African American soldiers;
  Brown, Henry Kirke; Colored People's
  Education Monument Association; eman-

cipation; Emancipation Proclamation; Freedmen's Memorial to Abraham Lincoln; Gettysburg Address; Hosmer, Harriet; Lincoln Memorial; Lincoln monuments; Lincoln tomb; Mills, Clark; National Lincoln Monument Association (Washington, D.C.); Ream, Vinnie; Rogers, John; Rogers, Randolph; Saint-Gaudens, Augustus
Lincoln Memorial, Washington, D.C. (French), 128, 212
Lincoln monuments
—Boston. *See Emancipation Group* (Ball)
—Brooklyn, by Henry Kirke Brown, 66, *67, 69*
—Chicago: *Seated Lincoln* (Saint-Gaudens), 126, 128; *Standing Lincoln* (Saint-Gaudens), 122, *123*, 124–26, 197, 203, 212
—New York, by Henry Kirke Brown, 73, 77, 81–82
—Philadelphia, by Randolph Rogers, 72, 76, 77, 81, 83–84
—Springfield, Illinois. *See* Lincoln tomb
—Washington, D.C.. *See* Freedmen's Memorial to Abraham Lincoln and Lincoln Memorial
Lincoln tomb, Springfield, Illinois (Mead): and African Americans, 94, 103, 114; design competition for, 101–3; final design for, 66, 101; fundraising for, 6, 66, 94, 103; proposed merger with Freedmen's Memorial, 100, 103, 114; rivalry with National Lincoln Monument Association (Washington, D.C.), 69, 103, 111. *See also* Freedmen's Memorial to Abraham Lincoln; Lincoln monuments; National Lincoln Monument Association (Washington, D.C.)
Lincoln's tomb. *See* Lincoln tomb
Livingston, Alabama, Confederate Soldiers Monument, *165*
Lossing, Benson, 166
Lost Cause, 130, 131, 132, 155, 161. *See also* Confederate commemoration
Lynn, Massachusetts, 183

Mahone, William, 138
Mall, Washington, D.C., 114, 212
manumission: iconography of, 75, 96, 98, 114; rite of, 74–75. *See also* emancipation

Marietta, Ohio, 90
masculinity, 30, *59*, 61–62, 77–78, 96–98, 117–19, 167–68, 181, 188, 207. *See also* African American body; African American soldiers; common soldier; common-soldier monuments; Douglass, Frederick; emancipation; *Freedman*; slavery
Massachusetts. *See* abolitionism; Boston; Lynn; Shaw Memorial
Massachusetts 2nd regiment, 195
Massachusetts 54th regiment, 194; commemoration of, 195–97, 200, 211; difficulties faced by, 196. *See also* Shaw, Robert Gould; Shaw Memorial
Massachusetts State House, 193
McDuffie, George, 36
McKim, Charles, 193
Mead, Larkin, 66, 101. *See also* Lincoln tomb
Mercié, Antonin: final design for Lee Monument, 146, *147*, 148; first design proposal for Lee Monument, 146; and Saint-Gaudens, Augustus, 146. *See also* Lee Monument
Michelangelo, 79, 106
Michigan Soldiers' and Sailors' Monument (R. Rogers), 86–87, 180
militarism, 164, 168, 177–78, 205, 207, 211. *See also* Howells, William Dean; James, William
Miller, Polk, 159–60, 161
Mills, Clark, 36, 217n.9; compared to Harriet Hosmer, 107–8, 145; as Confederate sympathizer, 107; design for National Lincoln Monument, 104, *105*, 106–13; monument to Andrew Jackson, 107; monument to George Washington, 109; as popular sculptor, 107, 109, 145; proposal for Lee Monument, 109; as slaveholder, 106–7. *See also* National Lincoln Monument Association (Washington, D.C.)
Mills, Fisk, 237n.60
Milmore, Martin, 249n.11
Minstrelsy, 12, 97, 160, 219n.19
Mitchell, John, 151–53
Mitchell, George H., 179
Monument Avenue: development of, 148–50; in 1907, *149*; in post-Civil Rights era, 211–12, 256n.1. *See also* Lee Monument; Richmond

monument industry, 164, 182
Morrison, Toni, 20
Murray, Freeman, 120, 161

Nast, Thomas, *Patience on a Monument*, *175*, 176
Natchitoches, Louisiana, *Good Darky*, 158
nation, American: interracial ideal of, 17, 70, 89, 94, 103–4, 112–13, 210; and "the people," 5; redefinition of, 3–5, 18–19, 54, 70, 89–90, 98, 103, 113, 122, 161, 208, 209–10. *See also* African American body; African American soldiers; emancipation; nationalism; public monuments; race; Reconstruction
National Academy of Design, 53
National Lincoln Monument Association (Springfield, Illinois). *See* Lincoln tomb
National Lincoln Monument Association (Washington, D.C.), 69; Clark Mills's design for, 104, *105*, 106–12; failure of, 113; fund raising of, 103–4, 110–12; origin of, 103; proposed merger with Freedmen's memorial, 103, 104, 111, 114. *See also* Freedmen's Memorial to Abraham Lincoln; Mills, Clark
nationalism, American: and citizen-soldier, 167; after the Civil War, 184; and common-soldier monuments, 183, 184, 207–8; and "the people," 6; and public monuments, 6. *See also* citizen-soldier; Civil War; common-soldier monuments; nation
Native Americans, 32, 58; in antebellum sculpture, 14; compared to African Americans, 14; cranial measurements of, 13–14; as ideal, 15, 223n.28. *See also* Catawba Indians
New England, and common-soldier monuments, 177
New-England's Freedmen's Aid Society, 94
New Orleans, 28, 29
New York, New York, 17, *52*, 67, 70, 73, 77, 81, 82, 128, 163. *See also* Lincoln monuments; New York 7th regiment
New York 7th Regiment (Ward), *195*, *206*; monument to, 162, *163*, 164, 176
Newport, Rhode Island, Common Burying Ground, 16
Niehaus, Charles, proposal for Lee Monument, 143, *144*, 146

Nora, Pierre, 215n.4, 216n.6
Norfolk, Virginia, 65, 187
Norton, Charles Eliot, 66, 70–72

Page, Thomas Nelson, 157
Pasquale, Paul D., 211
patriotism, 178, 211; African American, 111. *See also* nationalism
Patterson, Orlando, *Slavery and Social Death*, 15, 30, 74, 219n.25
Petersburg, battle of, 170, *171*, *172*
Pezzicar, Francesco, 87
Philadelphia, 72, 76, 77, 81, 84, 87. *See also* Centennial Exhibition; Lincoln monuments
Phillips, Wendell, 160
photography, 141, 149, 153–54; compared to sculpture, 9. *See also* war photography
Pittsburgh, Pennsylvania, 70, 72. *See also* Avery, Charles
Pittsfield, Massachusetts, 187
portrait sculpture, 106; essential to monuments, 66; limitations of, 67, 69; problem of, 122, 125, 141
Powers, Hiram, 23, 83. *See also* *Greek Slave*
Preston, John, 36
proslavery ideology, 27, 31, 41; after the Civil War, 150, 160; and the Confederacy, 129; paradoxes of, 43, 50. *See also* abolitionist ideology
proslavery imagery, 26–27, 31, 43, *44*, *45*. *See also* abolitionist imagery
Providence, Rhode Island. *See* Rhode Island Soldiers' and Sailors' Monument
public monuments: in cemeteries, 70, 72, 162, 249n.11; as conservative, 4, 211; democratization of, 5, 162; function of, 4, 6–8, 209, 210; fundraising for, 6, 91–92, 103–4, 110, 136–39, 188; to great men, 150, 176, 178; as high art, 66; as image of "the people," 7–8, 150–51; interracial, 70, 89, 117, 125, 211; as means to gain civic recognition, 6, 94, 111, 119–20, 161; as national self-definition, 6–7, 89, 103, 207–8, 209–10; national vs. local, 89; permanence of, 4, 8, 65, 75, 84, 117, 211; as popular expression, 6–8, 66; public for, 84, 89, 92, 94, 100, 110, 112–13, 136, 161; ritual of, 6, 7, 136, 138, 150–55,

188; siting of, 148; as unique, 181–82. *See also* African Americans; architects; common-soldier monuments; emancipation; Emancipation Proclamation; equestrian monuments; Howells, William Dean; Lincoln monuments; nationalism; public space; sculpture; war memorials; women; *individual entries for monuments*

public space: in nineteenth-century U.S., 5–6; as representational battleground, 5; as site of monuments, 65, 162; visibility of African Americans in, 17, 18, 88, 89, 189. *See also* public monuments; public sphere

public sphere, 209, 216n.6; in nineteenth-century U.S., 6–7. *See also* public monuments; public space; whiteness

Pujol, Paul, 147

Quarles, Benjamin, 7, 120

race: and classical sculpture, 8–9, 11, 61; definition of, 8, 217n.8; and dominant culture, 20; and human body, 8–9, 11–12, 15, 90, 119, 209; and idea of the nation, 4, 20, 113, 209–10; invention of, 8. *See also* racial theory; slavery

race relations, 88, 155, 191, 210; idealization of, 157–59. *See also* race; Richmond

racial equality, 84, 103, 104; allegory of, 111; failure to imagine, 113, 119; understood in the human body, 119

racial theory: and classical sculpture, 8–9, 11, 30, 217n.10; and facial angle, 30, 73. *See also* race

racism, 8, 20, 64, 81, 134, 201, 211. *See also* race; racial theory

Randolph, Sarah Nicholas, 139, 145, 148

Rauch, Christian Daniel, 66, 109

realism: literary, 59; reconciled with classicism, 54, 60; in sculpture, 54, 57–58, 106, 122, 125; vs. allegory, 108, 115, 183. See also *Freedman*

Ream [Hoxie], Vinnie: *Abraham Lincoln* (U.S. Capitol), 81, *82*, 83; and Lee Monument competition, 145, 244n.44. *See also* Lee Monument

Reconstruction, 18, 70, 102, 111, 103, 175, 209, 210, 213; as cultural challenge, 4, 17, 78, 113; failure of, 113,

121–22, 128, 152; and Freedmen's Memorial, 89–90, 92, 119; in Virginia, 135. *See also* Freedmen's Memorial to Abraham Lincoln; U.S. Congress

Regular Army soldiers: image of, 168, 169, 170; vs. volunteers, 164, 167–68. *See also* common soldier; volunteer soldiers

Republican Party, 72, 137, 152

Republicans, radical, 103, 107, 111, 113, 145

Revolutionary War, 70, 194; army, 167, 168; monuments to, 166

Rhode Island Soldiers' and Sailors' Monument (R. Rogers), 84, *85*, *86*, 180

Richards, T. Addison, 46

Richardson, Henry Hobson, 197, 198

Richmond, Virginia, 144, 160; and legacy of slavery, 130, 154; as modern city, 130, 149–50; in post-Civil Rights era, 211–12; race relations in, 151, 212; State Capitol, 130, 138, 148, 149. *See also* James, Henry; Lee Monument; Monument Avenue

Rochester, New York, 186, 189, 191

Roediger, David, 19

Rogers, John: proposal for Lincoln monument in Philadelphia, 72; *Slave Auction*, *16*, 17, 28, 53

Rogers, Randolph, 73, 249n.11; final design for Lincoln monument in Philadelphia, 81; proposals for Lincoln monument in Philadelphia, *76*, 77, 83–84. *See also* Michigan Soldiers' and Sailors' Monument; Lincoln monuments; Rhode Island Soldiers' and Sailors' Monument

Saint-Gaudens, Augustus: on jury for Lee Monument, 142–43, 146; life studies of African Americans, 201–2; Lincoln Monument, Chicago (*Seated Lincoln*), 126, 128; Lincoln Monument, Chicago (*Standing Lincoln*), 122, *123*, 124–26, 197, 203, 212; and merger of real and ideal, 125, 128, 203; racial prejudices of, 201; Shaw Memorial, 193, *194*, 197–98, *199*, *200*, 201–4, 206–7, 210. *See also* Lee Monument; monuments to Lincoln; Shaw Memorial

St. Louis, Missouri, 93, 116. *See also* Ladies' Union Aid Society; Western Sanitary Commission

Sandusky County, Ohio, Soldiers' Monument, *185*, 186

Scott, Charlotte, 90–91, 94, 120

Scott, Sir Walter, monument to, 66

sculptors: African American, 63; and monument sponsors, 7, 66, 69, 83–84, 110–12, 114–15, 118, 146–48, 198–201, 203. *See also* sculpture; *individual entries for sculptors*

sculpture: academic, 141, 143, 145, 146; canon, 9, 11–12, 53, 69, 81, 107; classical tradition of, 9–12, 14–16, 32, 53–54, 58, 177; and heroic body, 15, 23, 55, 58, 67, 69, 106, 108, 176–77; and human body, 8–9, 12, 14, 66–67, 78, 89, 90, 117, 119, 176; ideal, 28–30, 32, 57, 59, 127; ideal vs. real, 125, 128; language of, 66–67, 78, 89, 119; as monumental medium, 8, 66, 82, 84, 117, 120; national, 32; and naturalism, 57; and nudity, 30, 57, 58, 62; popular vs. high art, 107, 108, 145; and representation of racial "color," 16–17, 42, 81. *See also* abolitionist imagery; African American body; African American history; African Americans; allegory; commemoration; common soldier; heroism; Native Americans; photography; portrait sculpture; race; racial theory; realism; slaveholders; slavery; slaves; South Carolina; U.S. Capitol

Seward, William, 108–9

Shakespeare, William, *Titus Andronicus*, 178

Shaw, Robert Gould, 194; in African American memory, 196; early attempts to commemorate, 195; glorification of, 195–96, 204, 206; reputation linked to African American soldiers, 197; William James on, 206. *See also* Massachusetts 54th regiment; Shaw Memorial

Shaw Memorial (Saint-Gaudens), 193, *194*, *198*, *199*, *200*, 210, 211; design history of, 197–201; early campaign for, 196–97; as fusion of types, 194; inscriptions for, 193, 255 n.94; reception of, 203–4; relationship of commander to troops, 202–3; as representation of black diversity, 201; rhythms of, 202; and slavery, 204, 205; as unique war memorial, 194, 201; William James's oration on, 204–7. *See also* Massachu-

setts 54th regiment; Saint-Gaudens, Augustus; Shaw, Robert Gould

Sherman, William Tecumseh, 50, 106

slave labor, 31, 34, 38, 41, 154; in Clark Mills's foundry, 106; and consciousness, 43; gang system of, 43, 47; imagery of, 43, 45, *46*, 47–48, 157, 158–59; as representational dilemma, 45–48; and skill, 42–43; task system of, 47, 49

slave stereotypes, 28, 219n.23; abolitionist, 49; ambivalent, 46–47; in ancient theater, 12, 218n.19; compared to soldier stereotypes, 169. *See also* African Americans

slaveholders, 5, 29, 31, 35, 49–50, 169, 178; defense of, 150, 180; as patrons of sculpture, 29, 31, 35–36, 57, 107, 157; in South Carolina, 29, 36, 41. *See also* proslavery ideology; proslavery imagery; slavery

slavery: abolitionist emblem of, 21, *22* 52, 73; and African American body, 14; ancient imagery of, 23, 74, 224n.46; attempts to idealize, 31, 43, 47, 50, 157–61; in collective memory, 5, 101, 129–30, 138, 152, 154, 157–58, 161, 167, 181, 207; iconography of, 21, 23, 26, 34, 41–42, 90, 106, 221n.2; and masculinity, 30, 117–18; in Missouri, 93, 116; in personal memory, 129, 155, 157; and race, 3–4, 15, 42, 113, 119, 129, 211; and sculpture, 14–15, 17, 35, 50; as "social death," 30, 219n.25; in South Carolina, 42, 209. *See also* abolitionism; African American body; Civil War; Confederate commemoration; fugitives from slavery; *Greek Slave*; Lee Monument; proslavery ideology; proslavery imagery; Shaw Memorial; slaves; soldiering

slaves: ambiguous status of, 46, 50; in antebellum sculpture, 16–17, 32, 34, 38, 47, 52; and blackness, 19, 42; as heroic, 15, 17; as liminal, 15, 46, 219n.25; in postwar sculpture, 74, 77, 79–81, 83, 90, 96, 104–6, 114–19; as soldiers, 97–98, 170. *See also* faithful slaves; fugitives from slavery; slavery; women

Smith, Joshua B., 196, 197

Smith, W. L. G., 45

Society of the Cincinnati, 194, 196

soldier monuments. *See* common-soldier monuments

soldiering: compared to slavery, 168–70, 181; and discipline, 169, 177. *See also* Civil War; common soldier; Regular Army soldiers; volunteer soldiers; warfare

South Carolina, 209; patronage of sculpture in, 29, 31, 35–36, 107; as proslavery center, 31, 35, 41. *See also* Beaufort; Brown, Henry Kirke; Catawba Indians; Charleston; faithful slaves; Fort Mill; Fort Wagner; slaveholders; slavery; South Carolina State House; white supremacy

South Carolina State House, 31, 36, *37*, 41, 48; Henry Kirke Brown's pediment project for, 36, *37*, *38*, *39*, 40–43, 47–51. *See also* Brown, Henry Kirke

Springfield, Illinois. *See* Lincoln Tomb

Stebbins, Henry, 176

Story, William Wetmore: *Libyan Sibyl*, 59, *60*, 197; and Shaw Memorial, 197

Stowe, Harriet Beecher, 45; *Dred*, 15, 17; on *Libyan Sibyl*, 59; on Sojourner Truth, 15; *Uncle Tom's Cabin*, 40, 45. *See also* Story, William Wetmore

Stuart, J. E. B., 148

Sumner, Charles, 195, 196, 197

Sundquist, Eric, 20

Tacca, Pietro, monument to Grand Duke Ferdinand, 23, *26*

Taft, Lorado, 125, 179

Tennyson, Alfred Lord, 127

Terry, Mississippi, 137

Thermopylae, 196

Thompson, John, 186

Torso, Belvedere, 53

Truth, Sojourner, 15, 59, 87

Tuckerman, Henry, 64

Turner, Victor, 228n.17

Twain, Mark, 159

Types of Mankind (Nott and Gliddon), 9, *10*, 12, 13–15, 53, 218n.14

Union commemoration, 109, 142; and Confederate commemoration, 164, 178–79; and emancipation, 83–84, 96–97, 100–101, 124–25, 178–80, 205, 212. *See also* Confederate commemoration; emancipation; Lincoln, Abraham

United Daughters of the Confederacy, 158, 253n.64

U.S. Capitol, 54, 64, 114, 166; Henry Kirke Brown's model for House pediment, 32, *33*, 34–35; sculpture of, 41, 81, *82*, 83, 107, 145

U.S. Colored Troops, 186

U.S. Congress: and abolition of slavery, 62; and Freedmen's Memorial, 114; and National Lincoln Monument Association (Washington, D.C.), 103; and proposal for monument to African American soldiers, 189–90; and Reconstruction Act, 103

U.S. Sanitary Commission, 100

U.S. Supreme Court, 114, 128

Valentine, Edward, 133; proposal for Lee Monument, 134, 141, *142*

valor: African American, 188; civic, 206–7; military, 188, 206; white, 150–51, 157, 188, 209. *See also* common-soldier monuments; heroism; James, William

Van Rensselaer, Marianna Griswold, 69, 125, 131–32

Verhaegen, Louis, 70, 71. *See also* Avery, Charles

veterans: honored in common-soldier monuments, 162, 166; as monument consumers, 162, 187; as monument sponsors, 162, 178, 247n.1; opposed to allegorical monuments, 183; racial segregation of, 188. *See also* Confederate veterans; Grand Army of the Republic

Vietnam Veterans Memorial, 5

Virey, Julien Joseph, 10–11

Virginia, 131, 134, 136, 144, 160; politics in, 135, 138–39, 211–12; press, 145, 147; women elite of, 135, 139. *See also* Lee Monument; Norfolk, Reconstruction; Richmond; white supremacy

Volk, Leonard, 102

volunteer soldiers, 164, 170, 177, 181; African American, 194; vs. Regular Army soldiers, 163, 167–68. *See also* citizensoldier; common soldier; Regular Army soldiers

war memorials, 64; before the Civil War, 166; modern transformation of, 19, 162, 166. *See also* common-soldier monuments; Howells, William Dean; Shaw Memorial

War of 1812, 167

war photography, 57, 164, 165, *172*, 174

Ward, John Quincy Adams, 81, 122; on emancipation, 56; experience of slavery, 57; *Freedman*, 52, *53*, 54–63, 64–65, 81, 125, 209; *Indian Hunter*, 58; on jury for Lee Monument, 142–43; monument to Henry Ward Beecher, 65; monument to New York 7th regiment, *163*, 164. See also *Freedman*

warfare: and heroism, 170–71, 177; imagery of, 170–72, 183–84; modern transformation of, 173, 184; trench, 171, 174. *See also* Civil War; common soldier; common-soldier monuments; equestrian monuments; heroism

Washington, Booker T., address at Shaw Memorial, 193, 256n.103

Washington, D.C., 90, 107, 114, 212. *See also* Freedmen's Memorial to Abraham Lincoln; Howard University; Lincoln Memorial; Lincoln monuments; Mall; National Lincoln Monument Association (Washington, D.C.); U.S. Capitol; Vietnam Veterans Memorial

Washington, George, 67, 70, 131, 168, 169; as Cincinnatus, 167; Greenough's statue of, 54, 58, 62; Houdon's statue of, 130; Mills's equestrian monument to, 109

Waterbury, Connecticut, 180

Wedgwood, Josiah, 21, 22, 23

West, Cornel, 19

West Point Academy, 168

Western Sanitary Commission of St. Louis: dealings with National Lincoln Monument Association, Springfield, 100, 101, 103, 114; dealings with National Lincoln Monument Association, Washington, D.C., 103, 104, 107, 110–12, 114; membership of, 93; sponsorship of Freedmen's Memorial, 91–92, 114–18, 128. *See also* Freedmen's Memorial; Lincoln tomb; National Lincoln Monument Association (Washington, D.C.)

White, Captain Samuel, 155, 158–59, 160, 161, 162

White, Stanford, 123

white body, 9, 18, 47, 49, 162–63, 182, 186. *See also* African American body; whiteness

white supremacy, 134, 155; accommodating racial diversity, 138, 159; and commemoration of Lee, 132, 135, 150; naturalized, 135; and Shaw Memorial, 202, 204; in South Carolina, 51, 159; in Virginia, 135, 138, 211. *See also* Lee Monument; South Carolina

whiteness, 132, 150: and common-soldier monuments, 18–19, 162–63, 181, 186, 188; in opposition to blackness, 12, 18–19, 30, 47, 51, 117, 186, 203, 253n.59; in public sphere, 19; in sculpture, 9, 18–19, 30, 47, 181. *See also* African American body; common-soldier monuments; *Greek Slave*; white body

Whitney, Anne, *Africa*, 59

Whittier, John Greenleaf, 194

Williams, George Washington, 188, 190, 195, 196; *History of the Negro Troops in the War of the Rebellion*, 188, 189

women: in abolitionist movement, 94; as donors to monument campaigns, 90–91, 94, 188; as guardians of "culture," 139, 150; as monument sponsors, 135, 139–40, 150, 188, 253n.64; monuments to, 5, 111–12, 159; in national monument to Lincoln, 111–12; role in common-soldier monuments, 188; as slaves, 30. *See also* abolitionists; emancipation; *Greek Slave*; Lee Monument; Virginia

World War I, 187

Yeatman, James, 110, 111, 112, 114, 115. *See also* Freedmen's Memorial; Western Sanitary Commission

Yonkers, 180; Soldiers' and Sailors' Monument, *179*, 186, 189

CPSIA information can be obtained
at www.ICGtesting.com
Printed in the USA
LVOW10s1755150917
548875LV00003B/112/P